A Matter of Life

and Death

A Matter of Life and Death

Remarkable True Stories
of Hope and Healing

Rosemary Altea

Jeremy P. Tarcher/Penguin
a member of Penguin Group (USA) Inc.
New York

JEREMY P. TARCHER/PENGUIN
Published by the Penguin Group
Penguin Group (USA) Inc., 375 Hudson Street, New York, New York 10014, USA ·
Penguin Group (Canada), 90 Eglinton Avenue East, Suite 700, Toronto, Ontario M4P 2Y3,
Canada (a division of Pearson Canada Inc.) · Penguin Books Ltd, 80 Strand, London WC2R
0RL, England · Penguin Ireland, 25 St Stephen's Green, Dublin 2, Ireland (a division
of Penguin Books Ltd) · Penguin Group (Australia), 250 Camberwell Road, Camberwell,
Victoria 3124, Australia (a division of Pearson Australia Group Pty Ltd) · Penguin Books
India Pvt Ltd, 11 Community Centre, Panchsheel Park, New Delhi—110 017, India · Penguin
Group (NZ), 67 Apollo Drive, Rosedale, North Shore 0632, New Zealand (a division of
Pearson New Zealand Ltd) · Penguin Books (South Africa) (Pty) Ltd, 24 Sturdee Avenue,
Rosebank, Johannesburg 2196, South Africa

Penguin Books Ltd, Registered Offices: 80 Strand, London WC2R 0RL, England

First trade paperback edition 2008
Copyright © 2007 by Rosemary Altea

Most Tarcher/Penguin books are available at special quantity discounts for bulk purchase for sales
promotions, premiums, fund-raising, and educational needs. Special books or book excerpts also
can be created to fit specific needs. For details, write Penguin Group (USA) Inc. Special Markets,
375 Hudson Street, New York, NY 10014.

The Library of Congress catalogued the hardcover edition as follows:

Altea, Rosemary.
A matter of life and death : remarkable true stories of hope and healing / Rosemary Altea.
p.   cm.
ISBN 978-1-58542-553-2
1. Spiritualism.   2. Altea, Rosemary.   3. Grey Eagle (Spirit).   I. Title.
BF1261.2.A44   2007   2006039483
133.9'1—dc22

ISBN 978-1-58542-648-5 (paperback edition)

Printed in the United States of America
1   3   5   7   9   10   8   6   4   2

Book design by Chris Welch

ACKNOWLEDGMENTS

First I would like to thank my publisher, Joel Fotinos, and all those at Tarcher who were involved in the process of publishing this book, and who gave such enthusiastic support.

My thanks to Denise, for her ever cheerful and helpful presence in my office. Also for going, unselfish and caring, above and beyond the call of duty in helping the many who contact us. I am grateful that she is on my team.

I thank my team, both here in the United States and in England, for their unfailing loyalty and hard work on the various projects we encounter together as our spiritual journey continues. The RAHEF would not exist without them.

A special mention to Lynn and Peter, to Jane, Jean and Joan, to Kay and Nigel, and to Eileen. Love and kisses.

My gratitude goes out to all those whose stories are written in these pages, and to those who allowed me to use them here. I am so honored. My gratitude also goes out to those many, many fans who have written asking for more, and whose enthusiasm and trust have carried me along all these years. I thank you all from my heart.

It is impossible to fully express my thanks to my friend Joann Davis, for the help and expertise she has given freely, for her time and effort on my behalf, and for being there for me when I felt so lost, not knowing what to do next. Words cannot say how grateful I am. Thank you.

My thanks to my child, who has been my best friend, and without whom I would have no reason to continue. And to God, to Christ, and to Grey Eagle, who has stood by my side as I have told my stories, unfailing in his presence, in his inspiration, and in his encouragement. He sees for me when I am blind. He hears for me when I am deaf. He feels for me when it seems that I am numb. He feeds me when I am not capable of nourishing myself.

Through the writing of this book, and for the help and support from all of you, I am truly nourished.

As always, my child, Samantha Jane, is first on the page,
for without her, I do not exist. She is my light, my hope and
inspiration, and the reason for my life here on Earth. Her courage
and strength feed me, her love warms me and keeps me from
the cold and harshness that is sometimes our world, and her
unfailing loyalty holds me up and saves me from the sinking
of my heart, which threatens to drive me into the depths of
despair, in those times of my human frailties.

Do you love me, or do you not?
You told me once, but I forgot. . . .

Contents

PART III

CASEBOOK

PART IV

A PROMISE IS A PROMISE

PART V

THE GOOD, THE BAD, AND THE BEAUTIFUL

PART I

MEDIUM RARE

Accident or Murder?

I was in Wyoming, way up in the mountains, at one of those fancy resorts that offer all the amenities for the best of everything a mountain vacation could possibly be. There were walks, mountain biking, hiking, camping; in fact, every possible activity for the outdoors was provided.

It was one of those days, when the sun is bright, the sky is a perfect blue, and the mountain air is crisp and sharp and clean. The smell of pines was strong in my nose, and needles scattered the floor like a carpet, crunching under the boots of the group who were making their way along the pathway through the woods.

The younger of the two couples was walking ahead, uncomfortable and embarrassed by the older couple's insistent and heated argument, noticeably upset that their walk was being ruined by the continual bickering of the older couple. This should have been a day to enjoy, a day for all of them to take pleasure in the phenomenal beauty of the Wyoming mountains, which was, after all, the reason they had come on this family vacation.

The log cabin they had rented was great, with a large living room, modern kitchen, two spacious bedrooms with bathrooms en suite, and it provided all the comforts of a home away from home. The atmosphere of the resort was wonderful, and this should have been the perfect vacation, thought the young man, as he walked by his wife's side, but it was quickly turning into a nightmare. His father and stepmother, and their constant arguing, well, that was something that he and his wife had not bargained for when they had agreed to come, and they did not like it one bit.

As I watched them from my vantage point, I found it hard not to be saddened by their apparent blindness to the breathtaking beauty around me. I found it hard to understand how the older couple could ignore such an amazing and incredible sight as the range of mountains surrounding us, stretching for as far as the eye could see and beyond, and not be calmed by it. But they saw none of it.

The argument raged on. The man, an obvious bully, thought that all he had to do was shout the loudest and drown out his wife's voice, ignoring all her pleas for him to stop. Tears rained down her face, but he simply didn't see them; nor did his wife's misery seem to affect him in any way. He just shouted louder still until she couldn't take any more.

"That's it, that's it. I've had it!" I heard the woman scream at her husband finally. "I am not going to take your bullying any longer. I'm going back to the cabin to pack my bag, and I'm leaving you. It's over! I've had enough!" And with that, she turned and headed back down the path the way they had come.

The husband, arrogant and self-righteous, still indifferent to his wife's pain, shrugged and let her go. Ignoring for now, at least, the consequences of what this might mean, he began walking a little faster, now eager to catch up to his son and daughter-in-law.

"What the hell's going on, Dad?" the son demanded, rounding on his father angrily as the older man approached. "We didn't come all this way on vacation to listen to you two fighting. You're just not being fair to any of us."

"Well, she's gone. She's leaving, so we don't have to worry about it anymore, do we?" the father replied belligerently, irritated by his son's angry reaction.

"But you can't just leave her to go back by herself," I heard the daughter-in-law say incredulously. "These mountains are dangerous, for God's sake, and you know perfectly well that we should all stay together. You have to go after her. We all do," she added, tight-lipped, even more exasperated by her father-in-law's attitude, and fervently wishing she had never agreed to come.

"She's right, Dad," said the son, who was made still more angry by his father's indifference. "We have to catch up to her, and all of us should go back together. These woods, as you perfectly well know, are too dangerous for one person to be walking alone."

And still I watched. I watched from my vantage point, as the husband turned angrily away from his son. "Well," he spat out furiously, "the last thing I want is to ruin anything for you, so you two go on. I'll go back and find her myself."

It was easy for me to follow him as he stormed off down the path, hurrying to catch up with his wife. And it was easy to hear him as he began yelling at her once again, even before he had fully caught up to her, just a little way up ahead.

I was so close to them, close enough to touch, but of course I could not, and as I continued to watch, his wife, hearing his voice, turned in anger to face him and began yelling back, screaming that it was over, that she was going to divorce him. He screamed back that he didn't care. By the time he reached her, his temper was completely out of control, the cords on his neck were bulging, and he was practically apoplectic.

As he lunged at her, he thrust out his arms, grabbing at her, his hands closing tightly around her throat in his uncontrollable fury. She lashed out at him, punching, punching, hitting out at his face, then, in an effort to force his hands away, she grappled with him, struggling furiously, trying desperately to get away. He pushed, she pulled, and a real struggle ensued, both of them now completely out of control, mindless of the danger. Then, quite suddenly and without warning, she lost her footing, slipping on the edge of the path. For a moment it seemed as if she were suspended on the precipice, her arms flailing, balanced like a tightrope walker hovering in midair, and I had the impression of time standing utterly still. Then silently, and with no effort at all, she went down, over the side of the mountain, rolling over and over, until she was gone from sight.

In that sudden and eerie silence, he stood at the edge of the cliff, staring after her, shaking and pale, the horror of what he had done written on his face. As he sank to his knees on the ground, I heard him whispering over and over again, "Oh my God, oh my God, oh my God."

After a while, and slowly then, like a man in a trance, he turned to get back onto the path . . . and came face to face with his son and daughter-in-law, who were standing rigid and wide eyed, staring at him. How much had they seen? How much did they know?

And yet still I watched, the silent ghost, unseen and unacknowledged, the unknown witness, and I followed them as they walked together, quiet and shaken, back to the cabin. No more yelling now!

It was a while later that they called the police and reported her missing, but by now of course, the woman we shall call Rose was already dead.

Back through the hole I came, the scene I had just witnessed fading from my eyes but not yet from my mind, and I was back in my living room in Vermont, where I was speaking to Rose's daughter on the phone.

I had been contacted by a well-known politician, who is very involved with a missing person's organization. He had seen me on the Larry King show, and had been impressed enough to call my office, asking for my help.

"No one knows what happened," he had told me, as he described the situation. "It seems she just disappeared into thin air. It's a real mystery. Her husband and family—she has daughters from a previous marriage—are simply beside themselves with worry, and it has been three months now since she's been gone."

"What do the police have to say about it?" I asked. "Do they have any leads?"

"Well, they don't seem to know, but they have a couple of theories, of course. It could be that Rose and her husband argued and she just took off. Some women do that, you know. Or it could be that something happened to her on the mountain. The police are looking at the husband as the prime suspect, and they strongly suspect foul play. Apparently, he has shown nothing but a belligerent and aggressive attitude. During the several weeks the police questioned him, he has lost his temper many times and has actually accused the police of not doing their job. It would seem—at least from the investigators' point of view—that he is protesting his innocence way too loudly, and in their mind, he does not seem to be behaving like a grieving and concerned husband. However, Rosemary," he continued, "they gave him a polygraph, and he passed. They also gave the son and his wife a polygraph, twice. The son failed the first but passed the second, the daughter-in-law failed both. Now the missing woman's daughters have asked me if I can help, and I thought you might be able to tell us something, you know, see something, maybe, that could be helpful."

"So basically you want me to find out if she's dead or alive, and either way, if I can locate her, is that it?"

"Well, I guess so. Is that the sort of thing you do?" he asked hesitantly, wanting to follow the proper procedure but a little out of his depth, not quite knowing what the proper procedure was.

"Why don't we start this way," I suggested. "I'll speak with the family, and if I can come up with anything helpful, we'll take it from there."

So here I was, a few days later, on the phone with one of the missing woman's daughters, wondering where this conversation would lead.

I knew the girl's mother was dead the minute she spoke, for I saw her instantly, standing by my side, eager for the communication to begin.

She was about five feet, five inches tall, with dark brown hair cut short but not too short, a round, attractive face, and dark brown eyes. She gave me her name right away, which doesn't always happen, and I knew she was trying hard to be as clear in her communication as she possibly could. It was important that she let her family know what had happened to her. It was important to try to bring them some peace.

Surprisingly, she had not begun with the incident of her death. First she wanted to give her daughter proof, proof of her life after death. She wanted to give her daughter evidence that she could still see, still hear, still be part of her family's life, even though she was now in the spirit world. She also wanted to give her daughter proof that it was really she. So for the first thirty to forty minutes of our conversation, she described the small and intimate details of her family and their lives, over the past few months, since her death. We went from the most insignificant details—new curtains, a birthday party, alterations to the kitchen, a new stove—to details of one of her daughters' relationships, problems with her grandchildren and school, and an upcoming wedding.

The daughter was both saddened and delighted by the details, even though she was heartbroken by the confirmation that her mother had, indeed, passed. "But I already knew," she sighed, "I knew in my heart that my mother was gone." Then: "But can you tell me, Rosemary, what happened to her? Can you tell me how my mother died? Her new husband, his son and his wife, they say they followed her back to the cabin after their walk, expecting her to be there when they arrived, but the cabin was empty, and my mother's things—her clothes and suitcase— were still there. Her husband says the reason she went back on her own was because she wasn't feeling well, that she had a bad headache. Is that true, Rosemary? It's just," she added sadly, "well, it's just the not knowing that is the most difficult. I need to know. My family needs to know," and with that, she broke down and sobbed.

It was at this point in the consultation that I felt myself moving back in time, moving down through the hole, down and through the door into that other dimension, passing through time and space and going back to the place where it had all begun.

Rose, the mother of the girl, who, distressed by her daughter's distress, laid her hand on my shoulder. "I'll show you," she had whispered in my ear. "I'll take you back with me, back to the mountain, back to that day, so that you can see for yourself how things really were and what really happened."

And so we had gone back. And, just as you have seen, Rose did indeed show me what had happened.

"There is no proof," said Rose, as slowly we had come back through the hole, to the now, "no physical evidence you see, and only you and I, Rosemary, will ever know the whole story, for I don't want my daughter to know. Knowing the truth, my family would have to live with the fact that my husband got away with murder, my murder, and if they knew that, a vendetta would ensue that would only destroy all their lives.

"So I want you to tell them it was an accident, and you know, Rosemary, in a way it really was. My husband didn't mean to do it, and it doesn't make any difference to me now. It's really better if we leave it this way."

So that's what I did, just as Rose had asked, and I was able to give closure to Rose's children so that they could get on with their lives.

I didn't lie or make something up; I simply described the struggle I had seen. I gave most of the details, a man with his hands around her mother's throat, her mother fighting for her life, and how she had lost her footing and fallen over the side of the mountain. What I left out was the part about the man. I did not say that I had seen his face or that I had heard his voice clearly, and that I knew who it was who was responsible for what happened. I did not say it was the husband.

Now some of you may be thinking that it was my duty to tell, to make sure that justice was done. But I have to remember that my first and most important responsibility is to those in the spirit world. I am obliged to do as they ask and to honor their wishes. If I do that, my job is easier. If I do that, then I can live with my choices and the decisions

I must make in my role as a communicator. Very much like a priest, a doctor, or a lawyer, I hold many secrets, other people's secrets, and I am bound by honor never to disclose those secrets. I have seen and heard many things that will never be disclosed to another soul, and Rose knew this. And Rose also knew that if she told me a secret, then that secret would be safe with me.

It may seem, in the telling of this story, that I have already broken my promise to Rose, but that is not the case, for no one will ever know whom the story is about. The family will never know that the story is theirs, for there are so many families with just the same story, the same heartache, the same grief.

"And only you, Rosemary, only you and I will ever know the whole story," said Rose, a contented smile on her face, happy that her ordeal was finally over, that she had made contact with her precious children and could finally be at peace.

"Only you and I, Rosemary, will ever know the truth," Rose had said, and she was right.

Well, of course, Rose and I . . . and one other!

Taking Flight

We are not human beings having a spiritual experience.
We are spiritual beings having a human experience.

—Pierre Teilhard de Chardin

During the last seven years or so there has been an incredible surge of interest in movies like *The Sixth Sense*, *The Mothman Prophecies*, that wonderful Kevin Costner movie *Dragonfly*, and TV shows like *Medium* and *The Dead Zone*. Thousands of books have emerged on the subject of spirituality—the New Age section, it's called. The topic of spirituality is now commonplace. However, it was not that long ago that people like me were considered, at best, strange and, at worst, cheats and charlatans, who took advantage of susceptible individuals, people suffering a loss. Now we are accepted as part of a normal society, revered, almost, by many, and our gifts are valued. That's the theory, anyway, and for the most part, it's true. But there are those who still treat us with suspicion, who doubt our gifts, and who question everything we do . . . and it might surprise you to know that I myself would fall somewhere within that category.

Don't misunderstand me, I'm not saying that I doubt the gift, but I do doubt many of the people who claim to have that gift. I have to! The last thing I want to do is to mislead others into thinking I can do more than I say I can, and the last thing I want for myself is to be misled. So it makes sense to me to question everything, while keeping an open mind, of course. That way I can make a better judgment about the things I see and hear.

It does become old, though, I will admit, when I come up against those individuals who, no matter what you do, no matter how much evidence you might provide, will stubbornly refuse to accept that there just might be something in what you say.

Most of the time it doesn't matter, as why should I care one way or the other whether someone believes in life after death? As long as I can trust in myself, in the process of mediumship, and as long as I remain honest and forthright in the work that I do, that's all that counts . . . well, as I said, most of the time.

Over the years, I have had my share of having to deal with arrogance, rudeness, outright insults, and scorn. When I was in England, although these things mattered, I had my friends, people who stood by me during those times, ready to defend me, to soothe me, make me laugh and make me feel better. An old adage says that you're lucky if you can count on one hand the number of friends you have. Well, I am more than lucky, because I have more friends than I can count on two hands, and when I lived in England, when I felt lonely or sad, or had to face other people's intolerance—which in those days was quite often—my friends were always there for me.

The hardest part about leaving my country and my home to come to work in the United States was in having to leave those friends behind, and the hardest part of the last thirteen years, since I have been living and working in the States, is that those same friends are not able to be with me when I need them most, although since that time I have made more wonderful friendships all over the world, and have been incredibly lucky in meeting some beautiful and caring people.

There have been two constants in my life: one, my child, Samantha Jane, and the other, my spirit guide, Grey Eagle. It should be said that without these two I would have given up long ago. Their love and in-

spiration have been my main source of courage, and it has been because of them that I have been able to write this book at all.

Like many of us, over the years I have been tempted to quit, to give
up on my life and to give up on myself. And like many, just at that point
when I know I can't go on any longer, something happens . . . I hear
a song on the radio, or the girl at the checkout at the supermarket
makes some small comment, or I receive an unexpected phone call or
letter from a friend, and then somehow I find myself carrying on living the life I thought I had no strength or desire to live. In those moments, when God seems to interfere, and it is obvious to me that I am
not the one in control, I've had mixed feelings. Sometimes I get angry
with myself and others because I feel that the universe is holding me
back, forcing me to stay put, when all I want is to move on. Sometimes
I am grateful that those same forces, God forces, know me better than
I know myself, that I would hate myself for quitting, for seeing myself
as a failure, failing others as well as myself.

After the success of my first book in 1995—it seemed to take the
world by storm—for years my life became one long round of travel,
media hype, and people-pleasing. My gratitude to all those who were
inspired by my work and my life thus far, those who helped make me
a success, knew no bounds. I became even more of a workaholic than
ever, and I took any and every opportunity I could to bring the knowledge of the spirit world to the public. My spirit guide, Grey Eagle, an
Apache warrior, a Shaman, a Healer, and my greatest teacher, a highly
evolved spirit entity, watched over me carefully as he had always done.
Always constant, he did his best to show me in every way possible that
he was with me, that he was standing by my side as I went out into the
world. Helping me with my work, Grey Eagle guided me the best he
could in my life in every way. But his best was only good enough if I
was paying attention, and there were many times when I was not. It was
never a question of not believing in him, it was more a question of not
believing in myself. America is a big place, and as I traveled around the

country, meeting thousands of people and working almost nonstop, giving interviews everywhere I went, the whole thing became overwhelming to me. I went from living in a small village in England, having a small but very supportive group of friends, becoming a good and inspirational teacher, with a wonderful group of students, knowing where I was and who I was, to suddenly becoming a person in the spotlight, an enigma, a curiosity on a larger scale than ever before. It wasn't that I wasn't used to it. It wasn't that I didn't know the world, for many of my clientele were from overseas. It was just that now there were so many other people I had to listen to, it seemed. Agents, publishers, events organizers, all experts in their individual fields, all inspired by the gift, all having their own opinions, often disagreeing with one another, and often disagreeing with me. I became torn; my self-esteem, never strong, began to deteriorate. More and more unsure and uncertain of myself, I found myself allowing others to make decisions for my life that I should have made for myself. My personal life a mess, living with an alcoholic, I became even more reliant on those around me whom I soon allowed to take control of much of my life.

It was no one's fault but mine. There is no finger-pointing, no laying blame, not even a little, as I knew better, *know* better than that. Grey Eagle had taught me early on in my lessons that people can only do to you what you allow them to do. I had allowed my life to get out of control, I had let it happen. Grey Eagle's voice was lost to me; I was too caught up in what was happening around me, too enmeshed in the trials and tribulations of my human existence to pay attention to my guide. And yet, when I was working, when I was communicating with the spirit world, I would hear him loud and clear. I would reach out to him, just as I had always done, and just as before, he was always there. But in those times when it should have been important for me to hear him for myself, when it should have been his help and advice I sought in my personal life, I allowed the voices of my friends and colleagues to interfere with my judgments. I lost control; I gave it up to others and allowed them to overwhelm me with their demands. Con-

fused, afraid of being on my own, afraid of failing in my career, afraid
of being unloved, afraid of being abandoned, I abandoned myself, my
knowing self, my intuitive self. I abandoned my soul. I forgot to listen
to that still small voice!

"People can do to you only what you allow them to do!" Wise, wise
words!

In 1996, while I was on tour with *The Eagle and the Rose,* Grey Eagle came
to me one night and gave me a vision, a dream vision. This was not an
unusual way for him to communicate something to me, but I knew that
my guide used this form of communication only if he wanted me to pay
particular attention to his voice, to his message to me. It was his way of
shouting out, of making me listen, making me very aware. He was aware
of the danger I was in. He knew that I was giving up my power.

In this dream vision I was in a car, a passenger, and the driver was
someone I knew well, a person who was very influential in my life at that
time and for several years to come. We were driving in a forest, with
tall trees all around us, and the road, very narrow and uneven, snaked
through the dense growth of the woods, making it impossible to see
where we were going. The car leaped and bucked as we raced over the
rough terrain, and I tried many times to get my friend to stop, to let
me drive, to take a breath, and to figure out where we were heading.
But she wouldn't listen to me, so sure that she was on the right track.
She just kept on going. Just as I thought we were going to crash, the
trees disappeared; the road became less rough but narrowed down to
not much more than a footpath. I took a breath and tried again to persuade my friend to let me drive, but she stubbornly refused to give up
the wheel. It was the journey from hell, and as in all dreams of this nature, it seemed to go on forever. Then, suddenly, and with a jarring
thud, the car careened into a ditch and came to a standstill; we had
come to a dead end. Shaking and angry, I leaped out of the car, went
around to the driver's side, yanked my friend out of the seat, and took
the wheel. Trying to remain calm and reversing slowly, I inched the car
this way and that, working to get us out of the hole we were in.

Waking with a start, the vision firmly in my head, my hands still gripping the wheel, I knew that my guide was giving me a clear picture of what my life had become, and what it would be like in the future if I didn't do something about it. He was letting me know, in as clear a way as he could, that I needed to take the wheel, that my journey was mine to steer, my life was mine to decide.

Later that day, I sat my friend down, explained the vision, and explained the need for me to take back control, to be allowed to make decisions for myself. I told her that she could not and must not make any more decisions for me about anything, without talking to me first. It was a hard conversation, as anything so far that she had ever done for me had been out of a desire to help me in my work. Her intentions were only the best, but my life decisions were simply not her call to make. They were mine.

For a few weeks, things were better for everybody. But as often happens in these situations, where there are strong-minded individuals all wanting things their way, my dream vision became a blur. My message from Grey Eagle that if I didn't take control of the steering wheel I would be lost, that message became a distant thing, a memory which hung in the back of my mind, waiting until I was ready to face it again. And Grey Eagle, loving and patient as ever, also waited, knowing that I had chosen the hard way, sad for the pain I was to put myself through but refusing to interfere.

There is nothing about me that is rare. I am as ordinary as the next person, making just the same mistakes, acting out my humanness, following the normal patterns of a regular human being. It is mediumship that is rare, in any form, and is much rarer in my case, as I am a trance medium, I help rescue lost souls, and I can travel through time and space while standing still. It is my gift that is rare, which makes me seem unusual, even as I am simply mortal.

In my humanness, in my private life, I had forgotten that I was a spiritual being with a power that comes from my soul and that feeds me, sustains me, and makes me strong. In fact, I used my humanness as an excuse for my weaknesses, my inability to think straight, to do something about my life. I often told myself that I was "only human," which I knew perfectly well was not true, and I gave myself permission to use my frail humanness as an excuse for my poor judgments, and watched helplessly as my life spiraled out of control.

Fear is a funny thing. It can make us freeze; it can render us helpless; it can make us weak and oh so human! But only if we let it!

Eventually, after several years, I began to come to my senses and, slowly but with great determination, took the wheel again. In the process of doing this, there was pain and hurt, confusion and despair, not just for me but for others too. But I had no choice, except the choice to wallow in my misery . . . and that I would not do. I had had enough of the dramas and inconsistencies, of the constant draining of my energy, and of having to make the tremendous effort to keep some kind of unsatisfactory peace.

It was hard, taking the wheel again, and lonely too, but as I became more and more confident in myself again, I realized how I wanted to live. I have enough drama in my life, dealing with other people's pain, real drama, unexpected and life-changing drama. I realized that I cannot afford to have those unnecessary and often self-inflicted dramas in my life. Finally I began paying attention to my guide, listening to his voice again, trusting myself, and giving my life up to God. And about time too!

How many times, I wonder, must each of us go through the same lessons, over and over again, sometimes learning, sometimes not? How many times are we tempted to point the finger at someone else, to blame someone else, and to live in despair? How long does it take us before we really get it, before we really understand that the power is ours and that only we can give it away? How many times before we understand that the definition of madness is to do the same things over and over again, all the time expecting different results.

"Despair is a prison. Hope can set you free," is a tagline from the movie *The Shawshank Redemption*, and one that I have paid particular attention to as I have gathered the material for this book. In the coming pages, you will find these themes in stories that are meant to remind us of an ever-present and protective God, who has a plan for each of us, even when our lives seem painful and full of suffering. We will be shown that our angels are always close by, that we can find strength in our beliefs, that our believing holds energy which can be a source of power. There are stories that show how even the simple selfless acts of love, caring, and kindness can make a difference. You will find examples of faith, which I hope will inspire and move you and which I hope will touch your heart. There is an example of how faith is powerful but a warning to beware of blinding faith, as it can consume our lives. There are stories which I hope will inspire you to live your faith, to keep your promises, no matter how hard that can be, to own your power, to live life to the fullest, and to remember that grief is more easily tolerated when we share it with those we love. And there is a story that is so terrible, an example of such evil, that some of you may shy away from it. But if you persevere, the inspiration of our angels will give you an understanding that no matter what, we are never alone, and that goodness and truth will always prevail over those dark forces we know to exist.

Again and again we will be reminded that "Despair is a prison, and hope can set us free." This is a book of hope!

"We are spiritual beings having a human experience." Yes, we are, there is no doubt of it in my mind, and the phrase "I am only human" is a myth. But I will go further: I like to think that we are spiritual beings who are being given the opportunity again and again to live our lives *as* spiritual beings and to have countless spiritual experiences, in our human form, while we live on this incredible Earth of ours. So for myself, I try to look for that one spiritual moment in every day, that one opportunity to listen to the heartbeat of my soul. And the amazing thing is that as I look and as I recognize that one small spiritual moment, other moments present themselves, and my day becomes filled with light and with the power of God.

There are times still when it feels as if I'm in an ocean, struggling to swim, and I feel as if I'm drowning. I am often lonely and miss my friends in England. I still get homesick sometimes. That said, America is my home now, and there are so many wonderful things about being here that I would miss if I didn't have them. As for loneliness, well, that goes with the territory, I think, and part of the price I must pay for what I do.

Many years ago, my good friend and fellow healer Mick McGuire warned me that the price of my gift was loneliness, and he was right. It's not only that no one can fully understand what and how it is that I do what I do. It also has to do with the idea people have that if someone like me can talk to the dead, and especially if they have a spirit guide, then they have plenty of company and don't need much of anything else. Many people actually believe that all my problems are solved by Grey Eagle, that I am never alone because of my communication with people in the spirit world, and that all my needs are met by them. This is so not true; in fact the opposite is more the truth, and partly because of this, I have made some huge mistakes in judgment, when in my loneliness and neediness, just as all of us do in those unhappy times, I have entered into relationships that caused me a great deal of heartache over the last few years. So much for being psychic!

Like the rest of us, my human existence often weighs me down. Like the rest of us, I am on a journey, together with Grey Eagle, that will take me the rest of my life and way beyond my human existence.

In the last three years I have worked hard to change my life, to get rid of all the negative and harmful energy that was around me personally. So many things had to change, and I finally found the courage to make those changes, even though it was hard, and even though it meant that I had to say good-bye to some people it was hard for me to lose. But Grey Eagle was always present in my life, and now that I am finally listening to him again, I know that this is the way it has to be. And I know with certainty that I will not give my power away again.

With this knowledge, and feeling much more content, we take flight, my guide and I, as we work and play, as he helps me live my faith, as we work to keep our promises and remain always spiritual beings, living this human existence, and holding on to those spiritual experiences we so often have. I have an amazing life, a wonderful gift, and I am truly blessed.

There is a phrase from that incredible and most inspiring book *Hanta Yo,* written by Ruth Bebe Hill, which says in its simplicity all that I am trying to live up to in my life. "Continuous, habitual spirituality." So this is what I strive for, to be continually and habitually spiritual.

"Hanta Yo, Hanta Yo, clear the way, for I come . . ."

Hanta Yo, clear the way, for *we* come, Grey Eagle and I. . . .

Tomorrow's Children

Most of my pain in the last ten years has been of my own doing, caused by my unwillingness, for a variety of reasons, to make those changes that I so badly needed to make. The difference, however, between this almost self-inflicted kind of heartache and another kind of heartache is that I always had the choice to change my situation. I could improve upon it whenever I was ready to do so, which, thank goodness, I eventually did. But as we know, sometimes life throws us a curve ball that can bring an everlasting and devastating heartache that we can do very little to change. The loss of someone close to us, through death, and especially the loss of a child, will often result in that kind of devastation. No experience of mine, no matter how terrible, can be even remotely compared to this. So I think that this is the time to say, OK, enough about me, let's get down to the heart of things.

We are going to begin with Tomorrows Children's Fund, an organization that has chapters throughout the country, and this will not be the first time I have written about it. The Fund is, among other things, a support group composed of parents, siblings, and close family who have lost their children to a particular and extremely virulent type of cancer. Also involved in the organization are nurses, doctors, and caregivers, who give their time and energy to make this group a successful one.

It was not long after I made my home here that I received my first call from Tomorrows Children's Fund in New Jersey, asking me if I would visit and speak to a group of parents who had lost their children. Of course I said yes, and since that time I have visited several times over the last ten or so years. Usually the meetings are held in one of the conference rooms at a hospital, and somewhere between twenty to forty people might turn up, most of them family members of the kids who have passed, and always a couple of nurses and caregivers. This year, though, the meeting was being held at one of the larger hotels, the Marriott, in Teaneck, New Jersey. I didn't think much about this until I was in the car on the way there, with three of my friends from England who had been visiting, and my daughter, Samantha. Too late to do anything about it, it occurred to me that there might be a larger group than usual. I hoped that it would not be too large, since there would be no way that I would be able to connect to all the families and give them a message, which was bound to mean disappointment for some. Kicking myself for not paying closer attention to the arrangements, I sighed and asked Grey Eagle for as much help as I would need to do a good job.

Because I have never charged for these kinds of events, some of you might think that there would be less pressure for me than if people had to pay high ticket prices and expected great things for their money. But you would be wrong. A lot of people were relying on me that night, not the least of them were the children who had passed, the most important of my audience, and I didn't want to let them down.

As I walked into the conference room, I knew immediately that I was in trouble, as there were more than sixty people already there, and more were coming in. Every time I had done this before, it had been a much more intimate and personal experience for everyone. Tonight was going to be different, and I knew that some disappointment was inevitable.

There were so many messages given over the course of the next five hours, so many children giving messages of hope and love, giving evidence of their survival after death, inspiring and moving messages which brought us all to tears. There is only room to give you just a brief account of some of them, not necessarily in the order in which they came. Hopefully, this will give you a little taste of what it was like, and I hope you will bear with me as I tell the stories, for I could not leave them out.

Caitlyn, or Cattie as she liked to be called by those close to her, first described her illness. She was sick for a long time and had lots of tubes in her throat, she told us, which her parents had to clean out for her because they were often clogged with mucus, which made it hard for her to breathe.

She was a very pushy kid, in a funny and charming way, not yet a teenager but old for her years. From her attitude, it didn't surprise me that she would manage to be one of the first to be heard.

Talking to her parents, through me, about the way they were dealing with her death, Cattie told us how, without meaning to, they were pushing each other apart because they were not sharing their feelings with each other. While we were talking, she asked that her father put his arm around her mom.

Describing some of the events in her family's life since her passing, and there were many, she was able to give her parents the evidence they needed to accept that it was really she who was with them in the room. Young Cattie's final message to her mom and dad was, "Tell them not to be so sad, and to hold each other, and to share their grief. Then they won't be quite so lonely without me." And as they listened, Cattie's mom and dad clung more tightly to each other, their tears a mix of sorrow and joy. They were happy to know that their daughter was safe.

I moved my head, my vision adjusting slightly, as another girl, also young, pointed out her parents to me as she waited her turn.

"They're moving," she said, when I was ready to listen, "and there are boxes everywhere. They are worried about leaving the house, leaving all those memories, leaving my bedroom behind. They made it look so pretty for me, wanting to do something that would make me feel better because I was so sick." And she went on to describe her bedroom, full of lots of frills and girlie stuff. "They don't know what to do with it all, and they're afraid to let it go. But I think it would be nice to give it away to someone who needs it more than me. And they think that if they move, I might not be able to find them. But of course I will."

This sweet little thing, so concerned about her mom and dad, went on to talk of what she called her fairy dust, her magical and loving energy, and she explained to her parents how she could sprinkle them with it from her place in heaven. Then finally, "And tell them to keep my teeth," she chuckled, and the mother gasped, realizing that her daughter was showing her clearly that she could see her, as she had only hours before been looking at her daughter's baby teeth, which she kept in a box.

I turned my head again, now listening to Geoffrey, who had grown a little since his parents had last seen him. I saw him standing directly in front of his mother and father, and I marveled at the accuracy of his communication, as he told them that he knew of their plans to expand their business. Then, looking to his father, he explained that the plans could not possibly work out until his father became more organized, more disciplined, especially in the office.

"He can't manage things now," said Geoffrey, with a chuckle, "and when Mom tries to help him out, all they do is fight, so she won't help out anymore."

Both parents, smiling ruefully at their son's remarks, agreed that this was correct, and asked Geoffrey if he could give them any advice.

"Work at it together. Take some time out to do things together. Clean up the messy office, make a plan and stick to it together." Then, explaining further, "Dad," he said, turning to me, "would rather be in the truck than in the office. But Dad"—then turning back to look at his father—"you have to learn to do both."

Geoffrey then went on to tell his parents that he was still painting and that he was teaching some of the younger kids in the spirit world about art. He also reassured his parents that he was happy and would be reunited with them again one day.

The next connection was different from the others. At first confused, I thought I was not hearing him clearly. I suppose this was because I was expecting all of my communicators to be kids who had died of cancer, so when I saw the young boy who was describing to me how he drowned, at first I questioned whether I had heard right.

"My mom is over there, in the corner, and she helps the group."

As I repeated this, one of the social workers nodded her head in surprise. Like me, she had expected only those Tomorrow's Children to make an appearance, but recovering quickly, the social worker was thrilled to hear from her son, as you might imagine she would be.

He began by talking about his mother's health, her frequent hospital visits, and her stay in hospital and her recent surgery. Obviously concerned, he described how she had refused to listen to her doctors, and told us that even now she was ignoring their advice.

"The last time you were in hospital it was bad enough, but next time will be much worse if you don't listen and do what you're supposed to. You have got to lose weight, Mom. Your problem is that you're too busy looking after others, and you don't take care of you."

The youngster then talked to us about his passing, which was a great relief to his mom, who had always worried that he had been frightened and in pain. Her eyes filled with tears as she heard his final words. "It was just like being in a nice dream," he said. "I was floating, floating, and I was not frightened at all."

Moving on, I came to stand in front of a group of five people who were obviously together, from what my next communicators told me. One, a smiling woman somewhere in her fifties, began by describing how she had died, very suddenly, having spent years dealing with kidney problems. Her weight, she told us, had been a continual battle, be-cause of her many health issues, and she hated being fat.

"I know you, Rosemary," she said at one point. "In fact, you'll be surprised to know that I was the one who organized this meeting. But I passed two weeks ago. I wasn't worried though. I knew I would still be able to come.

"That's my daughter," she said, pointing to the young woman to my left. "And these," she said with a wave of her hand, indicating the small group sitting in front of me, "these are my family. My sister's boy is here with me, and he would like to give a message to his mother and his cousins, if that's OK." I smiled encouragingly at the young man standing beside his aunt and relayed his message. He had died, he told me, in a motorbike accident, and his head had been crushed. "It was a mess," he said, smiling ruefully. Then he went on to say that he was fine now and asked me to let his family know this, which of course I did. Then I went back to speak again with his aunt, who had a little more to say.

"I was ill for years," she told me, shaking her head sadly, "but my passing was still a shock to everyone, so can you tell them, Rosemary, that I'm OK, and—wait a second. Look!" I heard her laugh, as she did a twirl for me; then continuing, she said, "Will you tell them that I'm finally slim again."

So many people and so much despair—I knew there was no time to take a break. A young boy, a teenager, wanted to talk to his mom and dad. As I described him—short, skinny, with large eyes and a wide mouth—his mother caught her breath, recognizing her son, even before he told us how he passed. He was talkative, and after explaining the type of cancer he had and how it had affected him—how, when he was first sick, the doctors had misdiagnosed his symptoms—he began to tell his parents of other things, things most people would see as ab-solute evidence that what they were experiencing was real.

The boy's mother was totally accepting, acknowledging her son, but the father—well, that was a different kettle of fish altogether. He was a real doubting Thomas, wanting to see the holes in the hands, wanting more and more confirmation. No matter how much evidence his son gave him, he needed more. Still he refused to accept even the possibility that I might be real. For the sake of his son, I found myself spending more time with him than I should have, given the fact that there were still many others in the room waiting to hear from their kids. The boy had told his father how he'd seen him at the dentist that day. He had described his father's back upper tooth. He had explained how it had been causing his father a lot of pain. He told us how his dad had refused to go to the dentist until the pain had become so unbearable that he had no choice. After his boy had given such explicit information, and I saw that the father still stubbornly refused to see this as possibly coming from his son, I did something I rarely did.

"Why do you think I'm here?" I asked, upset and extremely frustrated by the man's attitude. "What is it you think I have to gain from this? I know it's not your son you doubt, I know you have had dreams and that your boy comes to visit you in your dreams, and you know it's really him. I understand that it's me you don't believe, me you don't trust, so I'll ask you again. What do you think I have to gain by being here?" And then, really on a roll and upset and frustrated for his boy, I added, "And how do you think your son must be feeling right now?"

My outburst had been unnecessary, unkind, and totally unprofessional, even though I had spoken softly. But I had no excuse for it. Angry with myself, I suggested we take a break. I needed to take a break, to take a breath and figure out what had caused me to react the way I had. It wasn't just that I hadn't been able to stand the look of disappointment on the young teenager's face, as he had tried and tried, unsuccessfully, to please his father. It was more than that, I reasoned. Here I was, sitting in a room full of kids who had died the most horrible and painful deaths. I was also sitting with their parents and families, parents who had had to stand by helplessly, sometimes for months, more often for years, watching their children suffer, not able to save their kids, and whose heartache at their loss was palpable.

I didn't blame the man for his doubting, even though he had taken it to the extreme. I was a doubting Thomas myself, so to a point I understood. So what was it that had tipped me over the edge, had frustrated me enough to allow my feelings to spill out? Well, the first thing to remember is that I am not a saint; just like everyone else, I can be worn down. Although I have tremendous patience, I can lose it at the most unexpected times. This was one of those moments, when the pain and suffering I'm asked to deal with on a regular daily basis, simply became too much for me. I was right in what I had said, even though I was wrong to voice my feelings. It was true that the father was suspicious of me . . . and I was used to it. It was my gift that he had doubted . . . and I was used to that too. But right then, with so much work to do and so little time to accomplish everything I needed to, and with so much suffering from both sides, the children and their families, the weight of it had born me down. Not an excuse, but at least it was an explanation, though it gave me little comfort at the time.

"I am one little person," I almost cried, "so give me a break—give your kids a break. They have no one else to speak for them right now but me."

The break over, a ten-minute respite, I took a deep breath and began again, immediately connecting with a small doll of a child, with blond, blond hair, skin almost as white as flour, and the biggest blue eyes. She was standing next to a man who was so opposite in looks, with swarthy skin, jet-black hair, and dark eyes, that when she told me he was her father, for a moment I wondered if I had misunderstood. But as she put her arms around his neck and clung to him, my doubts disappeared. I described her and was able to give him the details of her passing as she recounted them to me. When I explained my momentary confusion, he laughed, telling us, through his tears, how everyone used to make the same mistake. "But you see, my wife is very fair, as fair as my angel," and he turned his head to the side, feeling his daughter close to him, knowing that she was there. Then, barely able to speak for the lump in his throat, he whispered, "And they are my two fair-haired princesses."

Moving on again, not wanting to waste any more time than I had to, I pointed across the room to a woman somewhere in her mid-thirties. Describing her daughter to her and the way that she had passed, and receiving acknowledgment from the woman that it was indeed her little girl, I went on to give the message.

"Your daughter tells me that you are a very angry person and that terrible things happened to you when you were a child, which you have not been able to let go of, and that now your suffering has become unbearable with the loss of your daughter.

"You are a nurse, she tells me, a nurse's aid, and even though you are a sensitive and caring person, at work you are often short-tempered and intolerant because you are filled with so much pain and holding it all inside. You want to change your job and have been thinking of going back to school, to become a qualified nurse, your daughter tells me. This is a good idea, she thinks. But you won't be happy with anything, she says, until you let the anger go. She is asking me to tell you this because she loves you, and she won't be fully happy until you are.

"Please don't cry anymore. It only makes me cry, and then I get sad for you. It's going to be OK, and I am still with you," she told her mom, and her mom smiled as the tears fell, knowing that her daughter was right, and she told us all she would try. She was going to try to be a nicer person from now on, knowing that her daughter was watching.

Next, a boy, perhaps ten or twelve years old, who was wearing a bright yellow football jacket, his favorite, and the one, he explained to me, that his parents had dressed him in before they had placed him in the coffin.

"It was so full—the coffin, that is—by the time all our friends and family had finished"—he laughed—"there was barely room for me.

"I see you buy flowers," he told his parents, "and I go with you both to the graveside every week. But then I walk back home with you, and the flowers are left behind. Don't buy flowers for the grave anymore. Buy them and put them in a vase by my photo, so we can all enjoy them."

It was not the first time I had heard someone in the spirit world give this message, and I smiled as I saw the parents of the children, all of them nodding and smiling their agreement.

Another boy, a little older than the last but also a keen sports fan, described, as he stood in front of his parents, how he had seen his dad go out of the room during our break to check on the scores of the football game. The Redskins were playing, apparently, and the boy's father was just as keen on the game of football as his son was.

"I was really sick for a long time, and all I wanted to do was go outside and kick a ball around," he told us, "but I couldn't. I was too weak. Now I can play, and I'm a teacher, spending my time teaching the other kids who are here. We have fun. We laugh a lot, and you must never worry about me," he told his parents, as they held on to each other, savoring every morsel of information their son was giving them, as tears of sorrow, mingled with tears of joy, rained down their faces.

Now it was the turn of a mother and her sister, aunt to the child whose message of love was so profound, so moving for them. They were Spanish and could barely speak a word of English, and so had arranged for an interpreter to be present, just in case they were lucky enough to receive a communication.

She was a pretty little thing, this child, with a heart-shaped face, and after much talking, her final message to her family was this: "The scent of the flowers in heaven smells just like the blossoms on the trees where we come from. They smell just the same as the blossoms at home—just like our home!"

And as she said this, and shifting my gaze slightly to take in the scene, I saw a grove of trees I knew to be somewhere in a Spanish garden, the home of these two women, the home of this child. The blossom trees were filled with the most spectacular flowers, the petals filling the spaces between the leaves. And I could smell the perfume, incredibly abundant, the sweetest you can imagine.

I had been given a glimpse of a little part of heaven on earth and had been given a gift to pass on from a heavenly child.

All the while she had been talking to me, the child had danced between her mother and her aunt, flicking up her long hair, a habit, and one her mother recognized.

"They want to know why they can't see us," she said to me, turning to face the people in the room, and then giving a message to all of us. "You don't see us because you don't believe you can . . . so you have to start believing!"

There were more messages, more and more and more, the communications from the spirit world seemingly endless. And the pain and heartache was also endless, or so it seemed to me. Then, yet another boy, who, speaking directly to his mom and dad, described the many times he had visited them and the signs, the little things he had done to let his parents know that he was with them. His mother had understood and delighted in her son's visits, but his father still had doubts and was afraid to believe, in case he was simply fooling himself.

"How many times do I need to show you?" the boy finally said, sounding a little as I had earlier, frustrated and despondent, but not nearly ready to give up on his father and unwilling to accept his father's skepticism.

"In the back of the closet you will find a pair of my old sneakers. Tie the laces together and hang them on a hook somewhere high up, maybe on the ceiling. When you see them swinging, and there is no breeze, and no one can have knocked them . . . then you will know that it is me, that I am pushing them to show you that I'm here." As he said this, he turned to the room, to give all the parents there a message, just as the little girl who had spoken before him had.

"Give us a chance to show you," he said, smiling his encouragement to the room, "just give us all a chance."

After more than five hours, and a promise to come back before

Christmas, to spend time with the unlucky ones who had not received a message that night, I finally said my good-byes. Many people came up to hug me, to give their thanks and to express their gratitude. The father I had been so hard on gave me the biggest hug, telling me he would not be so stubborn the next time, and we laughed together, knowing how hard that would be for him. One of the nurses, who had known most of the children, told me how wonderful the evening had been for her.

"It felt like they were all back again. I could see them and feel them close to us all, and I could feel their love pouring over us," she sniffed, fighting back her tears, and overwhelmed by her experience.

At last I climbed into the car with my friends, my daughter snuggled in beside me. We too were overwhelmed, saddened but joyful, a mix of emotion, too difficult to absorb all at once. I was so exhausted and so sad, as I thought about the parents and their loss, and I thanked God, as I held my child's hand, that my burdens, my heartaches, and my loneliness were only small things by comparison to the suffering we had just witnessed.

Everything is relative, I mused, as the car began to move toward the city, and as hunger struck me, the realization dawned that it was past midnight and none of us had eaten dinner. As the unbidden thoughts of food and a comfortable bed invaded my painful wonderings, I thought for one last time, "How true it is, how true it really is. . . . Everything is relative!"

A Little Bit of Knowledge

Everything is relative, and as we have seen from the last chapter, pain and heartache come in many forms. Even though we can reason that the world is full of people who are worse off than we are, still, pain is pain, and no kind of heartache should be made less of, even if it is over the smallest thing.

Working as a spiritual medium now for more than twenty-five years, I have seen all kinds of pain and have had all sorts of experiences, and I find it remarkable that even the strangest, the oddest of stories are often duplicates of other stories, as are the stories from the Tomorrow's Children. Many of the children passed the same way. Their families had similar issues, and had I been in a different environment, in an audience of several hundred, it is easy to see how those families might think that the child coming through from the spirit world and describing his or her illness, was theirs.

I find it intriguing that there are few stories that are unique, that so many of us have parallel experiences, that somewhere in the world, at some point in time, someone else is going through the same things that we or our friends and family have gone through, or vice versa.

I see this all the time, especially during my lectures, when, in giving a message to one person, suddenly someone else will put up their hand and say, "I think you must be talking to me."

Even the little things—like kitchen renovations, a new oven, a wedding or an engagement party, a baby on the way, a new stair carpet just installed, a window broken, a front door just replaced—will often apply to more than one family. As I look around at my audience, trying to locate the one my spirit communicator is waiting to connect to, I will see several hands go up. All of them seem to know the person I have described, a man, five-ten, dark hair, slender build, who died of a brain tumor; a woman, mid-sixties, who died of lung cancer; a teenage boy, blond hair, six-two, broad-shouldered, who was killed in a car accident. Even the names will be the same sometimes. And it will be the smallest of details that will help me separate them out, find the right person, and give the correct message.

Very often I get frustrated with myself because I have such difficulty sorting things out, but almost always, my audience is much more patient than I. Often they will find humor in the fact that I am once again confused as, now having narrowed it down to two possibilities, I am still getting the run-around. Let me give you an example of what I mean.

"I have a man here who tells me he died in a car crash."

Several hands go up.

"He gives his name, Alfred."

Some hands disappear, but three remain up, all in different parts of the room.

"I can see him quite clearly, about five eight, a little on the heavy side, fair hair, slightly thinning on top."

Again I look to my audience. The three hands are still up.

"He tells me that your living room walls have just been painted a bright yellow and that you have had all new windows installed," I say, believing that I have finally narrowed it down.

One hand goes down; two remain. I repeat what I have just said, hoping that I can reach my goal, hoping to narrow it down still further. After all, I tell myself, how many people can there possibly be who have yellow walls in their living rooms?

I ask the man in the spirit world who is communicating through me to point out the person in the audience he wishes to speak with, and this is so simple a request that you might have wondered why I hadn't thought of it before. I have, and I did, and the same thing happens. All I hear is a response that confuses me, often because I will hear two people talking at once. So I ask for more detailed information, more evidence, which I get.

"I am being told that someone in the family has just had surgery on their foot."

Now sure that I have finally eliminated one of the two hands, I look up and see that the two hands still remain. Why, I wonder in frustration, scratching my head for the tenth time, am I not surprised?

I check with Grey Eagle, and yes, I have all the information correct. So what do I do now? I listen, I pay attention. I work hard. My audience is surprisingly patient, and eventually I see daylight. I see two men in the spirit world: Both died the same way; both are the same height, give or take a little; both have fair and thinning hair; and both have the same name. Unbelievable, I think, shaking my head, and what is more unbelievable is the fact that their families, not knowing each other, not living in the same area, but in fact many miles apart, seem to be living parallel lives. Everything about them seems to be the same. But then there are those differences, those small details that will tell them apart, and it is my job to find those little things, to hear those details, as my communicators in the spirit world talk to me.

Usually, things work out. I am able to separate the energies, to untangle the lines, so to speak, and to translate what I see, hear, and sense, and to do my job. But it is hard sometimes, and it is so easy to think that I am being told one thing when, in fact, I am being told something entirely different. This is when I must listen to Grey Eagle, who corrects me when I get it wrong. And at these times I am so grateful for the special and extraordinary gift I have, and for the knowledge that I have gained over the last quarter of a century.

It is said that a little bit of knowledge can be a dangerous thing, and there are many circumstances in which this old adage has been proved right. For example, we all know that an ill-informed doctor can unintentionally do great harm. But to the patient who has to live with the consequences of taking his advice, good intentions are often a bitter reward. A friend and student of mine recently had this experience. Many years ago Gary was in a terrible road accident, which left him with problems with his leg, and more specifically, with his ankle. After years of putting up with the way things were, the pain in Gary's ankle became more and more unbearable, and he finally went to the specialist, who told him that the only way to cure the problem was to fuse the anklebone. This procedure would certainly result in no more pain, but the downside of the surgery meant that Gary would walk with a terrible limp for the rest of his life. He would have no movement in his ankle, and once the surgery was performed, there was no way to reverse it.

Upset by the idea that he would be crippled but thinking that he had no choice—after all, the surgeon had great qualifications and a good reputation—Gary was about to sign the papers and have the surgery. Fortunately, he spoke to me first.

"Get a second opinion," I said. "Go back and talk to the original surgeon who fixed you up after the accident."

"He doesn't do this anymore," said Gary. "He only works with children now."

"Have you tried?" I persisted, and handed him the phone.

Amid Gary's protests and explanations—that he had already tried once, that the surgeon was never in his office, that he had been assured by others who "knew," that it was futile to try—I pushed the phone at my friend and insisted he try once more. It was no surprise to either of us when, after listening to Gary's inquiry, the surgeon's secretary said, "Hold on a moment. He's right here and would like to speak to you."

Having heard his secretary mention Gary's name, the surgeon had remembered him, and pretty soon an appointment was made.

There was, it turned out, no need for surgery, no need for any aggressive treatment. Gary now wears a molded support, very easy and comfortable to wear, he assures me, which he can take on and off at will. The end result is no more pain and no limp. You can't even tell when he's wearing it!

We have all heard stories of doctors, lawyers, accountants, professionals in every field, who "did not know," after the fact, after the harm is done, that harm was being done to those who sought help. People who relied on those who were supposed to know. Those whose job it is to know, but whose knowledge, for one reason or another, is limited.

In my own field, we see this all the time, people with some small measure of psychic ability, who, like Gary's doctor, are ill informed and whose knowledge is limited. I recently met such a group of people, who are good, kind, well intentioned, highly spiritual, and believing they are on a mission from God and their angels. When I think of them, I am conflicted, able to see both the potential for harm and for good.

There are thousands, if not hundreds of thousands of us who see, who hear, who sense in one way or another, who connect to the spirit world, who have some small psychic ability. There are also hundreds, if not thousands, who believe that their psychic abilities are more than they really are. This is a fact, and we all know it, but for those who desperately want to work in this field, who have the intention of doing only good, there is a major denial going on in that they are simply not good enough. And for those who want the messages, for those who are desperate to hear from the spirit world, there is also a denial . . . they believe. They *want* to believe, which makes it all the more easy for everyone to convince themselves that what they are doing is OK. But is it?

I was new to the neighborhood, and a friend had suggested I might want to try the local mission. As I walked into the church, I tried to keep an open mind. Even though Grey Eagle had given his opinion and even though I already knew I would not be a regular weekly visitor, still I hoped. I hoped I would find something wonderful, something fine, perhaps even something rare.

I was introduced to the couple who ran the mission as a friend, and as I walked into the main body of the church, I passed a room where I could see four or five people holding hands in prayer. This, I thought, was a good sign.

The atmosphere was peaceful and calming, another good sign, with soft music playing in the background. People began arriving and pretty soon the service began. The people I had seen standing in prayer when I had first come in, now filed into the room and stood on either side of the lectern. Each person stood behind a chair, and we were informed that if we wanted healing we should wait for an empty chair and then just go and sit in front of one of the healers.

So, I learned, they were healers, four of them, three women and a man somewhere in his early thirties. I watched eagerly, wondering about their methods, asking for Grey Eagle's opinion of each and also making my own assessments.

It became clear pretty quickly that the young man, the only one standing on the platform, was more involved with his performance, his act, than he was with his patient's needs. His hands and arms were everywhere. One minute he was doing an impression of a bird, then a butterfly, then a guru, hands together in supplication, bowing, stretching. On and on it went—his antics, his dramatic displays seeming endless—in his desire to be noticed.

In my intolerance I almost wanted to slap him, to sit him down and make him be still. The sad part, I felt, was that had he been more centered on his patient's needs, he could have channeled his energy in a more positive and constructive way, and then maybe he would have had more impact. But who was I to say?

I moved my attention away from him to each of the other healers, and I felt that in their much more humble and gentle way, each had a real talent, a real ability to give healing. I also felt that their intentions were only the best. I was delighted. Here was something good; here was something fine; here was something real.

My delight, however, was short-lived, my disappointment greater than it might have been had I not seen the real potential for a wonderful and productive place of healing.

After healing was given and a short sermon and a prayer, two of the healers, one at a time, began giving messages that they said were from the spirit world. This was their undoing. Going from person to person, many whom they knew, the weekly regulars, they said things like "They are telling me," "I feel," or "I sense that they want me to say." On and on it went, and I listened intently, hoping to hear evidence of some sort, hoping to hear something profound or inspiring, maybe a small but significant detail, something real. I was waiting for more, hoping that perhaps a real connection to the spirit world would actually be made. So far I hadn't seen one. When one of the women came to me with a message, I felt myself almost willing her to get something right, something real, just as everyone else there was. I wanted it to be real, I truly did, but it was not. It was terrible, just awful. It was imagination run amok. It was self-delusion and the worst display of how easily we can deceive ourselves.

I felt saddened, disheartened, disappointed, frustrated, and confused. I felt mean and intolerant, judgmental and harsh, and I didn't like myself for it. Back and forth, back and forth I went, telling myself that it didn't matter, that so much good was done in this place, so many people were helped through their healing prayers, through their kindness and good intentions. Then I would remember the harm I had seen done when people had been told things that were simply not true, had been guided on the wrong path by the overactive imagination of a would-be medium, influenced into doing things that would eventually lead to disillusionment and confusion, that would make their lives worse than they already were.

Back and forth I go, still pondering as to the greater good. Still, I am torn. Who am I to say? Who am I to judge, anyway? Since when did I become the all-knowing and all-seeing, the one who knows better than everyone else? So saying, it would be easy now for me to let it go, and I will—until the next time or until that next person comes along who has been the recipient of some well-meaning, kind, and generous yet totally delusional medium, who has put the person into turmoil, given messages meant to be comforting but that create a living hell.

Let me give you just a very few of the thousands of examples of such messages:

Message: "They tell me"—they, meaning the spirit world—"that your husband is having an affair and is probably going to leave you."

Result: The woman goes home, packs a bag, and leaves her husband of ten years. A week later, realizing that she has been stupid and gullible, she tells her husband she wants to come home. But all trust is broken. He was not having an affair and cannot forgive his wife for believing a stranger and for reacting the way she did. The marriage, which was a good one, is now over. She came to me for help, but the damage was done. That harmful little seed had taken root, and the cost was great.

Message: "They are telling me that you are going to start your own business and you will be successful."

Result: Believing every word, wanting to believe, he starts his own business, mortgages his house, certain of success. He goes bankrupt and loses everything.

Message: "There are spirits in your house trying to tell you something."

Result: She becomes frightened, can't sleep, is convinced that the house is haunted and eventually moves, leaving behind good neighbors and a house and location she once loved.

Message: "The person you have just met is no good for you."

Result: The end of a potentially good relationship.

Message: "You tell me you've lost your son, and I see him. He is standing in the middle of the desert, lost and alone, wandering around like a lost soul. I keep hearing him calling you, and he's crying because he can't find you."

Result: Devastation. Not only do this couple have to live with the heartbreak of losing their child, but now they are tormented by the image of their son wandering the universe, in some godforsaken place, lost, alone and crying out for help. And no matter how much I try to reassure them, when they come to see me several months later, that it is not so, that little seed has been set.

Message: "They are telling me—no, your mother is telling me she is very angry with you, but she doesn't say why."

Result: Confusion, hurt, despair, and helplessness.

Message: "They are telling me that you can be a medium, just like me."

Result: More of the same mediocre self-delusional, frustrated hopefuls.

Message: "I know you lost your daughter, and I see her. But she tells me she's busy and doesn't want to talk to you."

Result: The mother of this girl, desperately hoping that she would have been given some proof that her daughter had survived death, immediately realized the medium was a fake. Angry and bitter, she turned against the idea that anyone could communicate with the dead. All mediums were fakes, she believed, and we were just preying on vulnerable people like her. She became very vocal, fueled by her anger and disappointment, and when she faced me on a live morning TV show in England, I could see how that one bad experience had destroyed any glimmer of hope that she might see her daughter again one day. As if that was not bad enough, I saw the distress and sadness in the eyes of her child as she stood by her mother's side, listening to her almost screaming that there was no such thing as life after death.

As you read these examples, all of them true, you may well be asking, as I did, why didn't this mother try again, why give up so easily? The answer is simple. It hurts too much. It is too risky to hold on to hope; the disappointments are unbearable. And why, you might ask, was the woman in the first example so quick to leave her husband if the marriage was so good? Who knows? It was a ridiculous thing to do, as was the idea of risking your home, finances, livelihood, on the say-so of a psychic. We give advice, we give help, and we give comfort and hope and reasons that might help those who come to us to go on living. If we are truly in communication with the spirit world, that's what we do. What we don't do, what we cannot do, is to assume that we are all-knowing, all-seeing. I tell my clients not to hang on every word I say. I am fallible. I can get it wrong; make mistakes, just like everyone else. So here are a few examples of what I have said to those who have come to me, who want me to run their lives—as so many do, believe it or not, when they get it into their heads that I am more than I really am.

Client: My husband is dead and I have no reason to live anymore. I want to take my own life.

RA: (I see her husband, and have given her a great deal of evidence that he is truly here with us.) "Your husband wants me to tell you that none of us will die before our time, and that it is not your time to die just yet. I know that he wants you to get on with your life, to find a way to be happy, and to live your life to the fullest. He tells me that he will help you if you let him, and he wants you to start by taking his advice to seek help, see a therapist, visit your doctor, deal with your depression, and have healing on a regular basis."

Client: "You told me the last time I came that my father said I would have a chance to change my job. Well, the thing is, I've been offered two jobs. Which one does he say I should take?"

RA: "Although your father is there to help you, the last thing he wants is to live your life for you. This is a choice you must make for yourself, so do as your dad has advised. Weigh your options carefully and have faith in the fact that you can decide for yourself."

Client: "Will I marry this man I just met?"

RA: "I can't—won't—say, as ultimately the choice will be yours. My advice would be to give the relationship a chance. Don't judge him on your past experiences with men. Your mother"—again, we have already heard from her, and she has given very direct evidence of her survival after death—"tells me he is a good man, and she approves of him so far, but any long-term commitment has to be your decision."

Client: "I have three children. Will I have another?"

RA: "Not if you don't want to—it's up to you."

Client: "Will I have a baby?"

RA: "Your grandmother [after giving much evidence] is telling me that there is a child in the spirit world waiting to be born. This child is yours, part of your future, and is an inevitable part of your future plans. She also tells me that this is what you want, and you mustn't worry, everything will work out fine."

Client: "Will I be happy?"

RA: "Your mother [having eagerly and excitedly let her daughter know that she is really here] tells me you have a wonderful husband, two fine children and security, all the ingredients for a happy life, so yes, the potential is there, and there is no reason why you shouldn't be. But will you appreciate these things? Will you value what you have? Will you work to be content? Or will you want more? Will you find disappointment in the things you have? Will you harbor discontent? I am told by my guide [and at this point Grey Eagle is giving me this information] that you are often discontent for no good reason and can be very negative. It is this part of your nature that worries your mother. She is asking me to tell you that misery is optional, and the choice is yours. Happiness is often a choice we make, so what will your choice be? It's up to you!"

There are many times during a consultation when I know that "an inevitable," a situation that is unavoidable, is going to occur, when we don't have choices, except the choice of our attitude. As a responsible professional, I try to help people understand that each of us is responsible for our own attitude and that our attitude can help us overcome, or at least live with, even the worst of adversities.

Here are some of the rules I try to follow as a spiritual medium when I am imparting messages from the spirit world:

1. Never leave anyone without hope, and at the same time, never give false hope.

2. Never allow anyone to believe that they are powerless, and always try to make sure that they don't give their power away to anyone else. No one in their right mind wants the responsibility of running someone else's life.

3. Try to be as compassionate as you can. Remember, something that seems trivial to you can be huge to someone else.

4. Never be afraid to say: I don't know . . . I can't see anyone right now . . . I can't make any sense of what I am being told. I'm not infallible.

It is a wonderful thing to have people look up to you, to be in awe of the gift of mediumship, and for those who have that little knowledge, I can appreciate how easily we can convince ourselves that we know more than we actually do. I can appreciate how easily we can fall into the trap of self-delusion when people finally notice us, when we become of some value, when we become needed. I am one of the fortunate ones. I have had friends around me who help me keep my feet on the ground. I have a healthy skepticism, and I know in my heart when I speak some untruth. I have a conscience, which I am forced to listen to. I am a spiritual medium and a healer who has been blessed with an incredible gift, and through this gift, and with Grey Eagle's help, I have learned not to be afraid to say I don't know—in those moments when I cannot hear, or see, or sense as well as I would like; in those moments when I fail to connect as clearly as I would like; in those moments when to impart certain information would be to overstep my bounds, to make someone else feel powerless, or to do some small harm.

My Brother

As we have seen, a little knowledge can be a dangerous thing, and we all know it. However, when that small amount of knowledge is used with integrity, there can be very different results, as you will see.

Those of you who have read my first book will be familiar with Mick McGuire, a wonderful healer, and the first person to give me a message from my father, all those years ago when I was so uncertain about so many things, particularly about my gift and whether I should use it.

"I see a man, Rosemary, standing to the side of your chair. He is about five feet, six inches tall and is wearing a khaki uniform, a cap, and sergeant major's stripes. I can see him and hear his voice very clearly, and he tells me his name is William Edward, and that he is your father."

I will never forget this message for as long as I live or the impact it had on me. As I write, I am transported back to that time, almost feeling again the prickling heat on the back of my neck as I listen to this stranger describe my father. A sergeant, a professional soldier all his life, he would stand so straight, so tall and proud, that you would barely notice his height, for he was powerful, and his energy gave the impression that he was much taller than his five feet, six inches. His name was not William Edward but William Edwards.

I was immediately entranced, and who would not be, with such a startlingly precise and accurate message. It would have been so easy for me at this time to have hung on every word, be swayed by every piece of advice, give up my own power to Mick, as there was no doubt in my mind that he was speaking directly with my dad. This man had a gift. This man had a connection to the spirit world. This man had an ability to change people's lives. And this man had the ability to change my life . . . and fortunately for me, this man had integrity.

"I am not a medium," he argued, over my protests that he was amazing. "What little gift I have, what little you have just heard, it comes and goes. It is not consistent. I am not consistent. Sometimes I hear and connect with the spirit world with the most remarkable clarity, but those times are few and far between. Trust me on this," he continued, "I know that my true gift, my real calling, lies not in mediumship but as a healer. This is who I am, and healing is what I do."

Never did Mick allow me or anyone else to believe anything other than this, and in those moments when his clairvoyant abilities were clear, he would always make sure we knew that he was often confused by his messages and that we should not necessarily take his words too literally. He would always remind us that his "sight" was limited. Knowing this, those of us who were privileged enough, as I was, to be involved with him in his healing work, would listen respectfully to his messages, and then weigh them carefully before we allowed ourselves to be too influenced. Here is a story which shows just what I mean.

It was a Wednesday night, and I was at that stage in my life when I had finally come to accept my gift and to use it. Wednesday nights were my nights, when Mick; Paul, another healer; Adele, a friend who has since passed with cancer; and Brian, my self-appointed philosopher and friend, would sit with me to help me develop my gift. These were the times when we would ask the spirit world for their help and guidance, for their wisdom and their input. These were those sacred nights which lent courage, inspiration, and strength to my already remarkable abilities. I needed Wednesday nights and I needed my friends.

It was almost toward the end of the evening when Mick spoke up, telling us that my father was present in the room and that he had an important message for me.

"Do you know who Richard is?" Mick asked. "Your father is talking about Richard."

Well, I didn't know anyone by that name, but I knew enough to pay attention to Mick.

"Richard," said Mick again. "Your father is talking to me about Richard, and I feel from what he says that you really should know who this is, Rosemary, and your father tells me that his message to you tonight is very important."

"Well, could you ask him to give us the message anyway, even if I am confused, and we'll find out who Richard is later?" As I said this, I knew that what Mick had to say might come out in a jumble, that it might puzzle and confuse me, and that Mick would be the first to say he had no idea what he was talking about. But I had had enough real evidence of Mick's ability that I knew I would be foolish not to pay attention.

Mick: "The knives are out. Daggers—or is it, yes, swords are being drawn."

RA: "Mick, does my father say who or what he's talking about?"

Mick: "Daphne and Theresa, and . . . yes, Richard, he is giving me the name of Richard again."

RA: "Well, Daphne and Theresa are my nieces, my brother's children, but I don't know any Richard."

Mick: "Wait, wait, your father is repeating those names again. He says that everything is coming out into the open. He says he has drawn his sword and is on the battlefield. Richard, he mentions Richard again . . . and"—pausing slightly—"and Rosemary, I'm seeing bars,

bars at a window . . . no . . . wait . . . a prison cell. I hear your father say, don't worry about anything, Richard is going to prison and the girls will be safe."

I was confused. Mick was confused. Nothing of what he said made any sense, except, yes, those were the names of my nieces. But I hadn't seen or heard from them in years—in fact, since Theresa was five years old and her mother ran off with the delivery man, taking the four children, two boys and two girls, with her. It had been a terrible situation, and my brother had tried to get custody of his kids. When that failed, he had left the country, going to Rhodesia, now Zimbabwe, to work as a manager in the tin mines. I had not seen or heard from his ex-wife or the children since then.

How old would they be now? I wondered, as I thought about my father's confusing message. Daphne would be nineteen, and Theresa would be thirteen. Were they all right? Should I call? What, if anything, should I do?

Mick was as much in the dark as I was. We both knew better than to dismiss the message as coming from Mick's imagination. He knew the difference, had learned to tell the difference over the years, and he knew this was the real thing. But what should we do with this information now? I could do only one thing. *Stay calm, put it to one side, at least for now, and whatever you do,* I thought, *do not go galloping off to the family with it . . . it would only scare them . . . and wait and see.*

I knew my father well enough to know that whatever he was trying to tell me, I was not to worry. If he said it would be OK, then it would be. I did, however, call my mother the next day on the pretext of "just a chat," and partway through the conversation, I managed to ask casually if she had heard from or seen anything of my brother's ex or from her grandchildren. This brought a negative "Oh, I haven't heard from them in over a year" from my mother.

Meanwhile, in another part of the country, a real, live drama was being played out, beginning at almost the precise moment of my fa ther's message to me. This drama was to rock my family and to cause us all to make a decision I will wonder about forever, as the consequences of that decision would have a lasting effect on my brother's children.

Theresa was thirteen years old, and many who knew her thought her a brat, a troublemaker at school, known for making things up, telling lies, basically doing anything she could for attention. So when she confided to her boyfriend, who told his mother, who then went to the school board and to the police with Theresa's secret—that her stepfather had been molesting her since she was five—no one believed her. The police, of course, investigated, relying heavily on the reports from Theresa's teachers. Her mother and stepfather were furious. How dare she suggest such a thing?

Over the course of the next few weeks, all hell broke loose. Even though the investigation was supposed to be low-key, everyone at Theresa's school, the entire neighborhood, seemed to know. The result of that investigation, not to anyone's surprise, was that young Theresa was at it again. She was labeled by many in her family as a little troublemaker, who would do anything to get attention.

After several weeks, finally everything had quieted down. Theresa was grounded indefinitely. Her boyfriend broke up with her, her teachers barely spoke to her, and Theresa's mother and stepfather treated her like a leper.

Half-term came around, and Daphne, the oldest daughter, was home for a week from university. She had barely walked into the house when her mother began the tale of Theresa's lying and deceitfulness, the tale of how she had tried to wreck the family. Daphne said nothing, just sat and listened as her mother went on and on about her lying younger sister.

The next morning Daphne found Theresa in her bedroom, crying, sobbing, feeling terribly alone and desperate because no one had believed her story. Daphne was silent, saying only that Theresa was to get dressed. They were going out.

At the police station Daphne told her own terrible story, as her sister looked on in amazement.

"He's been molesting me since I was eleven, since he moved into the house, right up to the time I left for university, until I was eighteen years old. He swore he would do something awful to us all if I told." Then, turning to Theresa, she broke down. "I swear I didn't know he was doing it to you," she sobbed, "I swear I would have done something, stopped him somehow if I'd known."

When my mother called to tell me the story a couple of weeks later, I told her about the message from my dad. "Who's Richard?" I asked. "What does someone by the name of Richard have to do with this?"

Of course, by now you won't be at all surprised to learn that Richard was Theresa and Daphne's stepfather.

Did he go to prison as my father had predicted he would? Oh yes he did, just as my father had said, and for a good long stretch, although in my view not long enough.

The decision we all made as a family—me, my mother, my other brother and sisters—was to not tell my nieces' father. I weighed this decision carefully. What right did we have to keep this from my brother? What right had we to decide that he should not know? The consequence of this decision is that my brother's children believe that their father doesn't care, that he was not there for them in this terrible time of crisis. The consequence is that they have never forgiven him his absence.

But we who made that decision, even though we are by no means close, even though we were highly dysfunctional, we knew that had we told my brother, he would surely have returned home and committed murder. We who knew him well, who knew what passion he is capable of, we knew that he would not rest until Richard was dead. We were in no doubt that he would have avenged his children.

Sometimes, used in the right way, responsibly and with great care, a little knowledge works. That little knowledge, that confused and mystifying message from my father, through Mick McGuire, helped me understand that those in the spirit world cannot always stop bad things from happening and that the bad stuff is equally as important to our growth as the good stuff. Even though they cannot always save us from the bad things in life, at least they are there, watching, guiding, and protecting us the best they can.

And so, what of my brother's children? What if anything should I do for them? I've decided to send them this account as soon as I am able, and I hope they will read it and understand things better, and understand their father better.

My brother's life was terrible and sad. He had learned anger and hopelessness from an early age. He had fought bitter battles with my father, with my other brother, and the worst battles he had fought were with my mother. She taught him that he was worthless, that he was nothing. When he cried, he was not a man, she would say. When he learned not to cry, he was cruel and heartless. But the truth is, Terry has a heart as big as a house. He has always been a sensitive and caring man, filled with love but confused, never knowing how to deal with his emotions. He had no idea how to show his feelings in ways that were acceptable or understood by others. He is soft, gentle, and kind but capable of raging and fighting out of control, just as he had been taught. No matter what he did, no matter how he tried to communicate, it always came out wrong for him. He ran away from his home, from his country, and from his kids because he thought he had no choice. He thought that his children truly would be so much better off without him. He had never known self-worth and had come to believe that all he could bring to anyone in his life was trouble, that he would be nothing but trouble to his children. To leave them, to go away from them, he believed, was one of his finer acts, an unselfish although misguided act of love, and he greatly suffered their loss.

Deserting his old life, deserting his family, his children, having no skills with which to reason, not knowing how to compromise, he headed down a black hole. A journey that was to last him the rest of his life.

He was nearing seventy when he finally came home to England with very little money, no property, and only a few skimpy belongings. And AIDS . . . Yes, he had AIDS. And he also had cancer.

At the time of writing it will be two years since he passed. His birthday has just gone, and as I think of him, I realize that, like many of us, he was given from birth bad direction, bad example, and he lived in confusion for most of his life. But he was my brother. He was full of love and had no idea how to express his feelings. He loved his children enough to give them up, to give them what he believed was something better in life. I hope and pray that one day they will know it. I hope one day that someone, maybe it will be me, will tell them about his generosity, about his confusions, and above all about his many kindnesses and his passion for life.

And perhaps, thanks to that little bit of knowledge that my friend Mick imparted to me so long ago, maybe my nephews and nieces will come to understand that, in their time of need, their grandfather is watching and doing his best to protect them . . . and that now their father is doing the same.

"Forgive me my stupidity, my ignorance," my brother asks me to say to them, as I write. "And Rosemary?"

"Yes?" I whisper, as I see him standing in front of me for the first time since he passed and I see my tears mirrored in his eyes.

"Please tell them that I love them, and will never leave them again."

PART II

A MATTER OF LIFE
AND DEATH

Curiosity Can Kill the Cat

When I was a young woman, in my teens, I was very curious and full of questions, all kinds of questions about a whole variety of subjects. Luckily, in my school there were two or three teachers who encouraged questions and pushed us to think outside the box. One was my drama teacher, one my English/history teacher, and one my theology teacher. They were different from my parents, who never allowed me to ask questions about anything at home, firmly believing that children should be seen and not heard. Sometimes I went overboard with my teachers, and they would have to cut my hundred questions down to four or five in any given class. I was also lucky to have, in my church, a wonderful group of elders who organized extra classes and debate groups, where my natural curiosity was allowed to flourish.

It is a fact, and I have often said it, that it is my natural curiosity which makes me such a good spirit communicator, for as soon as I make a connection with the spirit world, my mind starts to race, and a dozen questions can spill out of my mouth in a heartbeat. Who are you? Where are you? What do you want? Whom do you want to speak to? What is it like there? How did you pass? Through the years, as I've matured, I have learned that there is a time and a place for such questions but there is also a time to be quiet.

I was infatuated with Elwyn, a much older boy who also belonged to my church. But he had a girlfriend, and there was no hope for me. Still, I would walk the streets, singing mournful love songs and ask the many questions I could not resist asking, out loud, to God, to the universe, and to anyone else out there who might be listening. Important questions, I had thought at the time, questions which were, to me, a matter of life and death. Questions like . . . Will I get married one day? Do I already know the man of my dreams? Will I have babies?

My favorite song by Doris Day was "Que Será, Será," whatever will be, will be. I liked the part about whether he'd be handsome, or rich . . . and there were those questions again . . . Will he be? Will I be? Will you be? On and on, a thousand questions and more. Rarely content with the answers I got, I always wanted more. There was always just one more question, my mind ever filled with curiosity, never quiet.

The older I got, the more I allowed my curiosity to spill over. Each question, each answer, would create two more questions. I wanted to know. I simply wanted to know. I wanted to know everything.

In my younger days, Christ was the one I pounded on the most. I trusted that He heard me when I called out to Him. I trusted that He loved me, and I trusted that He would answer me, guide me in all things, which He did and still does. Then came Grey Eagle, and along with him came more questions than I can count, as I'm sure you can imagine. Looking back, I am ashamed at my thoughtlessness, my constant need for information and for assurances in all areas of my life. I'm sorry for my presumption that those in the spirit world had the time, the inclination, and the energy with which to deal with my needy, selfish, and demanding ways. Although it was not a conscious thought, I assumed they had nothing better to do. The worst of it was that even when my questions were answered, I would then question myself about the way I had questioned. If I had phrased the question another way, would the answer have been different? Finally, after one such session with Grey Eagle, when my questions were endless and repetitive to the point of being ridiculous, my guide held his hand up to his ear and, with great patience and love, said kindly, "Rosemary, my little flower, your constant questioning is making my ear bleed."

I looked with horror, and sure enough I saw a small trickle of blood running from Grey Eagle's ear down the side of his face. It was then, at long last, that I got it.

Our loved ones in the spirit world guide us. They steer us, and they protect us as best they can from others and from ourselves. Those of us who listen, who listen to our instincts, to our intuitive inner voice, know this only too well. They want us to talk to them; they are happy that we question; they are thrilled that we make them part of our every-day life. But part of that guidance, part of their teaching, is about their helping us understand which questions are appropriate and which are not. I knew a lady once who was convinced that her angels were with her twenty-four hours a day. Her faith was strong, and her belief was a wonderful, inspiring thing to see. However, as I came to know her better, I wondered if her behavior might perhaps be just a little too extreme.

Before she left the house, first she would ask her angels which door she should use, front or back. Before eating or drinking anything, she would ask her angels for their blessing and to tell her if she was doing anything wrong. If she was closest to the back door, and her angels told her to use the front door, that's what she did. If her angels told her not to eat this or drink that, then she would not. One day she called me to let me know she was selling or giving away all the rugs in her house. "The angels have told me I must," was her explanation.

It was the same with everything she did. She would check with her angels—before picking up the phone, before going to the cinema, to a play, out to dinner, to visit a friend, in all things, in every aspect of her life.

I quickly realized that she had become fully dependent on the spirit world for everything. She had allowed her great faith to consume her, to control her life beyond that which is reasonable. We might call this blind faith, but I saw it as blinding faith, blinding to the extent that she really could not see anything as it really was. She had given away her power and had become powerless to act, to take any action or make any decision for herself.

I asked myself, as I asked her, "Do you really think this is what God wants for us? Do you really think that your angels do not want you to have a mind of your own, to be unable to make even the smallest decision for yourself? Do you really think that your angels have nothing better to do than concentrate their time on your every thought and action, even to the point of determining the time you go to bed and the time you get up? Is this reasonable?"

Her answer was that her angels were with her all the time and that she trusted them completely. I couldn't argue with that, as I too believe our angels, our loved ones in the spirit world, and our guides and teachers are often present in our lives. Just not at our beck and call twenty-four hours a day. Was she really hearing her angels, or was it her imagination, her neediness, that had created this situation? Who was I to say? But experience tells me that it was the latter.

Guilty myself of abusing the connection I have with the spirit world, I can see how easy it is for others to assume not only that the spirit world has all the answers but that they are beside us 24/7, waiting for those moments when we need them. Believing this makes us feel better. It makes us feel safe, and it gives us a certain kind of security. But in making these assumptions, we are also assuming that they have no life of their own, nothing better to do than baby us, that they are just as needy for us as we are for them. And worse, that they only have a life, a purpose, an existence through us, which of course is just not true. Through the years I have learned to be more respectful. I ask questions only when I have a real need. I try not to buy into my own neediness, and in those times when I lose a patient or friend, I try to let go. I try not to look for them or to call out their name. I try to remember that if they need me, or if they simply want to visit, they know where to find me, and I make sure that my door is always open.

I remember the younger of my two brothers, Malcolm, once telling me how guilty he felt about not visiting our mother more often. "I have really good intentions," he said, "and I often go, planning to spend an hour or so. But within five minutes of stepping through the door, I've had enough. Her constant questions, complaints, her neediness, I can't stand it. It drives me away. I find myself making excuses about how I can't stay, and then I bolt."

I think that most of us can relate to that, as we've all had those times when we feel that someone is just sucking the life out of us, and we have all had those times when we just can't wait to leave or when we just can't wait for our visitors to go.

I never want to be that person who is so insensitive to others' feelings that they just can't wait for me to go. I never want to be that person who causes people to groan when they see me coming. But I know there have been times when I have been that person. I have often been inconsiderate in my demands of my spirit guide and of others too; now I am more careful. I want the spirit world to welcome me, to be excited when they see me coming, when I call on them for something. I want them to respect me, and I want them to want me around. I never want to wear out my welcome, and I understand that if I am continually looking for someone else to solve my problems, then I will never learn strength and I will never learn true communication.

I would like to say that I will never allow my curiosity to make Grey Eagle's ear bleed again, but I am human and needy, and at those times when I have new people around me and my curiosity about them gets the better of me, I find myself slipping into my old ways, asking often unnecessary and trivial questions of the spirit world. Then I remember and I stop, at least most of the time.

But curiosity, as we well know, is a necessary ingredient for anyone who wants to learn anything. As a teacher, I need my students to be ready to question me, themselves, and the things they are learning about.

When I first came to America, I had no inclination to continue my teaching work. I felt dried up and exhausted from the effort teaching takes. Having to be available for classes, giving up at least two nights a week solely for that purpose, and having to make the effort not only to discipline myself but my students as well, had taken its toll on my life. It was too much, and after more than twenty years, I decided that I had had enough. It was time for me to retire from that area of my work.

"No way, no way," I would say when asked to take on a student. "Sorry, but I don't do that anymore."

Over the next three years I was asked, more times than I can count, if I would begin healing classes, and I would always refuse. I had made my decision and was happy about it. But even as I write, I can imagine the smile on the faces of some of you as you read because you know, as I do, that we are not the ones who decide these things. If the spirit world has other plans, then sooner or later, no matter how much you may struggle against the idea, they will get you.

It was at a lecture I was giving at the Arts Center in Manchester, Vermont, that I heard myself saying, after someone in the audience had asked if I took classes, "I'm thinking that I might begin teaching again, so if anyone wants to know more, after the lecture is over, give your name and number to my secretary . . ." and I realized, horrified, that I had been well and truly GOT!

Despite my initial reluctance, my journey as a healer—or should I more accurately say, my continued journey—has been remarkable. I have met many wonderful people, both students and patients, and have developed some great friendships. However, my methods of training are very different here in the United States. Since the foundation for our healing organization had already been laid in England, the type of intense training that the British healers had to endure was unnecessary.

The language barrier and the differences between the American and

British cultures also influenced my methods. It is often said that we are two countries divided by a common language, and it's true. You might be surprised at the misunderstandings that occur simply because I know I have said one thing and my students have understood me to mean something entirely different. This has been hard for me because I have always been a really good communicator and can explain myself, at least most of the time anyway, clearly and precisely, especially in the classroom, leaving no doubt in the minds of my students as to what it is I require of them. No matter how hard I tried, I could not seem to avoid those moments of confusion, as I would look around the room and await the responses I was hoping for, and just not getting. Finally, I realized that it was up to me to change. I was in another country and should not expect that everyone could understand me. One of the biggest mysteries I have faced over the years is the one where immigrants come into a foreign country and refuse to change the way they live or to adapt to the ways of the country they have chosen to live in. Whatever happened to the old saying "When in Rome, do as the Romans do"?

So, having chosen this new life, this new culture, I realized that it was up to me to change, to learn a new language, so that I could be heard. It was a bit like trying to teach an old dog new tricks, and I have still not entirely mastered the art of communicating in the American way. When I make blunders, they can sometimes be big ones. But on the whole, I think I am doing better, although I still confuse my team at times . . . but now they realize why.

As a result of my new training methods, I have a group of very special and dedicated students who get together at a local meeting place every Wednesday evening and offer their services as healers to anyone who wants them, giving their time freely and without charge, knowing that it is payment enough to be a part of something as special as healing is.

I can't pretend that I'm not exhausted by the process sometimes, and I can't pretend that I don't get frustrated and even angry sometimes at the fact that I have been asked to do what often seems an impossible task. But then I remember the tremendous bonuses that I am continually given, and I relent and am grateful that I have been chosen to be a part of a much greater miracle than most of us can even imagine exists.

As I have learned over the years, all of our experiences, the choices we make, well, everything, is a matter of life and death. Everything comes down to the way we live our lives, and what happens to us when we die. These next stories will illustrate exactly what I mean by this.

Cathy

Unlike many situations, where events occur suddenly and without warning, this is a story which tells of a family who were in turmoil for a long time. It tells of a husband who had a lot of time to come to terms with the possibility of losing his wife, but, as many of us would, remained in denial for as long as he could.

The phone call, like many I receive, was a sad one. A young woman in her thirties with terminal cancer, who had been fighting her battle for some time, was in hospital, and had taken a turn for the worse. The news was bad. Her body was no longer responding to treatment and was breaking down. Would I please come?

I had not known of Cathy before this phone call, even though, as I later discovered, she and her family lived only a fifteen-minute drive from my home. But they had heard of me and now were asking for my help.

"Which hospital is she in?" I asked.

"Burlington," the voice on the other end of the phone replied.

Having only heard of Burlington but never having been there, I

65

asked, "How long do you think it will take me to get there?" I was told, "Approximately two hours."

"OK, I'll be there as soon as I can."

A healer is never alone, and will always work as part of a team, both with those in the spirit world and, if he or she is lucky enough, with friends and helpers here on this earth plane.

I called Nancy and quickly explained the situation. "I need you to come with me if you can, as I've no idea how to get to Burlington hospital." I was asking my friend to drop everything, even knowing how busy she was, and to help me. Without hesitation, she agreed, and less than an hour later we were on our way.

This was Nancy's first time with me in such a situation. She was a new student, not yet having begun regular training, since at this point I had not begun to teach here in America. My students were all in England, as were most of my patients. Little did I know that all this was about to change. But I digress, so back to my story.

"What should I do? What should I say? How would you like me to handle myself?" These questions and what seemed to me hundreds more were asked by Nancy on that first two-hour ride to Burlington. She was nervous, excited, apprehensive, and desperately keen to do the right thing. I smiled, knowing that her fears stemmed from a tremendous generosity of spirit. Perhaps here was a healer in the making, but only time would tell.

I drove, Nancy directed, and on the way I tried to reassure her and explained that she should do nothing at this time but observe me closely, listen carefully, try to be keenly aware of my actions with my new patient and her family, and perhaps pray a little, or indeed, a lot, for as I have said so many times, the best way to teach is by example.

As we walked into Cathy's room, she and her husband had been expecting us. Both were nervous, not really knowing what to expect. Both were hopeful, and both were hoping for a miracle.

Newly married, a little over a year, Cathy had two sons from a previous marriage, and Dan had full custody of his children, a boy and a girl. Four young children, two people in love, and everything to live for. Then Cathy became sick.

We introduced ourselves, then Nancy went quietly to the chair in the corner of the room, and I perched myself on the bed, clasping Cathy's hands as I did so. And I began to talk and to ask questions, trying the best I could to put these people at their ease. At the same time, I wanted to help them understand the process of healing (something I feel I need not go into here, as I have written so much about it in my other books).

Grey Eagle was with me, close by my side, and over the next hour, as we talked, something became very clear to me. Yes, both Cathy and Dan were hoping for a miracle, but while Dan's idea of a miracle was for his wife to suddenly rise from her sickbed and become whole again, Cathy needed something different. She needed confirmation of her own belief in a life after death. That she would have a place to go, to be with God, and that she would be able, still, to care for and protect her husband and their children. Cathy knew that her cancer was incurable, and had already accepted that she was going to die. Her husband, on the other hand, had not. She was looking to me to help. For both of them, this was truly a situation where life and death lay in the balance . . . where their future was most obviously a matter of life and death.

It is strange, with all our knowledge of science and technology, our greater understanding of things, that we human beings, especially those of us in the Western world, have such little understanding of death and even look on it as a kind of failure. We should have done more. We could have done differently. We ought to have, might have, or perhaps could have prevented it. These are the feelings most of us have when someone we love either dies or is in the process of dying. And our feelings of guilt can often be overwhelming.

Death is something that happens to us all. Death is something that was happening to Cathy, and to her husband and children, to her family and friends, to all those who loved her. And even though many of

Cathy and Dan's family had gone through the process before, still they were lost, living a nightmare that couldn't possibly be true. After all, she was so young, so young, and too young to die.

For more than two weeks I visited, going each day, spending as much time as I could, with Nancy, a true friend, a part of my team, keeping me company on the ride there and back, fetching drinks, chatting with the family, showing support to all of us in every way she could.

For two weeks we spent time with Cathy and Dan and their wonderful family, who embraced us and helped us with our work. Each day was a different day, which brought with it many different experiences. Some days Cathy was fully awake and able to participate in everything around her. Family and friends visited almost constantly, and her room was never empty. There was always some loving soul watching over her.

Nancy and I were very quickly embraced by everyone, and I found myself in that rare position of intimacy with strangers. When I say rare, I mean rare for others, but because of who I am and what I do, not rare for me. Nevertheless, I was in a position of privilege.

Cathy and I had many long conversations, mostly about our belief in the afterlife, and we found ourselves on the same wavelength. She had so many questions. I had some answers. She trusted and so did I. It was like being on a train, journeying with a good friend, talking, listening, marveling at the scenes we saw through the window as they flashed by, not wanting the journey to end, but making the most of each moment, for we both knew it would.

All this time, Cathy's husband only wanted to listen, not to participate, for he was fighting to stay off the train, not wanting the journey, not for himself or his wife, and then, finally stepping onto the train, he began journeying with us.

Acceptance is a hard thing, especially when acceptance means loss, but as George Eliot once wrote, "It makes the mind very free, when we give up wishing, and only think of bearing what is laid upon us, and doing what is given us to do."

Finally Dan had joined the train, along with his family and friends. Finally he had moved forward, and Cathy, no longer concerned that he would manage without her, seeing him grow stronger, was able to let go and move on. It was almost time!

For two weeks I watched as Cathy's body became weaker, and her will to stay became less. For two weeks I watched as her spirit became stronger, and her will to move forward became more.

I knew she was making ready to fly.

It was during those two weeks that a strange thing happened. I don't know quite how to tell this story without making myself sound either totally crazy, or as if I believe that I'm the second coming. Each time I have recounted this experience, perhaps only twice before, to my students, both in the United States and in England, I became embarrassed at my seeming audacity. I can only tell you that I was empowered and humbled, both at the same time.

Cathy was sleeping, slipping more and more into a state of unconsciousness, moving steadily away from our earth world. It was a day that Dan, Nancy, Elizabeth Fisher, Cathy's minister, and I were chatting quietly in Cathy's room, when without warning, terrible screams filled the air. Startled, we looked at one another, and I began to rise from my seat to investigate. Before I could move further, however, Elizabeth, closer to the door, said, "Maybe I should go and see what's wrong." We all nodded, as the screams and shouts filled the room and corridors of the usually quiet hospital, and the sound was awful, making the hairs on the back of my neck stand on end.

Tentatively Elizabeth opened the door, but whatever it was she saw, it was obviously too much for the minister to take in, and she quickly closed the door shut and sat back down, her eyes wide and fearful. By this time I was on my feet. I had heard pain, piercing, terrified pain, and it struck at my heart.

"Maybe I should go," I said, knowing I would, but sensitive to Elizabeth's feelings and not wanting to tread on her toes. She, however, relieved not to have to deal with a situation obviously unfamiliar to her, nodded with relief, and so I crossed the room and went out into the corridor.

Quickly I took in the scene. There were two young women, holding onto each other tightly in a desperate embrace. One was screaming and screaming and screaming. Her screams ripped right through me, yet as I stood there, I became strangely still and unmoved. A calm had come over me, an unusual quiet had stilled my emotions, and I remained only purposeful. Standing apart as I did, time slowed, I slowed, and it was as if the world had stopped its turning. But all of my senses were acutely in tune, and I could see and hear everything, as if my brain had taken on a more intense awareness, and I could hear the very air around me breathing.

Slowly, and it seemed to me, without any effort, I turned my head, taking in everything around me. I noticed an older couple standing at the end of the corridor, gazing out the window, not moving, and there was a quietness about them, although their silent pain had found a voice in my head. They stood with their backs to the scene, seeming to ignore the screams, as if they were separate from the two young women. Yet I knew they were all related.

I stood, a stranger in their midst, and strangely grown, feeling as if I were ten feel tall, a giant, and with a power in me that was pulsing and propelling me forward. This driving force, indescribable but yet natural to me, it seemed, was a great and commanding power that I knew I had to own and to use. I felt not as if I were someone else, just a thousand times more of who I really was.

Without thought, I lifted my arms out to the girl, who was no more than thirty years old perhaps. "Come to me," I said firmly, in a voice that was meant to be obeyed. "Come here to me."

For a moment, just a fraction of a second, they were all startled, all quiet, all turning to stare at me, a total stranger to them. I stood, now feeling much more than ten feet tall, and it seemed to me that the power of God was raising me to incredible heights.

"Come to me," I repeated firmly, my arms held out toward the young woman who had been screaming so, and like a lamb, she came, and I held her in my arms and comforted her.

As she clung to me, her wailing increased in volume and intensity, if that was possible. I stroked her hair and for a moment made calming, shushing noises. Then, gently but very firmly, first I whispered into her ear, "Be quiet now, be quiet. You have to stop this noise. He can hear you, and he needs you to be strong for him. Be quiet now, be quiet. You have to think of him." Over and over I said this, and more besides, knowing through the power that God had given me that this young woman's husband, terribly ill and fighting for his life, lay only feet away from us, in the room opposite Cathy's. I had a knowing, an understanding of the situation, without any words from Grey Eagle, and I accepted that knowing, simply knowing that it was so.

All the while stroking her hair, I explained to the girl that her husband needed her to put her own fears and pain to one side, that she must muster all the strength she had, and that she must be strong for him. A totally selfless act.

"You can do it," I said finally, "I know you can," and I held her still, as she became quiet. The power I felt in me had in some way transferred to her and to her friend. I felt it. They felt it. Finally the young woman dried her eyes, blew her nose, and with a little lift of her shoulders and a small weak smile for me, she quietly headed back to sit by her husband's side and to hold his hand.

I too headed back to my patient. As I walked into the room where Cathy lay, a calm and a peace washed over me as I looked toward her. It would not be long now, I knew, for even though I couldn't yet see them, I had the sense of angels present, waiting, I was aware, for the right time . . . Cathy's time.

My work here was nearly done, I knew, and as I spoke my silent good-bye to Cathy, I heard the heartbeat of her soul, loud and clear in response, and I knew she would be fine. But before I said my good-byes to the family, before I left the hospital for the last time, I had one more thing to do.

His room was directly opposite Cathy's, across the hall, and as I made my way toward his bed, I felt Grey Eagle draw close to my side.

He was alone, his family gone, perhaps to the cafeteria for a break. Pale and extremely sick, he lay still in the bed, but he was conscious and looked directly into my eyes as I took his hand in mine, his eyes terrified and confused.

I smiled down at him and squeezed his hand tightly.

"You don't know me," I said, "but I have been sent here by your angels to give you a message, and it's really important that you listen to me now."

A small and almost imperceptible nod of his head told me he could hear what I was saying and that he understood.

"Fight! You have to fight this thing, this sickness that you have." Quietly but firmly I went on, "You are not going to die, not yet, for it is not your time. And you must fight to help your angels as they protect you now."

His eyes were wide but no longer fearful. I felt a small pressure as he squeezed my hand.

"And now sleep," I said, "a peaceful sleep," and gratefully, he did.

One died that night and was taken by her angels to a place of light, where her soul was set free, where there was no more pain and only love. One other, the stranger, to whom I was a stranger, began his road to recovery, his soul made stronger by his ordeal and by the light of his angels who had that day entered his heart and given him courage.

And I was truly blessed.

Picking Up the Phone

There are many ways to connect with our loved ones who have passed, and of course, our first choice would be to be able to do it for ourselves. To see and to hear our loved ones who have passed, in a clear way, unhindered by our belief that we can't do it, that it is simply our imagination, our wishful thinking, not confused by muddled sound waves, telepathic static so to speak—this is how most of us would choose to connect if we had our way. But as we know, that is rarely possible. Our second choice would be to have a one-on-one communication with a medium. However, trying to get in to see one, a good one that is, can be almost impossible, since the waiting lists can prove to be so long that our patience can run out. One way, often equally positive, can be a consultation over the phone, and this is how many mediums are working these days. It means that no one has to travel those great distances anymore.

I first began taking consultations over the phone more than twenty years ago, when my reputation had begun to spread far from my own country. Amazingly, it was way before I had published my first book, and the fact that people had begun to come to me from all over the world, spoke volumes for the power of word of mouth.

In this chapter, I would like to give a couple of examples of how speaking to people over the phone works, and you will see that the spirit world has no trouble at all with this concept. In fact, the only one who might be confused from time to time is me.

I am going to begin by describing my telephone consultation with Mary Jane K. The experience was so positive that it was one of those times when I bless the technology I so often complain about, as we all do, when the telephone rings nonstop and we just don't have time to answer it.

In all of my telephone consultations, I start the same way, asking, "Who do you want to connect to in the spirit world?" and "What are the issues in your life you would like help and guidance with?" Of course, those issues are always matters of life and death, matters which might concern our loved ones still on earth, whose lives are so important to us, their happiness so tied in with our own. Or we may want to know what has become of our loved ones who have died, often leaving us bereft, heartbroken. With Mary Jane K it was just the same, and I was careful to remind her that there are no guarantees, of course, that we would be able to do what she asked.

"My mom and dad and my son," she replied simply, when I asked my first question.

"And what are the issues in your life that you would like help and guidance with today?"

1. Are they at peace?
2. Can he (referring to her son) see his sister's wedding?
3. Can they tell us how we should handle our grief?
4. What is my son's legacy that he left us?
5. My son, can you tell me how he died?

I saw Andrew straightaway, standing in front of me in my upstairs living room. It was a clear communication, and I listened as he told me how he had been bipolar, how he could be either very up or very down, that he had been like that for most of his life, and that he had been very depressed at the time of his passing.

"But that wasn't it," he said, as I listened closely, trying my best to help him as he gave this very important piece of information. "You see, it seemed as if I took my own life, and I suppose in a way I did. But it was so much more than that, you see. I heard my name being called by my angels and by God, and as I listened, I felt them reaching out to me, and I knew that it was my time to go, that I was being called home. I want you to explain to my mom that I didn't kill myself, that I was gone from the earth, even before my physical body took its last breath."

Now, this was by no means the first time I had heard such a thing, but I knew that Andrew's mother might find it a little hard to understand. However, as I explained her son's message, Mary Jane immediately understood not only that Andrew had answered her most important question but also that he was giving her his evidence of survival in a way that was so overwhelmingly comforting.

"He didn't take his own life," she sobbed, a statement, not a question. "It was not his choice, but God's choice, that's what he's telling me, isn't it, Rosemary? He didn't want to leave us!" And I smiled at the boy and he smiled back, as we felt the guilt and the hopelessness in his mother begin to fade away.

Now that the hard part was over and Andrew was feeling more confident, more certain of himself, without pause he went right into the subject of his sister's wedding, laughing as he told his Mom that he knew about the panic with the dress.

"It doesn't fit," he chuckled, "and there's less than two weeks to go to the wedding day." Mary Jane began laughing, exclaiming in delight that, yes, her son was right and that she was going to the dressmaker with her daughter for a fitting that very afternoon.

Moving on, knowing that he had only so much time to say all the things he wanted to, and needing to send more messages home,

Andrew began talking of his other sister and the new baby who had been born after he died.

"Baby Andrew," I heard him say. "Baby Andrew—they named him after me," and I felt the tears sting the back of my eyes, as Andrew's mother gasped, thrilled that her son had seen the baby.

He then gave a personal message to his mom, a message which was much needed, as it had seemed to her that one vital part of her life and her family was missing, and she didn't know what to do about it.

"You are so sad because you think that I won't be there, that I won't be at the wedding, but I will, Mom, I will. I will walk by her side down the isle, and then I will sit next to you so that together we will hear her say her wedding vows. At the reception," he continued, "I want you to hold baby Andrew in your arms and dance with him. I will be right there, and dancing with you too. I am the baby's angel and will always be with him through his life. . . . He's teething and giving everyone a hard time right now, but mine is the hand that rocks the cradle."

"Who is Mickey?" I asked Mary Jane. "Andrew wants to give Mickey a message, something about his bad tooth, and to get it fixed." Mary Jane laughed again, overwhelmed by the information she was being given. "Mickey is another son," she replied, "and he needs a root canal."

"You need to share your grief," Andrew went on more somberly, addressing another of his mother's questions. "Dad doesn't know how to express himself very well, and he has to learn to share his feelings, his grief, with you. You are all thinking the same thing, that you should have been able to do something to stop the tragedy. It's worse for Dad because he feels he let the whole family down, that it was his job to protect me and he couldn't. Tell him that it was God's plan, that it was my time to go, and that I am truly happy now. And please, Mom, try to talk more about these things. Don't hold your grief in. Tell the family that I want them to share their feelings and that I will always be listening and doing my best to show you all that I am still around. My legacy is the baby, baby Andrew, and I am his angel, his guardian, and I will walk with him always."

Suicide is a terrible thing, and when someone takes his or her own life, that act will leave the family with guilt and devastation which can haunt them all their lives. Andrew was able to explain to his mom how it was, that he had heard his name being called, that he was gone even before his physical body had taken its last breath. This meant that it was out of his hands and therefore there was nothing for anyone to feel guilty about.

In allowing me to share this story with you, I know that Andrew's mother hopes that those of you who have had a similar experience of a loved one passing to the spirit world, having taken his or her own life, that you will be comforted and helped, having a better understanding of how things work, and that a healing will begin to take place. And that is my hope too!

My next story came from a telephone consultation with Danielle G, and shows how hard it is when we are forced to make the decision to take someone we love off life support and how wonderful it can be when that person is able to reassure us that it was the right thing to do.

When asking who she would like to connect with in the spirit world, Danielle had no hesitation at all. "With my mother and first husband," she answered firmly.

"And what questions would you like them to answer?"

1. Can you tell me about my mother's death?

2. My in-laws?

3. Children? As I hear this question, I also hear Grey Eagle say, "Two and one . . . Two to first marriage, one to second."

4. If you can, could you ask, Is there a message for my daughter, from her dad?

I saw Danielle's mother even before Danielle had finished giving me her list of questions, and she began her communication by describing the hospital room she was in, prior to her passing. As I listened, it was easy for me to go down and through that time travel space and to see her, as if it was happening right then. As I watched, I saw lots of tubes, and I could see that she was, or rather, had been, hooked up to a life support machine. Coming back to the now, I glanced in her direction, as she stood before me, and encouraged her to keep talking, even as I recounted what I had seen to her daughter. "It was so awful for them," I heard her say, "but the worst part came when they had to make the decision to pull the plug."

As I said this, Danielle and her sister, who had been listening on the extension, both cried out, remembering that terrible moment of life and death as their mother's life lay in the balance, and although they were extremely emotional, they were excited and thrilled that their mother was communicating so well. "Yes, yes," they both said at once, and their mother, also thrilled to be talking at last with her girls, continued, telling me how her family had been so worried that they had done the right thing and reassuring them both that it was her time to go. They were to stop their worrying, because it was exactly what they were supposed to do.

As I was listening to Danielle's mother, I became aware of a man standing by my right shoulder. I knew straightaway it was Danielle's husband, and as he saw me glance his way, he began speaking, not realizing that I was unable at the moment, to give him my attention. "I went very fast," I heard him say, but then, hearing two voices, those of the mother and the husband, speaking at once, I became confused.

"I have your husband here with me," I said, and recounted what I had heard him say about his passing, that he had gone quickly and without warning.

"But now I am being told about an accident, and I'm not sure if this connects to him."

What I had done, and although it is an easy mistake to make, I know better, was to make an assumption, which was that Danielle's husband had died from an accident. But I was wrong, and if I had been a little more patient, Danielle's mother would have straightened things out. As it was, Danielle, her sister, and her young daughter, all on the phone together, laughed at my confusion and told me not to worry, that they understand perfectly.

"We understand, we understand," they said in unison. "It was our mother who had the accident." Then I heard their mother's voice clearly again as she described how she had been raced to the hospital by helicopter and was immediately placed on life support.

"Teeth," I heard the mother say, "teeth, my teeth. Tell them I know about my teeth," and somewhat taken aback by this sudden change of subject, or so I thought, I told the girls what their mother had said. More evidence, more than they could believe was possible, and the two sisters were beside themselves with delight.

"Before we took her off the life support, I put her teeth in," said Danielle, laughing. Her mother, hearing her say that, said, "Yes, and you had a dreadful time doing it, didn't you? You couldn't get them in for ages. It was really hard, but"—she now joined in the laughter with her girls and turned to me—"they wanted me to look my best when I went, but the truth is, I was already gone, and so all that hard work was for nothing." At this, we all laughed together, and after a while, Danielle's mom continued, while her husband waited his turn patiently, knowing that I would get to him soon enough. "They sold my house, sorted out the paperwork, but there were arguments with their brother, as he doesn't trust the girls to know what's right. Stop fighting. Let it go. Life's too short, and small niggles will mar your life. Don't let small misunderstandings spoil your chance for a good life."

Now it was Danielle's husband's turn, and he began by explaining to me again how he had passed, apologizing for jumping in and causing my confusion. The messages he gave to his wife and children were wonderful, and he made a point of including the third child, not his, but the child born to Danielle and her second husband, saying they were all one family. He liked his wife's new husband and said that he was a good man, who was taking good care of them all. "And as for your in-laws"—and he explained he was talking about the parents of Danielle's second husband—"well, they are good people, just inter-

fering. Don't let them get to you, don't play games, and try to understand that they mean well, even if they do drive you crazy sometimes,"
he laughed. Danielle laughed too, and agreed to try to have more
understanding, even though it would be hard to do. As Danielle's
husband spoke, once again I caught a glimpse of this man's life, his
past, as peering down and through the hole, I saw a boat, a small
vessel, which, he quickly informed me, was a sailboat. "As you can see,
Rosemary, I was never happier than when I was sailing," he said, knowing that I was glimpsing a part of his life on the earth plane. "I never
felt more free than when I was on the water," he said, and he went on
to explain how important it was to him that his children learn how to
be free.

"My son is too anxious," Danielle's husband continued, "and he
worries too much. He needs to learn how to let go. Teach them to sail,
teach them to sail free." He smiled, knowing that his wife would understand that his use of the term sailing was just a metaphor. "I want
them to learn to be free. I want you all to live life, to make the most of
each moment. Life is so short, so don't waste it." And to his daughter,
listening in, he said, "Don't worry about the braces on your teeth, you
only have a couple more years to go," he chuckled. "And you will always be beautiful to me."

It was time to wind up, and I looked to Danielle's mother for her
final words, but before I could go on, her sister, realizing that we were
about to finish, jumped right in with, "Just one final question, please.
I need some financial advice."

It would have been more appropriate for Danielle's sister to make
a further appointment. However, answering quickly, the girl's mother
began talking of her daughter's investments, describing a large pot of
money, and a question of whether she should take some out to invest
elsewhere. "Property—she's thinking of investing in property overseas," said her mother, quickly. "Tell her it's a good idea, but make sure
she gets some sound investment advice from someone she trusts."

"And now," I interrupted, knowing that I had to put a stop to any more last-minute questions, as we could have gone on and on, and fully understanding how hard it is for everyone to end a connection such as this, "and now, let me finish by telling you that your mother and your husband, Danielle, that they love you all so much. And I see them standing together, and they are blowing you kisses. They want me to tell you that they will always be around, whenever you need them, and all you have to do is call."

So, as we can see, the spirit world has no trouble at all communicating by any means open to them. All we have to do to hear them, to connect to them, is to make the call, to reach out to them with our heart and mind, and trust that they are listening to us.

You don't need me, or someone like me, and you don't have to be psychic, but it helps if you believe. All you have to do—metaphorically, that is—is just pick up the phone.

A Conversation with Bob

I could tell that he was skeptical the minute he walked into the healing center with his wife, Lesley, looking fit and healthy, a typical outdoor type, a true Vermonter in every sense. Little did I know then the effect that this man would have on my team and me! Little did I know how inspired my team and I would all become by our new patient!

Bob had been diagnosed a few months before with a particularly fast-growing and malignant brain tumor. He had been taken to the hospital with massive head pains, had collapsed on arrival, and after a brain scan, the tumor had been discovered.

After two major surgeries Bob was given the bad news. The surgeon had been able to remove much of the tumor but not all, and the chances were that it would grow back again, and fast.

Now, Bob was a builder used to constructing things, used to making things work. He also had a passion for biking, skydiving, any daredevil sport, and the one thing he loved best in the world was a challenge . . . so now, here he was, facing perhaps the biggest challenge of his life.

I was soon to learn that Bob would face this challenge as he did all the others, with courage, fearlessness, and determination, and absolutely head-on. No wasting time on self-pity, no time spent wondering how this had happened to him or why him (as so many of us might do), and no wasted time spent idly sitting around waiting for someone else to find a solution.

With his wife's help and support, Bob had explored the Internet, looking for every bit of information he could find about his cancer. He had called numerous hospitals, spoken with many experts, tried a number of experimental drugs, and was given the option of further surgery. No guarantees, no promises of a full recovery but a way of giving him a few more months. Eventually, Bob decided that a few more months were not worth the pain of the surgery, and so he declined. Now he was willing to try something different, something new. Now it was time to try healing for the first time.

Not only did Bob not believe in healing, or even understand what it was, he also did not believe in God. But as a builder, as an explorer, and a very curious individual, he thought he would give us a try . . . and as he would say, it never hurts to try, and after all, what did he have to lose?

He was hooked from that first night. Not on God or on the possibility that healing might work. No. Bob was hooked on us as a team, a group of sane, smart, reasonably educated people, not what he had expected. He had thought we would be more "way out," perhaps a little "off the wall, a little spacey, New Age," wearing New Age clothes and hairdos. The fact that we were nothing like he had imagined surprised and confused him. Over time, as Bob got to know us better, he became fascinated with the concept of energy and with the way we as a group talked about how we could use energy to help us heal. Our acceptance of a higher power, of God energy, of a universal source of healing energy, intrigued him, and our obvious dedication to our work also intrigued him. Our other patients, their stories, and their positive experience with us, all of this intrigued him too, and he decided he wanted to know more.

As the weeks went by, Bob began to realize, to his surprise, that his healing was helping. He found that he was able to relax more easily. He began seeing colors, and skeptical as he was, he thought that maybe this might be due to the tumor. But none of the rest of us thought so. He was also beginning to feel a sense of peace, which he knew was coming from his Wednesday-night sessions with us. He soon wanted more and, before long, asked for my healing CDs, which he played at least three times a day, amazed and thrilled at the response he was having to them, how easily, through the guided meditations, he was able to feel free, to feel calmed, and to feel healed in his inner being.

With all of this new experience came questions, flooding his mind thick and fast, and the more questions I was able to answer, the more questions he had. He was coming to believe . . . in what, he wasn't sure—but he was coming to believe in something. He was coming to believe in some kind of energy, something outside himself. And he began to understand that maybe there was something to this life after death thing after all. However, he was not ready yet to accept such an idea as anything more than an unexplored possibility.

Every week Bob came to the center, no matter how sick he felt and, in doing so, acknowledged the benefits he felt. He always had a smile, a curiosity, a drive to learn more, a kind and always positive word to say to our other patients. He made them feel as if they were special to him, and I believe they were. I never heard him complain, no matter how ill he felt. I never heard him angry or desperate, and he would always tell us how lucky he felt, what a good life he'd had, and that he was not afraid to die.

It was impossible not to be inspired by his attitude, and as he became more frail, my team and I went to his house, at his request, to give him healing on a daily basis. This was not an uncommon thing for us to do, but what was uncommon was the way we would all feel afterward. It felt as if Bob was giving us something rather than us giving something to him. There was never a shortage of volunteers, and my team seemed to go out of their way to find extra time to visit Bob. It was as if none of us could get enough of him. He made us all feel so special, and each of us could see how special he was.

Over the course of the next few months, Bob and I had taken to having long and in-depth conversations, just the two of us, sometimes over the phone, but more often during my visits to his home, and it was not unusual for him to call just to see how I was doing. There was just such a call the day before I was to do a marathon radio show, and I began to tell Bob how I would be totally tied up the next day, since the marathon started at five A.M. and wouldn't finish until around seven P.M.

"You mean you'll be on the phone the whole day," he said, incredulous that such a thing could happen. "Well, who's going to take care of you?"

I laughed. This was so typical of Bob, and I reassured him that my assistant, Denise, would be there until five, to make tea and to make sure I didn't starve.

"Well, what about dinner? Who's going to make dinner for you?"

I replied that I hadn't thought that far ahead, and told him not to worry, that I had done this many times before, and although it was grueling, it was no big deal. Ten minutes later the phone rang again. "You're coming here for dinner tomorrow, no arguments, about seven thirty, OK! Something simple. Let me know in the morning if there's anything you don't eat."

The next evening I drove to Bob's house, tired from my day, my voice hoarse from talking for hours, my ear numb from the constant pressure of the phone against it. I was looking forward to a nice relaxing dinner, good food, a glass of wine, and good conversation. I felt completely burned out and ready to just chill out. Little did I know that "they" had other plans, little did I know that I was not done for the day, and that I had more work to do. Little did I know that I was walking into an ambush, that the plan was in place, and that "they" had set me up!

The food was good, steak done on the grill and a delicious salad.

Perfect, just what I needed. Bob was feeling particularly good that evening, and was chatty, full of stories about his life, his exploits. Lesley and I listened as he recounted one tale after another, making us laugh as he described some of his more daredevil episodes. Obviously, his friends were important to Bob, which became clear to me the more he talked. Even more important to Bob was his background, his upbringing, his ancestry. He was enormously proud that he was a fifth-generation Vermonter, and it was as he began telling me about his grandparents and great-grandparents that "they" saw their opportunity and took it. It was no surprise to them. They knew it was going to happen. And it really should not have been a surprise to me. This had happened so many times in the past, and in such a natural way, just as it was happening now. But I had been tired, and not thinking.

As the room filled, my tiredness left me, and I began paying attention to Bob's family, wondering for a moment which one would be the spokesperson. I knew there would be one, for there were too many for me to speak to them all. The two closest to Bob were his grandparents, the ones he was speaking about at that moment, telling me where they were buried. He was oblivious for now that they were standing by his side, paying close attention to what he was saying and adding their own thoughts, joining in the conversation, and filling in the parts that Bob had left out or simply didn't know. It was only as I began to join in, to add those small pieces of information that Bob's grandfather was recounting to me, in a way that seemed perfectly normal, just part of the story he was telling, that Bob slowly began to realize that something was up. Finally he asked, after I had recounted one small detail he had left out of his story, "But how do you know that?"

My reply, as you might have guessed, was that his grandfather was standing by his side and that it was he who had told me these things.

"You mean that he's here now," said a bewildered but excited Bob, "and that he's actually joining in our conversation?"

"They have been waiting for this opportunity you know." I smiled. "But I'm not going to continue unless you tell me I can."

Well, the truth was that Bob's family, those who were in the spirit world, were not the only ones eager and ready to communicate. Bob and Lesley had talked about the possibility previously. Had discussed asking me if I would do it. Now there was no need. Here we were and everyone was ready.

That night Bob and Lesley received many messages from Bob's grandparents, messages of hope and encouragement. Information that I could not possibly have known was given, proof beyond proof that there was indeed life after death. Of course, Bob being Bob, he began asking questions, lots of questions, not of me but of his grandfather and grandmother, and they answered as best they could, satisfying Bob's curiosity for a time, giving him answers that led to the inevitable. More questions.

My tiredness forgotten for a while, we talked for the next couple of hours, until suddenly, weariness overcame my enthusiasm, and now exhausted, I told them all I had to stop.

Bob and Lesley were overwhelmed by their experience and over-awed by the things they had heard. As I said my good-byes, I noticed a glow about my patient, a renewed determination. That amazing spark that I had seen in the beginning was returning. When Bob had first come to us, that spark had begun to diminish as he struggled with his illness, becoming weaker and a little frailer. It was not that he felt he could now beat the cancer. On the contrary, his grandfather had made it clear that Bob would be joining him soon. So no, it was not the hope that he would be cured that made Bob sparkle, not at all. It was more about how beautiful he realized his life was, even with his sickness. It was about his recognition that his life had not been in vain, that it was not nearly over, and that a new adventure, a new challenge, was about to present itself to him.

As I was thinking about Bob on my way home, I began to wish that others could in some way experience what my students and I had. Rarely had a patient affected so many in my team; rarely had I seen so many people inspired in the way Bob had inspired us all. *If only I could bottle it,*

I thought, *if only there was a way to preserve and to share whatever it was that Bob had been able to give us.* It was then that I had the idea.

"How would you feel about making a CD?" I asked him one day when we were up at the farm. We had been sitting on the knoll, look-ing out over the Green Mountains of Vermont and talking about Llewella, whom I have not yet told you about and whom Bob had never met but had heard a lot about. As I looked at him, I could see that he was much more frail than I wanted him to be. Watching him as he sat on the bench marveling at the view high up in the hills, and listening to him talking to Llewella now as if he could plainly see her, and I felt he could, I knew that his life here was coming to a close much faster than I wanted it to. There was not much time left, and I knew that if Bob agreed to my suggestion, then we would have to do it quickly.

I had called and spoken to Ryan, the young man I had worked with on my other CDs at the recording studio I used, and had explained Bob's condition to him. We had decided to play things by ear, to take as long as was necessary, and just see how things went. Bob's memory had begun to fail, just a little and only every now and then, but I knew he was worried about it, and as we drove to the studio, I reassured him that everything would be OK, that it would all work out as it was supposed to.

"But Rosemary, you didn't give me the script, and I haven't studied any of the questions."

"What script?" I asked, for a moment taken completely off-guard. "What script are you referring to?"

"Well, you know, the questions, the things we are going to talk about today."

I laughed. "Oh, that." I smiled. "I rarely have a script, Bob, and today we are just going to hope that the spirit world can inspire us. Don't worry," I continued, patting his hand reassuringly as we neared the studio, "you'll see. It will all work out."

The introductions over, Bob and I settled into our chairs, and Ryan seated himself behind his desk, in front of an impressive array of equipment.

Ryan, who knew me well by now, since I had worked with him on my other CDs, was not surprised when I told him we were going to ad-lib, to simply have a conversation and see how it went. He simply took it in his stride.

For the next couple of hours that is exactly what we did. We had a conversation, pausing every now and then to take a break or to let Bob add to or amend an answer to a question if he was not satisfied with his original response. But for the most part, we simply chatted, or so it seemed, and Bob forgot to be nervous. He stopped worrying whether he had made a mistake and he became Bob, the Bob I had grown to admire, the Bob I had grown to love, the Bob I knew would truly inspire everyone who listened to him.

As we left the studio, Ryan and I were concerned that we had gone over time. Neither of us wanted to cut or to change any of the conversation in any way, but we knew we would have to. The CD simply wasn't long enough. We arranged to talk the next day, and so saying our good-byes, I drove my patient home. Bob was tired but elated, and the thought that he was doing something positive to help our organization had given him the extra boost he needed to complete the project. It was with a smile and a warm hug that I dropped him at his house.

The next day Ryan called. "Rosemary, you know that I told you the CD time would probably not be long enough, that we would likely have to cut some of what we recorded," he said, hesitating just a little. "Well, you'll be as surprised as I was to learn that all of what we did, just and only just, mind you, well, it all fits. We don't have to cut or change a thing!"

I smiled when I heard this. I couldn't pretend that I knew. I didn't. I hadn't known. I had thought that we might have to cut some stuff out too. But was I surprised to learn that our conversation had lasted exactly the right amount of time as the CD would allow? I think "awed" would be a more accurate description. In awe that, once again, the spirit world could plan things so precisely!

It was only a few days later that Bob had another relapse and was rushed into hospital. This time, his family and friends thought, would be the last time. The prognosis was not good and no one expected Bob to come home.

When I went to see him, he was conscious but weak, and he knew his time was running out. I stayed for a while, but so many of his friends had come to say their last good-byes that I decided to leave for a while, and come back later. It was as I was leaving that Bob reminded me of the promise I had made him a few weeks earlier. He had read, in one of my books, a story of how I had traveled with one of my patients to the spirit world. Margery had been frightened to make the journey alone, and so, after seeking permission from Grey Eagle, I had been allowed to accompany her as she passed. Bob thought this was a pretty neat thing to do and had, of course, asked many questions about the way it worked. Then one day, out of the blue, he asked if I would go with him when it was his turn, not because he was afraid but because he thought it would be special to share the journey with me. I had agreed, checking first with Grey Eagle, of course, and Bob and I had a few conversations about what it might be like.

I asked Grey Eagle how much time Bob had left. My guide reminded me of something Bob's grandfather had said on the night I had gone for dinner, that Bob had more time than we would think. Nodding my thanks for this reminder, I drove off, assured that my patient would be fine for a while, and reassured that I would be able to keep my promise to him.

I wanted to give some support to my team, who were working on the renovations at the farm I'd inherited, which was just a fifteen-minute drive from the hospital. While there, I made dinner for my crew and arrived back at the hospital at about eight.

Lesley was waiting for me in the parking lot, and as I stepped out of the car, she grabbed my arm. "Thank God you're here," she said breathlessly, "he's going! He's going! He's said his good-byes to me, told everyone to go home, and he's asking for the 'witch'!" As she was saying all this, Lesley was dragging me toward the hospital. "Hurry, Rosemary, hurry, he's going and he's calling for you!"

As we raced to the elevator, I held on to Lesley's arm and tried to reassure her that everything would be fine. At the same time, I was asking Grey Eagle if this was really it, if Bob was really going now. My spirit guide shook his head no, and reminded me again what Bob's grandfather had told us. OK, I thought as we headed for Bob's room, but in my humanness I wondered if perhaps I could have misunderstood.

As we entered the room, Lesley held back, not wanting Bob to see her there. They had agreed that she would not be present at his passing, because Bob, trying to protect her, didn't want his wife to suffer any more than she had to, and she had agreed to abide by his wishes.

The curtain was drawn around his bed, but he felt my presence and immediately tried to sit up, to come toward me. As he called out for the "witch" again, his nickname for me, I reached him, pulling him, with some difficulty, back into the bed.

"I'm here," I said gently. "It's OK. I'm here."

At once Bob became even more excited, telling me over and over again that it was time, that the train, as he put it, was pulling into the station and that we would need to board pretty soon. Holding on to me, his arms felt like a vice, and he began pulling me down onto the bed with him. I reassured him that we had time and slowly extricated myself from his grip. I moved around to the other side of the bed, indicating silently to Lesley, who was standing frozen by the door that she should take the sofa, which was next to the bed but hidden behind the curtain. Holding her son's hand, Bob's mother sat silent beside the bed, but as our eyes met, she gave me a wavering smile. Bob and Lesley had both agreed that his mother should be with Bob and me when he passed, and as I moved to the other side of the bed, she gave me another tired but warm smile. Was she about to lose her son? She thought so, I knew, and I wondered briefly if she might be right.

I climbed into the hospital bed, wriggling into the small cramped space next to my patient, knowing that this could be a long slow night, and immediately Bob grabbed hold of me.

"It's time," he said again, and with such conviction that I couldn't help wondering again if I'd misunderstood my information. I decided that it didn't matter. We would just play this out and see what transpired.

All through the night Lesley lay on the sofa, dozing on and off. Bob's mother, Marilyn, sat in the chair, holding his hand, or, when he moved, with her hand on his legs. I lay next to him in the bed.

All through the night Bob talked incessantly, asking me questions about the things he was seeing and hearing. Was that really his grandfather? And yes, without my reply, he knew that it was. And "What, Rosemary, are all those colors?" And could I see them? And here's the train, and "Why, why, why is it taking so long?" On and on the questions went, on and on Bob talked about what was happening to him. Excited beyond belief, thrilled by the experience, and impatient to start the journey, he wanted desperately to begin this new phase of his life. He just couldn't stand the waiting. Try as I might, I could not get him to be still, although I did encourage him to be quiet and to listen, more for my sake than for his, I realized, as I was getting desperate myself, desperate for a little sleep. Each time I nodded off, he would wake me with yet another question or a demand that I should try to hurry the process. One such moment I woke with a start to find my face pressed hard against the side rail of the hospital bed, with Bob's elbow in my back. Oblivious to anything other than the journey, he was so happy to think that at last his time was here. I turned to him, doing my best to satisfy his questions, drawing on my strength as a healer, encouraging him to talk to me and to the people in the spirit world who had come to visit him. Somehow we got through the night.

The light had just begun to creep through the blinds of the hospital windows, and as my eyes opened, I saw a nurse come to the side of the bed to check on her patient. She must, I am sure, have thought it a little odd to find a strange woman in Bob's bed, while his wife was sleeping soundly on the sofa. She crept out of the room as quietly as she had come in. I carefully lifted my head to see Marilyn asleep with her head on the bed next to her son, and Bob, finally sound asleep, curled up next to me. The crisis was over. He had managed to come through the night, and I knew for sure that he would have a few more weeks left to him, that he would be able to go home, to sit on his porch and look out once again at his beloved mountains, that he would be able to sleep in his own bed, with his wife next to him, and that he would have his wish . . . which was that he could die at home.

Disappointed as he was, and he made his disappointment clear to us all, Bob accepted his fate. I had explained to him that it was not yet his time, that for some reason he, his soul, was not yet ready to leave, that there were still some things to be done, maybe some things to be said, another experience to be had. Although he was still impatient, I convinced him not to waste the extra time he had wishing for something that could not be but to be joyful that he had been given some precious time, and that he must cherish it, make the most of the gift he'd been given.

During the following few weeks, Bob did exactly that. He learned to cherish his extra time, seeing it as a bonus, and although his body became weaker and weaker, his spirit found a new strength. He began telling his friends of his experiences, not just with me and my team, but he told them about all those things he had witnessed for himself. Some of his friends, those who had been, like Bob, not wanting to believe in any such thing, put Bob's stories down to the fact that Bob had a brain tumor that was obviously distorting his thinking. But those friends who knew Bob the best could see, had seen throughout his illness, a new Bob, a stronger and more inspired man, a man they should listen to, a man who could teach them something, something worthwhile, something valuable. Those who knew him best knew that Bob had been touched by a higher power. Even if they didn't understand it or couldn't give it a name, they still knew that that power existed, for they could see its existence in the eyes of their friend.

In those last weeks, I visited Bob every day, often going two or three times a day. Sometimes I would find him out on the porch, a blanket wrapped around his shoulders. Sometimes, if it was late at night, I would find him in bed. He would always wake when I came in, even if it was three or four in the morning, which it often was, as if he could sense my presence in the house. Always we would have our conversations, talking quietly so as not to wake his wife, his mother, or the friends who had come to sleep overnight just in case they were needed. Bob would store up his questions, keep hold of his thoughts, his experiences, and as soon as I would arrive, he would begin picking my brain. I like to think that I never disappointed him, even when I couldn't answer or didn't know the answers to some of his questions, and he never disappointed me either. Even at the end, even when the pain was so great it hurt to move even a little, I never once heard him complain. He was always trying to make it easier for the rest of us.

At long last the journey was over. I had left the house in the early hours to return home, knowing that within the next few hours, I would be traveling with Bob for the last time. The journey was remarkable, as it always is, as silently I moved with Bob into that other place, leaving behind the earth world, and venturing into that other world, that other time and space. Bob really didn't need me there with him, as his angels wrapped him in their arms and lifted him up, carrying him to that place where so many others were waiting. I quietly watched as he was reunited with his family, and I witnessed the joy on his face as all his hopes and expectations were realized, and tears fell softly on my cheek as I said my silent good-bye to my friend.

My work was not over yet. I still had Bob's family to support, and as dawn was breaking, I drove back to Bob's house to be with Lesley and Marilyn in what would be their darkest hour. I wanted to repay some of what Bob had given to me and to try to bring a little light and hope to them in their time of need, to tell them of Bob's journey, to describe his smile and his joy, and to let them know that Bob was safe and that, finally, he was home.

Always taking responsibility for the way he lived, always trying to live his life to the full, Bob died the same way.

I wanted to tell his mother and his wife that yes, of course, remaining just as he had always been, their beloved Bob was already making plans for his next challenge, his next adventure, the first in his new life, and one of the many to come!*

---

*To learn more about Bob's CD, *A Conversation with Bob,* go to www.rosemaryaltea.com. All profits from sales of the CD go to the Rosemary Altea Healing and Education Foundation.

PART III

CASEBOOK

Preface

Everyone likes a good story, especially a true story, and everyone likes to get a glimpse of other people's lives, particularly when the spirit world is the main theme of the tale. Whenever I meet someone who has read my first book, I hear the same things: "It's wonderful. How brave you were. What a gift you have. Oh, how I loved those stories!" So I thought it would be appropriate to do the same thing here, to have a casebook section, to compile a group of stories about ordinary people who have had extraordinary experiences. Some stories are sad. Some are funny or intriguing. All are enlightening and give us hope.

Even though I have been working as a professional medium for more than a quarter of a century, and have long ago accepted that some things simply defy explanation, still I cannot help my natural instinct to seek and to question each and every incident of what we know as the paranormal or the supernatural. I look for answers I will never find. I am *the* biggest doubting Thomas of all time and doubt myself the most. This has its upside in that I strive all the more for perfection in my work.

Each of the following stories has an element of the unusual about it, and if, like me, you are inclined to doubt, you will find plenty of room here to do so. As for me, because I was present and an integral part of each of the stories told here, seeing meant believing.

Inspiring and often beautiful, each of the stories is, in truth, an example of what has already happened to some of us and what is waiting for the rest of us. Each is an example of life and death. Each shows us how, eventually, in one way or another, all of us "take flight."

God's Plan

I knew they were there, somewhere in the audience, and I had decided not to look for them but to wait and see if I was directed there. It was a hard call, and by no means an easy decision to make, because it could have meant they would not get a message from me. "And who," I mused, "would need one more than they?"

Not knowing them by sight, and only having heard a little of their story from my assistant, I had decided to be steered by my guide and not take matters into my own hands. After all, it was more than possible that someone else could need me more, could need a message from the spirit world more. And who was I to say? God's plan, I reminded myself again, God's plan, and anyway, it was not for me to decide these things. It was not my responsibility to choose. This was not Rosemary's plan; this was not the audience's plan. Only God's plan was important here.

It was winter in Vermont and a snowstorm was in progress. I had been with a patient all day, since early morning in fact, when I had gone to the hospital, arranged for her transfer home and for nursing care, and then stayed with her, talking with her friends John and Esther about her situation.

The day before had been a nightmare. It had begun when Cheyenne, Llewella's friend, had called in a panic. Llewella had been vomiting badly and was complaining of real pain in her stomach, Cheyenne had said. I knew immediately that it was serious, for, since I had known her, I had never heard Llewella complain about anything.

"Call the nursing service and get someone out to the house," I instructed the young woman who had been taking care of my patient. "I'm leaving right now and I'll be there in about forty-five minutes."

When I arrived, the visiting nurse was already at the house, and had given Llewella a thorough examination. "She's dehydrated," she said in a low voice, coming to meet me as I walked into the kitchen. "We have to get her to the hospital right away."

"No," boomed the voice from the bedroom. "No, I said. I'm not going to any hospital. I'm not moving. I'm staying right where I am."

The nurse and I and Cheyenne looked at one another, and the nurse shook her head in frustration, and explained how important it was that Llewella should be moved and receive proper care.

"She's stubborn," said Cheyenne, obviously upset, "and you won't make her do what she doesn't want to do. No way, no way."

I knew she was right. One of the things I loved most about Llewella was her cantankerous stubborn streak. It was what had helped her survive as a hill farmer. She had kept the farm going against all the odds, just as she had done all her life, living there on her own since her parents died thirty years before. I sighed, took a deep breath, and went into the bedroom, closing the door behind me.

"You have to go, you know," I said, taking Llewella's hands in my own. "You're dehydrated, which is why you feel so bad and why you're throwing up. You need treatment."

She looked right at me, her eyes like flint and her jaw set hard and determined, and I knew she was going to fight me on this. For the next ten minutes we talked it through, she giving me all the reasons why she shouldn't go, and I, giving all the reasons why she should. The bottom line was that Llewella was afraid. She was not afraid of dying, as some of you might suppose. No, she had come to terms with that probability a long time ago. But she wanted to die at home, where she belonged, where her heart and soul were, among things that were familiar to her, where she felt safe. She was afraid that if she went into hospital, then she wouldn't come out. And the last thing in the world she wanted was to die in a hospital bed. So we compromised, Llewella and I, two Warrior Souls, each trusting the other, each loving and caring for the other's well-being, each having respect for the other. Finally, reluctantly, she said, "I'll go, but only on one condition." Looking me straight in the eye, she said, "You have to promise me you'll have me back here within twenty-four hours. I don't want to die in that damn hospital."

"Twenty-four hours?" Could I possibly manage that, I wondered, and immediately I felt Grey Eagle's hand reassuringly on my shoulder, and so, trusting, I promised my friend, and I made her another promise too. I promised her that she would not die before she came back to the farm.

Llewella had been my patient for more than a year, not long, in the scheme of things, but over that period of time, as often happens with my patients, we had become very close. We both knew her cancer was terminal. For reasons of her own, she had allowed me into her life, an unusual thing for her, and together, we had worked on improving the quality of the time she had left, rather than the quantity. That had been an easy task because Llewella was a strong and stubborn individual, who, if she set her mind on something, would not be easily persuaded otherwise. Being an extremely spiritual woman, knowing the Bible by heart, as she had read it more than once a day for most of her life, Llewella had a great faith in God, and she believed that He had answered her prayers and had sent me to her. Having that same great belief myself, I knew that God had given me Llewella for my benefit rather than hers, for rarely had anyone in my life inspired me as she did. She had taught me so very much about so many things, and in particular, she had taught me about living my faith.

It was a terrible ordeal for Llewella at the hospital. As I helped turn her on her side for yet one more X-ray and heard her cry out in pain— as even the slightest movement caused her distress—I wondered for the tenth time if I had made the right decision. Finally, as she muttered in my ear, "No more," I told the nurse that this would be the last X-ray, even though she told me there were three more to go. Eventually they got her into bed and put an IV in her arm, and as I left for the night, finally she was sleeping peacefully.

The next morning I was at the hospital early, with only a little over two hours left to keep my promise. Llewella's oncologist had already been in to visit her and had given her the news that she had very little time left. Weeks, he had said.

As Llewella's health care executrix, I was informed of this by Dr. Eisemann when I called to get her released. The doctor told me that he wanted Llewella to stay in the hospital, where she would be taken good care of. Of course, Llewella had her own plans, and I told the doctor about the promise I had made.

Dr. Allan Eisemann had been Llewella's oncologist since she had first become sick two years previously, and knew her well enough to know she was not a woman to argue with. "Twenty-four hours," he mused. "Well, we'd better get moving, then. I'll arrange for an ambulance and a hospital bed to be sent to the house right away."

I followed the ambulance back to the farm less than an hour later, and miraculously the bed had already arrived, and had been set up in front of the window in the living room.

After a few more hours, it was time for me to leave. As I tucked the blankets around my friend, wanting to make her as comfortable as I could, I adjusted the angle of the bed one more time, making sure it was close enough to the window for her to see out onto her beloved farmland and her horses. As I looked down at her, it broke my heart to see how weak she had become in just the last forty-eight hours. Still, as I reached across to pull the covers up and under her chin, she managed one of her incredibly bright smiles and stared into my eyes.

"You kept your promise," she whispered softly, almost too weak to speak, and I nodded, a lump forming in my throat. It was true, I had kept my promise to her that she would die at home, and I had taken her from the hospital just in time. But I didn't want her to die; I didn't want her to leave me. As I squeezed her hand, I knew that this was Llewella's last day and that these would be our last few moments together. *What am I going to do without her?* I thought selfishly, holding back the tears that were welling behind my eyes. *What, dear Lord, am I going to do?*

It would be fair to say that this tough old farmer with big muddy boots, her pants held up with string, a cap always perched on her gray-blond head, the peak pulled down over her weatherbeaten face, her gait, until just a few short days ago strong and purposeful—it would be fair to say that Llewella was an inspiration to everyone who met her. She was more than an inspiration to me.

Leaving as late as I could, knowing I had a lecture scheduled that evening and that the drive home would take at least an hour, probably more with the weather as bad as it was, I finally said my good-bye. I knew I would not see her again on this side.

The drive home was difficult. It was snowing hard, and the journey was made more troublesome by the fact that halfway home I developed a really bad headache. My friend, Joan, who was visiting from England, helped a lot by keeping my mind on the positives of dying rather than the negatives of losing a friend. Still, by the time we finally reached home, my headache had grown to mammoth proportions, and was on the verge of spilling into a really bad migraine.

"Oh God," I groaned, as I reached for the Advil. "Please don't let this happen. How will I be able to work tonight?"

"We've got less than an hour," I heard Joan say, as I headed toward the bedroom.

"OK. I'll take a quick shower and hope these pills kick in," I muttered hoarsely, feeling worse by the minute.

"Fifteen minutes," said my friend, now seeming like the voice of doom. I sat on the bed, holding my head in my hands, rocking myself backward and forward, gently, trying to ease the pain in my head. Tears spilled down my cheeks, as I wondered: *How am I going to work? What am I going to do with all those people who have traveled so far? What am I going to do?*

Somehow, with Joan's help, I got dressed and headed to the school where our event was to take place. The whole thing had been organized by the husband of my patient Cathy, whose story I told earlier. Dan had asked me to do a charity event to aid a local children's facility, which I had been glad to agree to. But now, having driven through the snowstorm and arriving with less than five minutes to go, I was getting myself into a real panic.

The hall we were using was full, I could see, with more than five hundred people present. I knew that many would be excited, that some would be nervous, and that all of them would be anticipating the best.

And my headache raged on, pounding in my ears. I could barely see. My eyes were misty and out of focus with the pain. As I stumbled backstage, my assistant, who knew nothing of my day except that I had been with a patient, and nothing of my now really near-migraine, pushed her way through the curtains to tell me, "They were here."

Confused and in pain, I muttered, "Who? Where?"

"The family I told you about yesterday," she said, keeping her voice to a whisper. "You remember," she repeated, as I just stood and stared, "the three survivors. Rosemary, don't you remember I told you about the survivors of the family who were killed in the fire last week? They called to see if you would see them."

I nodded vaguely, trying to remember what I knew and realizing that I actually knew nothing more than what Denise had just told me. I knew only that and the fact that the family was fairly local to the area and that I had agreed that I would, of course, see them sometime soon.

Dan came with the microphone. "It's time," he said, and looked at me closely. "Are you ready, Rosemary?"

Was I ready? Now there was a question. Of course I was not ready. My head still throbbed painfully, I could hardly see, and my assistant, Denise, was waiting to see if I needed her to do something, although I had no idea what. Feeling desperate and out of control, I saw an image of Llewella suddenly flash in front of me. Absently nodding at Dan, I began to think of the three people out there in my audience who had so tragically lost their family.

I won't look for them, I decided, stepping out onto the stage as I heard Dan's introduction come to an end and my audience applauding, my cue to get going. *Maybe today is not their day. Maybe someone else will need me more. God's plan. That's it, remember God's plan. That's what I'm going to do.*

As cold and snowy as it was outside, the warmth of my audience was a startling contrast, and as I began the evening, it became very clear that more than a third of the crowd were people from all over America. Some had flown in, some had driven for hours despite the appalling weather conditions, and even the locals had given up their log fires and cozy armchairs to spend the evening with me.

As always, I immediately felt my guide's presence, and even though the headache still raged, I began to calm, to trust, to live my faith, as Llewella had taught me to do. *Whatever will be, will be,* I thought, *whatever will be, will be.*

I saw her quite clearly, standing next to her parents, and as I walked toward them, she described the brain hemorrhage, the suddenness of her passing, and the ease with which she had passed. She was so pretty, with dark curly hair, shoulder length, pale olive skin, dark brown eyes, and a smile that lit up the room. "I'm a nurse," she told me brightly. "I'm a children's nurse, and I really love my job."

Holding on to her father's hand, gently squeezing her mother's, I relayed all I saw and heard. They nodded and laughed and cried, as their daughter gave them evidence of her survival.

A tap on my shoulder came from the row behind. "What about me? Can I have a turn now?" Looking back over my shoulder, I saw a young man about twenty-two or twenty-three years old.

"Of course," I said, smiling, still holding the hands of the young woman's parents. "Of course, go ahead. But who is it you want to speak to?"

"My mom," he replied boldly, "but you'll have to turn around because she's right behind you." And so turning, sure enough, he showed me his mother, who was looking at me wide-eyed and incredulous that she had been chosen.

"Your son tells me that he died in a motorbike accident, that he hit a brick wall and died instantly, is that right?" I asked. She gasped and shook as tears flowed down her face, and she nodded that she understood.

"Your son is here, standing right in front of you, trying to let you see that he didn't die," I said softly. Once again she nodded her understanding.

A tug from behind me, and now again the young woman who had died of a brain hemorrhage was speaking, and standing next to her was a little girl, maybe five years old.

"She's one of my children," I heard the young woman say, "and she has only been here a few days."

The young woman's parents were extremely confused, as I relayed this piece of information. For a moment, so was I, but confusion quickly passed as the five-year-old, quite determined to have her say, squealed loudly, pointing to the front of the audience: "There they are. There they are." And quick as a flash, she made a dash to where her brother and sisters sat.

"Follow her. Follow her," Grey Eagle said. "No time for thinking, Rosemary, just go with the flow."

The walk down to the front was simultaneous with walking through and down, down and through the hole. "Go with the flow. Go with the flow," Grey Eagle urged, and the flow took me to a time and a place not so very far away.

I could smell the burning before I saw the glow. I could see their spirits, their energy, before I saw their bodies, which had been burned and blackened by the fire. They were a family of eleven—parents, grandparents, siblings, and two grandchildren. One was the determined little five-year-old girl I'd seen. The other was just a baby a few months old, a little boy. Eight had died in the fire, and I stood and watched from my place in that netherworld as their house turned to ash and rubble, with them inside, until nothing was left.

Again, a tug at my sleeve, and coming back through the hole to the now, I saw the two sisters and the brother, just seventeen years old, and they held each other and cried, as I recounted what I saw.

"I was a bus driver," their mother proudly told me. "I drove the school bus, drove it for years." As she spoke, she cradled the baby gently in her arms and, pointing to her daughter, said, "Tell her we're keeping him safe, and that one day she will see her son again."

As I repeated what I'd heard, the young woman in front of me clung more tightly to her sister, a great wail of anguish escaping her lips.

My audience too was weeping, held captive in that moment, as I was, by the horror and pain that these three young people were experiencing.

I spoke with several others in the family who had died in the fire— the father, an aunt, a brother and sister, all of them wanting to give messages of hope and of love, and I knew I would be meeting with them all again a few months from now, when these three young people would come to see me for a consultation.

The five-year-old was impatient, and before I knew it, she had dashed back up the aisle to the young woman I had first spoken to.

"Tell them she's my nurse, and we laugh and play and have lots of fun."

Now, moving on—and where was I going now? Everything was happening so fast. There were so many voices wanting to be heard.

In the midst of it all, I saw Llewella's face, I saw it so clearly, yet I knew she had not yet passed. She had a few more hours to go, I knew. Then, going with the flow . . . "I'm her sister and I was sick. Meningitis, a fever, my head hurt so badly, and then it was over," I heard another young woman say. Clutching her husband in disbelief, amazed at the accuracy of the message, the young woman I'd come to stand in front of nodded her head.

"I've been asking and asking for a sign, for her to show me that she's with me," the sister said, almost breathlessly. "Could she give me a sign that it is really her?" Straightaway, with barely a pause, and before I even had time to ask, her sister replied, "The bird, I was the bird. I am the bird, the bird that has been coming to the kitchen window every day for the last few days. This is my way of showing you that I didn't die. I am the bird that flies to your house and taps its beak on the window to let you know that I am always here for you." And the sister gasped, knowing for certain that it was true!

"Go with the flow, go with the flow," and I follow Grey Eagle's guiding hand as we go to the next and the next and the next. Not thinking, just working, making the connections and letting it happen.

I am listening and relaying a message, my head tilted to one side, my eyes focusing on what is beyond my normal vision, and then focusing on the person I am giving the message to. I move my head just a fraction to the right and catch my breath.

I see him standing next to his wife, a big smile on his face, excitement in his eyes.

I can't believe that I see him, and my heart does a leap and the lump that comes into my throat is huge. It seems so unexpected. "But why would it?" I knew that she was coming. I gave her the ticket myself. I feel the tears threatening to spill down my cheeks, and I bow my head, biting my bottom lip hard, trying to gain some control over my emotions. Slowly, head down, I walk up and down the aisle. With luck, my audience will not see my distress. They will only think that I am listening for more voices, searching for more communication. In truth, though, I am merely a tiny human being, who right now is floundering in a sea of mixed emotion.

Sheldon, it was Sheldon. He had taken care of me, my property, my dogs, and my home. And he was my friend. I had been in Europe when he became sick, and had returned home to find him in a coma that lasted two weeks. Every day I had gone to the hospital, staying close by, trying to be of some help to Mary, his wife, and the rest of his family, and doing whatever I could to make things easier. Sheldon and I had a very special and unusual relationship. We were very close, and his story is told later on.

At the time of the charity event, Sheldon had only been gone six weeks, and although I had not actually seen him, I had heard him quite clearly on several occasions, particularly when he was asking me to get his wife's Christmas gift.

So here we were, my audience and I, and now here was Sheldon, standing next to his wife, waiting his turn, wanting to give her a message. I took a deep breath, struggling for composure, and as I became more in control of my emotions, I took another peek, wondering briefly if it had been my imagination, and yes, he was still there, the smile still on his face.

"Tell Mary," I heard him say, "just tell her I'm here. She's hoping for a message from me tonight."

It was all I could do to get the message out, and Mary was overjoyed to hear from her husband that he would not leave her side until such time as she didn't need him anymore.

And then, once again, going with the flow and moving on, the adrenaline flowing free and fast, the evening almost at a close, I went walking with my audience, stopping in front of two women and a young girl, a teenager, not yet knowing what I was going to do or indeed, if I would do anything.

They told me afterward about their journey to Vermont. The mother, Cindy, and her daughter, Bridget, had made plans to fly out to Vermont with their friend, Linda. The three of them were making their way to the Chicago airport, a two-hour car ride, when about half an hour from their destination they were involved in a terrible car accident, and their car was totaled. Fortunately, no one was injured, but Cindy was frantic, with only one thing on her mind. She must not miss her flight. Somehow, she just knew she had to get to my lecture. She knew that something important was waiting for her in Vermont, and so, leaving her car in the middle of the road for the tow trucking service to clean up, she managed to persuade the police officer on the scene to drive her, her friend, and her daughter to the airport, where they just, and only just, made their plane.

As I've explained, the hall was full, a packed audience, despite the terrible weather conditions, and let us not forget that other audience, those from the spirit world who were filling and spilling over into the room, just as eager, just as nervous and expectant, an unseen audience, unseen by all perhaps but me. So many, too many to count, but I could see the ones I was to speak with next.

He smiled and, stepping forward, placed his hand gently on his wife's shoulder, a small tear slipping down his cheek as he did so. Turning his head, he reached behind him with his other hand and brought forward a young boy about ten years old. "My son," he said quietly, motioning to the child. "My son and I, we passed together, but Bridget"—and he lifted his hand from his wife's shoulder to stroke the young girl's hair—"my daughter Bridget had to stay behind."

"What happened?" I asked, already moving into that time travel space. "What happened?" I asked Grey Eagle, and then, moving down and through the hole, I saw. There were two children, a boy and a girl, riding with their father in the car. I watched from my place as the car and its passengers drove along the not-too-busy road, and I could clearly hear the sound of their voices, the laughter and chatter, the friendly bantering as the children played some kind of game. Happiness is a wonderful thing. I saw the father smiling as he listened to his kids, occasionally joining in the fun. This was a normal family outing.

This could be anyone, I thought, for a moment finding myself caught up in the fun they were all having. *This could be me and my child.* Then my thoughts were cut short as my senses shifted, and I felt it coming before it ever appeared in my vision. The crunching of metal was loud in my ears as the sound of two vehicles collided at speed, and all I could do was watch as the car rolled over and over, and over again.

The boy and his father stood together to one side, watching with me as the accident was played out again, and as we watched, it seemed to me that they were almost hovering above the wreckage. The girl seemed to be floating, too, but in a different way and separate from them. Then came the light, an intensely bright, bright light, and I heard the familiar sound of whispered wings. The air about me moved, a subtle movement, and my hair lifted briefly in the breeze that they made as they scooped up the man and the boy. How many there were, I could not tell, but angels were all around. They had come for their charges, and there would be no turning back for them now.

Moving, moving, I came back through the hole, back to the now and to my audience. The two women and the girl were crying and laughing, thrilled that the messages were so clear and understanding everything that I'd said so far. There was more, so much more, as the man and the boy, wanting to say so much, talked on and on, giving evidence of their survival after death. It was thrilling for all of us, for everyone there, but then, I felt that, some small thing was not quite in place. I was missing something, and I was not sure what it was. I looked to my guide with a questioning gaze. What was it? What was it that I had missed? *Something, something,* I thought, as I felt myself moving back again into that other time. Through the hole I went, and once more I watched and saw the accident, repeated again as if for the first time. There was the man, there was the boy, and the girl—I could see her clearly too. All of them floating, hovering it seemed. But wait, one separate, not yet her time to go. So what had happened to her, and why had I seen her floating that way? I knew there was more, and I needed the rest of the story. I knew there was more to see.

I watched, patient and sure that it would be shown to me. The ambulance lights were bright and the sirens were loud. There were two of them, the man and the boy who both lay dead, and the other, the girl, was in critical condition. She lay small and crumpled and bloody, and I watched as they placed her in the ambulance and drove her away. Then, *wham*—time moving forward fast—I saw her as she lay in a coma, no one knowing if she would live or die. Severe head, neck, back, leg injuries, and if she made it, the child would be damaged for life.

Back through the hole, looking at the child and knowing the struggle she must have had, the treatments, the physiotherapy, the incredible pain she must have suffered, I reached out and took hold of her hands.

Bridget's father and brother drew close, giving words of comfort and hope, giving inspiration to the child, now thirteen years old, who still had such a long way to go to combat the disabilities the accident had left her with. She smiled as I gave her the messages from her father and brother, and the smile was wide, lighting up her face. "Do they know I made it?" she asked. I nodded. "They do indeed," I replied. "They do indeed."

The evening was over, and what a spectacular evening it had been. My headache had dissolved like magic the moment I had begun to work, and I had not let anyone down, or at least I hoped not. It was two in the morning when I climbed into bed, and thoughts of Llewella came once more into my mind.

"You have done all that you can do," Grey Eagle whispered reassuringly as I lay my head on the pillow. "It will not be long now, just an hour or so, and before you wake up, she will be home with us. Angels are there with her, and she can see them now, so go to sleep. Don't worry. She is safe."

And so I closed my eyes as tears ran down my face, and I asked, "What am I going to do now?"

"Trust little one, trust, for we keep you safe, too. Trust, little one, trust, and you'll see."

So I slept while my friend passed, and in my dreams she called my name. And I hear her words now as I write. "God's plan . . . God's plan . . . God's plan!"

Lightning Never Strikes Twice

Lightning never strikes twice in the same place . . . or does it?

I bought a small house in Florida on the Gulf Coast, with exactly that thought in mind. The original house had been almost completely demolished by a hurricane several decades earlier, which meant, by the law of averages (this was my reasoning anyway) that it was unlikely to happen again.

Of course, I knew differently, for as my experience as a spiritual medium has shown, God can throw us a curveball at any time, and reason, or at least our human way of reasoning, does not apply.

Over the last twenty-five years I have come to understand one thing, and that is that I rarely truly understand anything. For instance, I ask myself, "Why is it that some families live a seemingly charmed life, while others face tragedy after tragedy?" To lose a child is bad enough; to lose more than one is beyond tragedy.

In this chapter, I'm not talking about those awful disasters where an entire family can be wiped out in a fire, as in the last story, and I'm not talking about earthquakes, accidents, and so on, where a whole family can be lost. I'm talking about one tragedy that follows another tragedy, separate and seemingly unconnected incidents that can and do destroy families. Lightning that does strike twice and even sometimes three times in the same place.

It is easy for me to remember those people who have come to me with such stories, easy for me to remember their faces. It is not so much what they look like that I remember, but the pain they carry is an unforgettable thing, and the heartache that is reflected in their eyes.

I clearly remember the woman who came to see me after she had lost her eighteen-year-old son in a motorbike accident, even though it must be more than twenty years ago since I've seen her. As I spoke with her son, two other boys came forward and stood one on either side of him. These two, it turned out, were two more sons she had lost. One had died as a baby, a "crib death"; the other was hit by a car when he was eight years old, as he was playing, right outside his house. Through that consultation, I discovered that she had lost three children, three of four siblings, all of them dying in separate and unconnected incidents. Added to that, after her eldest son had been killed, the woman's husband had suffered a massive stroke and had become an invalid, living his life in a wheelchair.

When I think of her, this lady whose name I have long since forgotten but whose story is vivid in my mind, I wonder about God's plan. I wonder, *How much pain is one person supposed to bear?*

"At least I still have my daughter," I remember her saying to me, bravely trying to find a reason to hold on.

And I also remember the woman in Italy at a workshop I was holding who could still say that her glass was half full, even though she had lost her only two children, one to cancer and one to an accident. Both, obviously, were separate and unconnected incidents.

Then there was a man in a wheelchair two years ago, at the first conference I attended at the Akwesasne Family Violence Center. He was a native of the Mohawk Nation, whose one son had taken his own life.

The other, high on drugs, had driven his car into the side of a mountain and died instantly.

In another example, I remember a man who was in a live TV audience in Rome. One of his sons had died in a car accident, a second had later died in another car accident, and his third son had died of a brain tumor. All were separate and unconnected incidents. This man's wife had also died of a sudden and massive heart attack, leaving him alone, his entire family wiped out, lost to him. I remember his pain, and I can also remember his joy, when I was able to contact them all, and to give him messages from them, messages of love and hope.

I have seen this so-called phenomenon too many times, and as you can imagine, I have been asked countless times by grieving and confused parents why God, and what kind of God, would want to take not just one but two, or in some cases three or four of their children, at different times and in different ways? Why God would want to wipe out an entire generation of kids? And the only answer I can give is that I don't know. I just don't know.

Kathe Parker had come to our workshop in Vermont with her friend the first weekend in October 2005. On Friday evening, the audience was large and friendly. An air of anticipation filled the room as I began my walk through the crowd, asking if anyone had a question. Dozens of hands shot up, and I could see that I had no need to worry about my audience participating. Everyone was ready to go, and as the evening wore on, I was able to give so many wonderful messages from the spirit world. There were lots of tears, lots of laughter, and we all had a wonderful and inspiring time.

Our all-day seminar began on Saturday morning with my asking what expectations, if any, people had and what agenda they were hoping to follow. I was amazed at the response I received, as from every corner of the room, people spoke up. Some wanted messages from the spirit world; some wanted to learn about healing. There were others who wanted to learn how to communicate with their loved ones who had passed. One woman, who raised her hand tentatively, not knowing why she had raised it, said meekly, as I pointed to her indicating that it was her turn, "I don't want to do this."

The audience laughed but kindly, thinking she meant "ask a question," but something in her tone, and the way that Grey Eagle drew a little closer to me, made me pay attention.

"You mean live, don't you? You mean you don't want to live," I said as gently as I could, and my audience, suddenly quiet, realizing there was more, immediately connected and empathized with the questioner's pain.

Barely nodding, she began to cry. "I just don't want to go on living." Her words, barely above a whisper, were heard by every one of us.

It was clear to me immediately that whatever problem this woman had, it would not be solved easily, that it would take time to help her, and it would take more time than we would have that day, so I told her that I would speak to her later on and see what, if anything, I could do.

Saturday moved quickly into Sunday, which was to be our healing day at the foundation's center. Surrounded by mountains and the breathtaking views, the sun unusually hot for the time of year, we spent the day learning about and giving healing. There were many who came bringing their animals for healing, and there were those who had come for healing for themselves. Of course, there were many who wanted to learn how to give healing, how to become students of the healing arts. It was a wonderful day with a great mix of people from all walks of life. As the weekend drew to a close, I looked around at everyone, strangers at the beginning, now with new friendships forming, and I thought back on the last few days. I thought about all the messages we had received from the spirit world, all the healing we had all received, and the teachings that had brought us all closer together. *Was I satisfied?* I wondered. *Had I done enough?* I would never know. All I would be sure of was that I had done the best I could.

It was almost time to end our time together, and I was about to ask everyone to join me in a closing prayer when a hand tapped me on my shoulder, breaking through my thoughts.

"The lady over there, the one with the blond hair, you promised to talk to her, Rosemary."

It was my friend, Joan, reminding me about the woman who had told us she didn't want to live.

I headed across the room, an apology already forming on my lips. It was not that I had forgotten, exactly, but there had been so much going on that she had slipped to the back of my mind.

As I began to apologize, she was so sweet, so understanding, telling me that she was quite happy to wait, that her experience of the weekend had been tremendous, and that she had gained much comfort just listening to other people's stories.

Looking into her eyes, and again feeling Grey Eagle draw close to me, I understood that she had lost a child. I knew she was desperate to make a connection, but I also knew that she had been willing to put her needs to one side, to be considerate of me and of mine and other's needs.

"How far away are you?" I asked, "How long did it take you to get here?"

"About five hours," she replied, a small glimmer of hope lighting her face.

"Call Denise." I smiled. "Call my office next week. I'll fit you in as soon as I can."

It was about two weeks later that Kathe and Jim Parker arrived at my home. It was Thursday October 20, 2005, 10:30 A.M. The sun was shining, hitting the golds, reds, and oranges of fall leaves, seeming to hold a promise of something special. But would that promise be fulfilled? We would know very soon.

I had already given my little speech, the usual warning that I could promise nothing, that I may not be able to connect with their child, and as I ushered them up the stairs to the sitting room, I still didn't know how well we were going to do. But I shouldn't have been worried, for as soon as I sat down, he was there, standing in the middle of the room, in front of his parents, a smile playing around the corners of his mouth, his eyes fixed on mine, and I could see that he was eager to begin.

Jim and Kathe sat together on the sofa, holding hands, excited and nervous at the same time, and as I began, their hands clasped a little tighter, the thrill of the moment, the promise of the day, taking shape before their eyes.

"We have a young man here, a little older than you might remember him, but handsome, eager, and as excited as you both are," I began. Then, before I had time to take another breath, I felt myself moving, slipping into that other time, that other place, down and through the hole, to be present at the scene of this young man's passing. It was as if it was happening in that "now" moment, yet I knew that I was somewhere in the past, still present in my living room, having one foot in one time, one foot in another, and able to recount everything I saw and heard.

I found myself on a field, a sports field, and I knew, don't ask me how, that it was a school's sports field. There were a number of boys, I could see, running this way and that, all of them dressed in kneepads and fancy shorts. Was it a uniform of sorts? But what were they playing? Was it football, soccer? No, it was a game I was unfamiliar with. What it was I wasn't sure. But it was a ball game of some kind—that I knew. There was a lot of running and shouting on the field, and searching, I saw him, the young man who was standing in my living room. As I watched him playing with his teammates, he looked strong, healthy and happy, and very into the game. Then suddenly, without warning, as I watched, he fell, or seemed to fall, dropping to the ground in an instant. At that moment, as if someone had hit the pause button on a DVD player, the whole scene froze, all sound ceased, all movement halted, and even the air seemed to become freeze-framed.

"I hear my name called." I could hear his voice, like soft sound on snowfall, reaching across the space between us, then a pause, and, "I heard my name called." I nodded, smiled at Jeff, understanding exactly what my young visitor was telling me. Fully back in the now, back in my sitting room, I turned to Kathe and Jim, and repeated what their son Jeff had told me. I described the playing field, the fancy shorts Jeff was wearing that day, the ball game.

"Lacrosse," said Jim. "He was at school, and he was playing lacrosse."

I described the way that I had seen Jeff fall, and as I spoke, Jeff explained how he had passed immediately, having heard his name being called by his angels.

"It was my time," he explained to us. "There was no fear, no pain, nor any chance that I could be resuscitated. It took just a moment, an instant, and I was with God.

"My heart stopped," he continued, "although I was perfectly healthy at the time. The doctors tried to find the cause, but they couldn't. There was no physical explanation for what happened. It was simply my time to go."

Jim and Kathe listened quietly as I recounted all of this to them, nodding their understanding. In the spring of 1996 their eighteen-year-old son, Jeff, a senior in high school, collapsed on the school playing field for no apparent reason and died instantly.

So far, the consultation was going well. The communication with Jeff couldn't have been clearer, and although Jim and Kathe were deeply saddened by their son's passing, they were thrilled that he was able to communicate so well.

Now the worst was over. The hardest part of any communication is the beginning, when that person from the spirit world describes the way he or she died and relives the experience for the family, as evidence that it's really their relative. The sadness and pain for the parents as they relive their loss is almost unbearable. So now I turned to Jeff, expecting him to speak to us on a lighter and more positive note, and asked him what he would like to talk about now.

"Times two," he replied simply, "times two."

I was confused and asked him to explain, and I repeated to his parents what he'd said. They nodded, seeming to understand but giving me no insight as to what their son meant. I was still confused.

"Times two," Jeff repeated again, laughing this time, and before I had time to ask, I saw another boy standing next to him, not quite as tall. The resemblance was unmistakable; it was obvious they were brothers. So now, here was Jeff's brother, Will, who told me his story. "Times two." He smiled and, pointing to his brother, said, "Just like him."

As impossible as it may seem, in the spring of 2004, Will, also eighteen and a senior in high school, collapsed on his school's playing field while playing Frisbee with friends. He died instantly, just as his brother had, eight years and twelve days earlier.

"I heard my name," said Will, speaking for the first time without his brother's help. "I heard my name called. It took only a moment, an instant, and I was with God. And of course"—now grinning wickedly and pointing to Jeff—"with him."

Jeff had told me Will's story, and had taken me to that playing field so that I could see for myself, and once again I had recounted all that I had seen and heard.

"Times two, times two." Two sons, two absolutely identical tragedies, with no medical reason to explain why, totally unconnected, eight years and twelve days apart! How could this be? I looked at the parents of these two boys and wondered how in the world they had been able to stand the pain of these two unexplained tragedies.

The change happened so quickly I was caught off-guard for a moment, as the heaviness of the last hour disappeared. The energy in the room lifted, and it was as if the sun, streaming through the windows, had become even brighter than ever. The two boys had moved, almost without my realizing it, and were now standing behind the sofa, closer to where their parents sat.

"We are entwined," they explained. "Our souls are entwined. This was our plan before we came to the earth plane, before we were born.

We have always been connected and could not be apart from each other for long."

As they spoke, both at the same time, stumbling over their words in the excitement of finally being able to talk to their mom and dad, it was obvious to me that they were happy and complete now that they were together.

Then I heard it again, as in unison, they said, "Times two," and my heart sank for a moment as I fleetingly wondered if there might be even more tragedy to come.

"It's OK, Rosemary," both boys said, sensing my concern, and laughing. "We just want to send messages to the two boys we left behind."

Will and Jeff went on to talk about their other brothers, Jim, aged thirty, and Charles, twenty-five.

They told us they had seen the ring, and that it was beautiful. Brother Jim is newly engaged and designed the ring himself.

They talked about the bride-to-be, Brenda, requesting that she wear a long veil or train, explaining that they wanted to carry it for her as she walked down the aisle.

They described their brother Charles, portraying him as an extremely sensitive young man, a naturally gifted healer, particularly so with children. He was still studying. They told us they believed he would make a good teacher or counselor.

The message they gave their mother, however, was a tough one, for they had watched her in her grief and had seen her sadness and her inability to move forward. They had seen how this has affected their brothers and, in particular, how it was affecting their father.

"We love you," they told their mom, "but we don't like to come and visit you at home because there is such a pall of sadness around you both, and it is so hard for us to take. We see you wallowing in your grief. We see Dad not wanting to go home because he hates the misery he feels when he walks into the house. We hate it too." Painful as it was for Kathe to hear, when the boys talked, telling us how they both felt, she understood them perfectly, as did her husband.

"We want you to look in the mirror every day, to find one positive thought, to work at being happy, and to remind yourself that one day you will see us again, be with us again, that you haven't lost us, and that life is still good."

Kathe cried and Jim cried, as much from relief as anything. As unpleasant as this message had been, this was what they had needed to hear and what they wanted to hear. Now they knew, without a doubt, that their boys were still around and still part of the family.

Their message to Jim was very different, as now, and on a much lighter note, they described their father's home office in the greatest detail—small, cramped, with stacks of papers on every surface. This was Jim's sanctuary, the place where he went to be alone, to think, to meditate, to cry.

Describing another room—larger, more spacious, and more organized—the boys talked of boxing things up, rearranging the room, making a bigger office. "More room for us when we come to visit," they joked. "Hey, Dad, we'll help you. It'll be a boys' project. Mom has to stay out of it. And Dad, put a rack on one of the walls, where we can hang our hats." At this Jim and Kathe began to laugh, telling me they had just begun to move Jim's office into a bigger room, and that, yes, there were boxes and boxes of stuff, and Kathe had already called the painter.

It was wonderful to see everyone smiling and happy at last, and just as I thought things couldn't get any better, I saw a young girl standing next to the boys. She was small, very petite and very pretty. Telling us briefly how she passed, she asked Kathe to give a message to her mom.

"Tell her I'm OK, will you please, and Kathe, will you tell her I'm still dancing and that I'm happy."

This was the daughter of Kathe's friend, the one she had come with to our weekend workshop in Vermont. Kathe and Jim knew right away who she was, and were delighted that they could take this message back to their friend.

Jeff and Will's final message to their parents was that they, too, were happy, happy to be able to make this communication, happy to be able to show how close they still are to their family. Laughing, both talking at once, they told their parents how much they were growing, how much more handsome they were now. As they talked, both boys made it clear that they would always be around and would be there to meet their family when it was their time to cross over.

A few weeks later, wanting to include this story in the book, I e-mailed Kathe and Jim to ask if they would help. One of my biggest problems in recounting stories, as I've said before, is that I see and talk to so many families that it is very easy for me to confuse or even to get mixed up about which story is which. Kathe and Jim immediately responded, sending me all the details of their experience with me and adding this final piece.

"No amount of grief counseling could do for us what the words from our boys have done," they wrote. "To know that they are close to us, well and happy, together, and they will be there when we cross over, has done more for us than any amount of grief therapy, marriage counselors or anything else we have tried. The pall of grief has lifted. We will continue to miss them every day of our lives. . . . We will cry. . . . we will grieve . . . but in a different way . . . with hope and thankfulness for the beautiful souls that surround us here on earth and in our life to come."

So, as we can see, lightning does strike twice, but why, I just don't know. To lose a child is bad enough. To lose more than one is beyond tragedy.

Tragedy following tragedy. Separate and seemingly unconnected incidents that can and do destroy families. Lightning that does strike twice, and sometimes more than twice, in the same place but at different times.

I do not understand it; I have no explanation for it, except that when God calls out our name, we willingly and with great joy return home.

I hope, in the telling of this story, that for those of you who have not had the same opportunity as Jim and Kathe had, an opportunity to connect with your loved ones in the spirit world, to hear them tell you that they are OK, and that they're still a part of your lives, that at least their story will help and inspire you along your path. Like Jeff and Will, your children will be together; they will come and visit you and will still be part of your family and your life.

I hope that for those of you who have had to suffer that terrible tragedy, tragedy beyond tragedy, I hope you can let Jeff and Will, their words and their story, be an inspiration for you to go on, to live your lives in a good and positive way.

As Jim and Kathe wrote . . . "We will continue to miss them every day of our lives. . . . We will cry . . . we will grieve . . . but in a different way . . . with hope and thankfulness for the beautiful souls that surround us here on earth and in our life to come."

The Akwesasne Experience

It was Monday, October 24, 2005, and we were on our way to Cornwall, Ontario, for a three-day workshop. The "we" were Denise, my secretary; Joan, my friend from England; Gary, a good friend and student; Chris, another student and chairperson of our healing organization; and me. We were all excited about spending the next three days with the Mohawk community at their Celebration of Life conference. We were looking forward to hearing the other speakers and enjoying the dancers and singers we knew would be there. Although we were all aware that the next few days would be hard work, still it was an adventure we could not pass up.

This was my second time as a speaker, and I pretty much knew what to expect. As we drove to the event, Gary, Joan, and I reminisced about our very first experience, when we had visited the year before. It had begun with a phone call from the Akwesasne Women's Group. They were looking to hold an event to raise money for the women's center and for the children's and family violence program they had begun. I was in the office when the call came in and happened to pick up the phone—a surprise for all of us, since I rarely do that.

"Who are you?" I heard myself ask, as the young woman on the other end of the line, obviously nervous and unsure, gave a garbled speech about her organization and its needs.

As soon as I heard the details of the program, I was onboard and agreed to go. This was to be an educational program, dedicated to helping people understand empowerment, empowerment in even the most hopeless situations. This was an opportunity to help so many who felt disabled, both emotionally and physically, born into a culture that seems, to the world outside, to be handicapped, to be destroying itself, with a high rate of suicide, drug and alcohol abuse. Perhaps this was my chance to make a difference, however small, to some of the people in the Native American community. Maybe this was my opportunity to learn more about a people whose history and way of life fascinates me.

So here we were, on our way to the conference, for the second time around, hoping that this experience would be as good as the last.

We arrived in the early evening, around seven o'clock, and after checking into the hotel, we had a light supper in the restaurant. There were people milling about everywhere we looked, and I realized that the conference would be packed. I recognized a few faces from the last time, but most were new to me, and I could feel lots of good energy bouncing off the walls, a real buzz in the air.

The conference began the next morning, Tuesday, at eight, with the opening ceremony and welcoming speech. Shirelle Jacobs gave the introduction and history of the conference, introduced us to a few of the staff, and then to Chief Jake Swamp, a fascinating and funny speaker, who has traveled all over the world and spoken before many famous audiences.

The conference was off to a good start, and the days flew by, the mornings taken by other speakers, the afternoons by me, and the theme of the conference remained the same throughout. Empowerment!

John Sardella, a favorite of mine, a man of great humility and an incredible speaker, gave wonderful insight and inspiration as he talked about addiction and healing. I listened, fascinated, as he recounted his experiences to us. Another speaker, Diane Longboat, inspired many by the telling of her own personal story, and then, of course there were the dancers and singers. It was on the second day, just before I was about to speak, that three of the singers gave a performance that was to blow me away. Explaining the prayer they were about to sing and the meaning of it, they began the song. The beauty of it, the beauty of their voices in unison, the emotion, the feeling I experienced while listening to them, is indescribable. The fact that their voices were incredible, stunning, added to the experience, and as the song went on, I closed my eyes to better connect with the moment, and an unexpected thing happened. I felt myself being transported to another place, one I knew well. It was Llewella's place, her farm in Ira, Vermont, and the home of our healing foundation.

I found myself on the knoll, one of the higher places on the property, with an incredible 360-degree view of the Green Mountains all around me. Standing in front of me was my guide, Grey Eagle, gazing directly into my eyes. He didn't speak, for the emotion of the moment was beyond words. But I felt his heart embrace me, and the power of his love was palpable, overwhelming, and his message very clear. I was doing everything I was supposed to be doing, I was being told, despite my doubts and fears.

I opened my eyes, and the mountains were still there, Grey Eagle was still there, and the singers were still singing their song.

Then, a small movement to my right caught my attention, and to my surprise I saw Llewella, standing next to me, by my chair, enthralled, I could see, by the music, by the song. Turning, she looked at me, tears filling her eyes and spilling down her cheeks. Although she didn't speak, I could feel that for her too, the emotion of the moment was beyond words. I felt her heart embrace me, and the power of her love was overwhelming, and her message, like Grey Eagle's, was very clear. I was doing everything I was supposed to be doing for her, too, her heart called out, despite my doubts and fears.

I closed my eyes, connecting once again to my spirit guide, connecting to Llewella, and connecting to the prayer and to the Mohawk singers, and it was a magical moment.

Now it was my turn to speak, my turn to connect with my audience and with those in the spirit world wishing to give messages. The emotion of the moment was beyond words. The hearts of the spirit world embraced me, the power of their love was overwhelming, and their message was very clear. I was doing everything I was supposed to, I heard them call out, despite my doubts and fear, and they knew that I was doing the best I could.

They know me, I thought. They know me so well. They know that, despite my many years of working with them, despite all the evidence, all the thousands of messages, despite the fact that people see me as an expert in my field, still I wonder. Each time I give a message, each time I give healing, still I wonder. Is it enough? Did I do enough? And the answer I give myself is always the same. It is never enough, no matter how good it is, and even recognizing that I am only one small person, and doing the best I can, still . . . it is never enough. There is always more to do. Still I doubt and still I fear. I doubt myself and I fear that I will always come up short of what I have to do!

As I felt their reassurance, tears filled my eyes and spilled down my cheeks, and the sound of the music filled my head as the prayer came to a close.

The events organizer was announcing the next speaker, and I heard my name as I was called to the rostrum. I lifted my hand to my face and brushed the tears away, took a deep breath, stood up, and began to speak.

The accounts you are about to read are longer and in some cases a little more detailed than some you have read so far, taken from the transcripts of the day, and given to you in just the way they were given to me. I have taken the crux of the message, leaving out the evidence we received beforehand that the person giving the message is who they say they are, presuming that by now you realize this is information that was already given.

The first message came fast and from a young man, not more than a boy really, who had died in a road accident and who wanted to connect to his mother.

RA: "I see him clearly, standing beside you. He has great teeth, which he is very proud of. He has a thing about his teeth, which he tells me, are perfect."

At this comment, his mother laughed, instantly connecting with her son, through his vanity.

RA: "He tells me he was going a little too fast, that it was really sudden, really quick, and there was no chance for resuscitation. He wants to tell you why he was going fast, although it might confuse you, but he says that he was in a bit of a hurry.

"He heard voices, many, many voices, and they were calling out to him. He saw light and shadows, and it seemed that there were angels appearing through the light, and he was so excited by what he saw and heard that he didn't feel the impact. He was so thrilled by what was happening to him, he says that he was sailing, flying, being lifted up, even before the accident happened. He was already on his way and was not even present on the earth plane when the car hit the wall."

Some of you as you read, may be wondering, "How can that be?" But I have heard this said many times before, often by those who have seemed to take their own lives or who have passed due to an accident. You may be surprised to learn that it is not at all unusual for those who have died not to be present, on this earth, that is, at that moment when the cord is severed and the physical body takes its final breath.

RA: "He was already transforming to another way of life, he tells me, which he says is wonderful for him, but not for you. For you, this is a terrible tragedy, and you don't know how you will ever get over it. You won't [I say gently], we never do, those of us who have lost a child, but you will learn to live with it, and your son tells me he is going to help you.

"He is excited for you, too, and tells me you have found someone to share your life with, someone new, a good man, and he can see that you're happy with him. He wants you to stay on the path. He says that he is pulling you along the path because you have begun a new journey, a good journey, and he is so proud of you. He wants you to know that he is your inspiration, your guiding light. He is laughing and tells me that he is alive and well, that he walks with you every day, and he wants you to take this message home to the rest of the family, and oh, yes, just one more thing . . . Please get your teeth fixed, will you, he laughs, so that when you smile, he will be happy that you are as beautiful as him!"

The mother laughed, we all laughed, as we heard the boy's final message. But for me, there was no time to dilly-dally. I had more messages to give.

RA: "I have a lady here, and she tells me she's your mother."

I was now speaking to a young woman, describing to her how her mother had died, what she looked like, and letting her know that she was right by her side, waiting to give her messages.

RA: "What is that saying? 'Lucky at cards, unlucky in love,' or something like that. Your mother tells me you feel that love eludes you at every step. You stand here, crying in front of us all. I know how painful this is for you, how painful your life is for you."

As I say this, I reach out and take her hand in mine, recognizing a familiar pattern, one that I myself once followed, and I know that the message this young woman's mother is about to give is not going to be an easy one.

RA: "Just as soon as you think you've found the right person to spend the rest of your life with, everything backfires, and this happens to you again and again. It's tough, it's horrible, your mother knows, but—and then a bigger BUT—she is not going to tell you what you want to hear. She is going to tell you what you need to hear.

"Let's start at the beginning, she says. It's not you, at least, it's not you in the way you think it is. You think that something is wrong with you, that you must be unattractive or just the kind of person other people don't like. That's not it, that's not it at all. This is what the real

problem is. You're in love. You're in love with love! You love the ro-
mance, you love the feeling of falling in love, and even when you tell
yourself to go slow, your heart starts to race and you are in too much
of a hurry to fall.

"Afraid to be yourself, you do what he likes to do, or what you think
he likes to do. You bend over backward to please, to be someone you're
not. So, what happens? Six months later, when you can't keep up the
pretense anymore, when the real you starts to emerge, he sees a different person, not uglier, not more or less controlling, not meaner or
spottier, just different, and he's confused. You're not the person he
fell in love with, he doesn't know you, and he feels cheated and runs!

"So, here is some excellent advice from your mother. Be you, she
says, be who you really are, from the start. Let him see YOU! It will only
work this way. Stop being afraid that you are not good enough. Stop
being afraid that no one will like you just as you are, that no one will
love you, just as you are. Just be you!"

More and more messages were given, as one after the other, those
in the spirit world came through to talk to us, showing us over and over
again that they had survived death, and were still a part of their families' lives. One such message was given to a woman in her early forties,
with two young children, whose husband had been murdered, stabbed
to death with a knife.

RA: "He begins by telling me that he felt no pain, that his passing
was quick and easy. He is talking to me about your family or, more precisely, his family, his mother, his sisters and brother, and his father.
He refers to the 'family fights' and is describing to me how difficult it
has been for you since he passed, as there are some in his family who
have been mean to you, cruel, who in some way blame you for your
husband's death, even though you had nothing to do with it and are
suffering his loss greatly. You miss him, he tells me, and you are in
such pain.

"There are two in the family who have always been jealous of you,
and they take great pleasure in stirring the pot, going out of their way

to make life miserable for you. You feel you should stay with the family because of the children. You don't want to turn your back on what used to be. You feel that you don't belong anywhere since he's been gone, and this is a natural way to feel, but why, he asks, do you let them hurt you this way, these people who are so mean to you? Why are you listening to them? He loves you very much, and he wants to give you a little piece of advice if he can. Why, he asks again, are you listening to everyone else? Why aren't you listening to your heart? Why don't you do what you want to do? Follow your heart, he tells me to tell you. Listen to your heart. Other people can be mean and they can be cruel, but you can stop them. Don't let a couple of people ruin your life. Don't let them make you feel guilty because I am dead and you are alive. Life is too short. Let others do what they want and you start doing what you want. Start living your life. I will always be around to help."

The theme of the program was family, and when I gave this last message, it reminded me of the many times I have seen families fall apart because someone dies and someone else feels the need to blame. One of the worst stories I ever heard was of a young woman who had lost her husband in the 9/11 Twin Towers tragedy. It was the husband, communicating with his wife from the spirit world through me, who told me what had happened.

She and her husband and their two small children had been living with her mother-in-law, renting the upstairs apartment of the family house, which had been a fine arrangement, and had worked very well . . . until her husband died. The mother-in-law had apparently never liked her daughter-in-law. Embittered by the loss of her son, at the first opportunity, just two weeks after his death, she gave her daughter-in-law one month's notice to find somewhere else to live. She turned her back on all of them—her grandkids, her daughter-in-law, and, if she had only known it, also her beloved son.

Death does funny things to people sometimes, and it isn't for me to judge the rights and wrongs of things. After all, I'm only the messenger. I do know, however, that meanness, cruelty, and discontent will only bring loneliness and heartache. The opposite of those things—generosity, kindness, and contentment of heart and mind—will produce only an abundance of good things. But when life appears cruel to us, when we suffer a loss, it can turn the nicest of us into people we don't really want to be.

It is not just in my experience with the Native American culture, as little as that has been, that I've seen families torn apart through drugs and alcohol. During my time with the Mohawk community, it was so apparent, and on a large scale, that substance abuse often results in family violence, and generation after generation suffer the consequences. What, if anything, can any of us do? I will leave you with this final but by no means last message, given from a young man who was killed on a motorbike. He was drunk at the time and high on drugs. He had gone out with his friends for a joyride, ignoring his family, ignoring all those wise counselors, his elders and the many wonderful people in his tribe who had seen him going on the wrong track and had tried their best to help him.

His girlfriend was at the conference, intrigued by what we were doing and by the many messages from the spirit world. But for some reason she believed she would not be singled out by me—and boy, was she surprised.

RA: "He tells me you want to drop out of school, that you think it's a waste of time, even though your parents want you to stay on. When he was here, he says that no one could tell him what to do, that he didn't listen to anyone, and that you're just the same."

The young teenager grinned, throwing back her ponytail as she did so, proudly agreeing that he was right.

RA: "He says you think you're not bright enough, and you don't believe in yourself, that you don't think much of yourself, and that all your cockiness is bravado."

The girl's smile slipped a little. She didn't like this. She didn't like being singled out, and she didn't like having other people know her true feelings. Her bravado had become a way of life, a way of hiding her insecurities. Now she was feeling vulnerable. But this young man loved her and wanted to show her a better way, a better way than he had taken. He was not about to let a little bit of embarrassment stand in the way of saving her, for there was more to come, and she knew it and had begun to be afraid.

RA: "I see that your mother, your aunt, and your friend are sitting with you. I know that they love you very much. He tells me so, and even knowing that they are here with you, he wants me to tell everyone your secret."

She began to cry, and I saw that she was just a child, after all, and my heart went out to her. But I knew that I must give the message in its entirety, no matter what, for the consequences of what she was doing were far greater than the repercussions of telling her secret. I reached for her hand, and she pleaded with me with her eyes, and I asked Grey Eagle for the third time if this was necessary, but I knew the answer in my heart.

RA: "You're taking drugs. Not just a little but every day, and just as this young man was, he tells me that you're hooked. You just can't seem to stop. He is asking you to get help, and says that there is a man in this room who can help you to stop. He wants you to go into a program, to begin to live a more positive life. He promises that he will help you to do it."

The girl was crying openly now, and her mother and friend, though shocked by what they'd heard, for they had no idea, had come to put their arms around her, to hold her tight, and to show her their support.

I walked to the other side of the room, not quite knowing where I was heading, and came to stop by a man in his fifties quietly listening to everything that had been said. It was one of those moments when, guided by Grey Eagle yet unaware of any voice, any light to show the way, I followed the lead of the spirit world, for they knew where they were going, and it was enough for me to follow.

I asked the man to stand up and tell us who he was. He replied that he was a counselor who worked with teenage kids in drug addiction and that he would be glad to talk to the young girl. Later, he got together with her and her family, and I like to think that he was able to help in some way. Was she saved? The young man who had been killed on the bike had certainly thought she could be, for it was he who had led me in the right direction.

I believe that is always the case. I believe that those in the spirit world will always lead us in the right direction, just as they had led me, and, you know, the only thing we have to do is learn to follow.

Simply out of Love

C an I give you a hug?"

I smiled and held out my arms to embrace him, and he came to me, his arms holding me tight, until gently I moved back and broke the connection between us, aware of the long line of people waiting patiently for me to sign their books.

"Never be the first one to break away from a hug," he whispered in my ear, and chuckling to himself, he waved farewell and disappeared into the crowd.

The next morning I was up bright and early, my thoughts going over the last two days. This was my first experience with the Omega Center in New York, an organization that plans and arranges speaking engagements. So far, everything was going well. Saturday and Sunday we'd had a great turnout, and I hoped my audiences had enjoyed me as much as I had enjoyed them. Now it was Monday. An all-day intensive, they called it, lasting from nine in the morning until four in the afternoon, and we were expecting several hundred to attend.

"A lot of people for a workshop," I mused, as I put on my makeup. But I was not too concerned, knowing that the spirit world has its plan. I trusted completely. Perhaps we'll talk about healing, and maybe I'll give a demonstration of how it works . . . and a voice broke into my thoughts . . . "Never be the first one to break away from a hug" . . . and the sound and the thought lingered a few moments, until, shaking my head, I let go the sound, laughing a little at the idea, picturing myself in a constant hugging mode. When people hug me, they feel they in some way become closer to their loved ones in the spirit world. Therefore they hold on to me for as long as they can. "Just not possible," I said aloud to whoever might be listening, and giving a final and hurried glance in the mirror, I headed out the door.

The room was full, and I could feel the energy bouncing off the walls and ceiling, as the sound of excited voices reached my ears. I was excited too. Here was another chance, another opportunity for me to share my gift, my wonderful and precious gift. Grey Eagle, as always, by my side, I stepped up onto the stage to the sound of great applause, lifted by the obvious enthusiasm of the crowd.

This was to be a whole-day, a whole-day intensive. So, where to begin? *With healing,* I thought, *let's talk about healing.* And so, for the next hour I explored the art of healing with an audience who were, for the day, my students. We explored the potential power and energy of healing, and the possibilities of combining our natural-born healing energy with that universal God force, God energy. We talked about how to go about doing just that. After telling a couple of my favorite healing stories and sharing my own feelings about the gift that healing brings, not only to the patient but also to the healer, everyone warmed to the subject. Questions and comments came thick and fast. The audience warmed to the idea that we can all own the power to heal in some form or another.

Toward the end of that first hour, it became clear to me that it wasn't enough to simply discuss our theories, but that we should put them into practice. This, of course, requires the use of guinea pigs (said with the greatest respect to said guinea pigs), and so I began my search around the room. Led by Grey Eagle, I made my way through the crowd, finally lighting upon a bearded gentleman, whose hand I took, lightly pulling him to his feet. "You can be our first patient," I said, smiling. "Come with me." Little did I know I'd just made this man's day. It wasn't until I stood with him on stage that I realized he was vaguely familiar to me.

"Do I know you?" I asked rather hesitantly, knowing my inability to remember names and faces, even five minutes after I've been introduced to someone.

"My name's Larry," he replied with a broad grin. "I'm the guy who gave you a hug yesterday."

I grinned back. "Oh, I remember now, you're the 'never break away from a hug' man." I went on to explain to the audience how Larry and I had had our brief encounter the day before.

"So, Larry, how do you feel about being our first patient?" I asked, pointing him to the high chair, which had been placed center stage.

"I've been waiting for this moment for a long time," he replied as he sat, and as I placed my hands on his shoulders, I understood why Grey Eagle had chosen him. First, I felt his pain and loneliness, his sickness; the feeling was overwhelming. Then I felt his need, his great need of something to help sustain him. His battle had been a long and hard one, a battle not yet over, not nearly over, and there was a long way yet to go. There are no accidents, no coincidences, and it was obvious to me that Larry had been chosen for a reason.

Standing behind him, handing him a microphone, I put my arms around his shoulders and gently asked him if he would like to share his story with us. There may have been some in the audience who might have wondered at this, because Larry, in his mid-forties, looking fit and tanned, was the picture of good health and well-being. But as we all know but often forget, looks can be deceiving, and as Larry told his story, he broke our hearts. More than fifteen major surgeries, malignant tumors, mastetic cancer, a horrible and insidious disease, and a battle he had been fighting for more than six years—six long, lonely, painful, and terrifying years. When was it going to end? Even now, even as he sat with us, and shared his story, he was about to make yet another decision. Another tumor had appeared; this one under his arm. Should he have more surgery or just give up? "There are days," he said, with tears running down his cheeks, "when it would be just so easy to give up and let nature take its course." Then, lifting his head to look at me, he said, "You know, Rosemary, thanks to you I'm ready to die, if that's what God decides."

"Well, Larry, what do I have to do with this?" I smiled.

"Ah," he said, unable to contain the twinkle in his eye, despite his pain, "I know you very well. I've read all your books and have listened every day for a long time now to your healing tape, which, by the way"— he added with a laugh—"I've copied and sent to hundreds of people."

"Copied my tape!" I exclaimed in mock horror. "Don't you know that's illegal!"

"So sue me," my new patient replied with a grin . . . and on that note, our friendship was cemented, and my audience took Larry to their hearts. It was incredible to believe that such a man, with such an unbelievably heavy burden, could still have such a great sense of humor. It was perhaps this sense of humor that had helped sustain him so far. Now, I knew, he was at the end of his resources. He needed something more, something that maybe my audience and I could help him find.

We began his healing, not with drama and fanfare but in quiet and loving prayer. All the people in the room giving something of themselves, a part of them, a thought, a moment, a piece of their energy, to a perfect stranger. Simply out of love. Each person's energy, combined with that of every other person, growing in strength, combining with the love of God, filling the room. It was a palpable thing, moving, embracing not just Larry but each of us. If any of us had ever spent a moment in paradise, in the presence of God and His angels, this was that moment. And all of us there knew it.

As if that was still not enough, as I watched the light of God grow bright in that room, I became aware of a presence, someone from the spirit world standing close by on the stage with us.

I became still, looking through and past the light, all of my senses finely tuned, knowing that Larry was about to be given one of the greatest gifts any of us could possibly be given.

Larry's father had died several years ago. Quite suddenly and out of the blue, his heart had given out. He and his son had been close, and there had been no chance for either of them to say good-bye, to say those things we all would like to say if we knew this would be the last time we might see those we love most in the world. Now he was here, the father who had so much to say to the son who needed so desperately to hear.

At first, it was barely more than a whisper, emotion getting in the way of things. "I'm here, son, I'm here," I heard Larry's father say, as he choked on his tears, his pain an obvious thing.

Silently I sent my thoughts, my power, my energy, out, out, out, trying to give him strength and support. I saw Grey Eagle standing close by and knew that all we had to do was to be patient and to listen and to relay Larry's father's words to his son.

"Larry, it's me, son. It's Dad. Don't cry, don't cry. I'm right here by your side. I know that you're sick, but everything is going to be just fine. You will be strong, and you will win. And I will help you. Just remember that I'm always here for you and that we will fight this thing together. You have much more time than you think."

As I held Larry and relayed his father's words, it seemed to me that my audience held their breath. Not one of us wanted to disturb the magic of the moment. Everyone wanted to do the right thing, behave the right way. We all knew we were being given a gift.

Larry's father had come to give his son a message, many messages in fact. He had come to give his boy all the things he would need to sustain him through the many trials, which he knew were to come. On and on he talked with us, with his son, giving messages of hope and encouragement, giving his son a clear understanding that it was not yet Larry's time to die. He was not saying that his son would beat the cancer, that he would have a miracle cure, but he was saying that whatever Larry's future was, he would win through. He would find whatever strength he might need to face that future and to conquer his adversities.

If ever a man needed to hear these things, Larry did. If ever a man needed help and inspiration to fight the fight of his life, Larry did. If ever a man needed to hear from his father that he was not alone, Larry surely did. What a gift. What an amazing and incredible gift we were all given that day.

Larry flew back to his hometown at the end of that day with his hopes renewed, his determination to win strengthened, heartened, his courage greater than ever before. He also left having made many new friends.

Since that time, over the last few years, Larry has undergone more surgery. It was not just physically excruciating for him but mentally tough also. There were several more surgeries, more treatments, and time after time, Larry came through, conquering his cancer over and over again until finally it was time for him to go.

I spoke to him the day before he passed. His voice was weak, and he had difficulty breathing, but despite that, our conversation was good. Larry still had his sense of humor and was still able to joke a little. He was finally ready to join his father, who he had no doubt was waiting for him.

Larry's courage, his refusal to give up even in the most extreme circumstances, is remarkable, to say the least. His story is an inspiration to all who know him, and now, perhaps, his story can be an inspiration to you too.

I will remember him this way. One time, during one of our many conversations, Larry and I got into a fairly in-depth discussion about life and death and God and so on. Larry was telling me about his search for truth. He talked about all the wonderful and interesting people he had met on his journey and about the vast amount of inspiration he had gained since having found what he called his new path in life.

"It has been really hard at times," he told me, "and I've often wondered whether I've been doing the right thing—you know, fighting so hard, not giving up. But now I have no doubts. I know I'm on the right path, and I feel that I'm in a good place." Then, laughing, he added, Larry-style, tongue in cheek, "Of course, Rosemary, as we well know, even if you're on the right path, you'll get run over if you just sit there. . . ."

Ghost Busters

Kim Cool is a writer of some note, a well-known figure in the town of Venice, Florida, a witty and intelligent woman of sixty-five, who looks more like fifty-five (good genes, she tells me). Kim is a kind of ghost buster, you might say, or perhaps more of a ghost hunter. Having written a series of books about ghosts, all Florida-based, and as a serious investigator, Kim has hunted high and low searching for truth, seeking out anyone who has had an "experience." She investigates, going back in history to try to verify, or otherwise, some of the stories and encounters people are willing to share. In her books, stories of hauntings and history go hand in hand, as Kim tries to tell it like it is, in her down to earth and very realistic fashion.

We became friends after I had been interviewed by her for the local Venice paper. I was holding an event in Sarasota, some thirty miles away, and Kim, ever intrigued by such as I, wanted to check me out.

As we sat together in my little house, amid builders, painters, and the like, Kim began her interview, asking all the usual questions that most journalists ask, not offering her own opinions, trying to stay neutral and unbiased, as all good journalists think they must.

As far as I was concerned, this was just another interview. I knew nothing of Kim at that time, other than that she was a reporter for the local paper and that she had contacted my office for this interview. I had known nothing of her history, or the fact that she too was a writer. That was soon to change, for during our time together, as often happens under these circumstances, Kim's husband and father were waiting patiently in the wings, knowing that soon now, it would be their turn to speak.

Amid tears and laughter, I learned about Kim, as her husband, Ken, described first his illness, then his passing, and then his darling wife's life since he himself had been gone. Soon Kim's father joined in, and they both had so much to say, so much information to give, and so much love, encouragement, and inspiration to share.

"This is the first time I've ever taken my family to an interview," Kim joked. "And this," she said, blowing her nose and wiping her eyes for more than the dozenth time, "this is the first time I've ever cried during an interview."

"Well, don't let it worry you," I replied, recalling the time that Elaine Louie, one of the toughest and most highly acclaimed journalists from *The New York Times,* had used up two boxes of tissues and three toilet rolls during her interview with me. "Almost everyone cries around me." I smiled. "And why not? You've had to wait fourteen years to hear from Ken and your dad. A few tears are in order, I think."

After our session, Kim realized that I was the real deal, and it didn't take long for her to connect the dots. She was a ghost hunter, a ghost writer, so to speak, and I could speak to the dead. Now, was that a magical combination, or what? But wait, maybe this was not something I would be interested in.

"Have you ever been on a ghost hunt?" Kim asked tentatively, as she scribbled furiously in her notebook, ever the professional, while trying to maintain her composure. After all, she was a reporter on the job.

I knew where she was going, and not really sure if this was something I was interested in, I was a little cautious in my answer.

The truth is, I've been on many a ghost hunt, although I prefer not to use that term. For what is a ghost anyway, other than someone in the spirit world trying to make his presence felt, for one reason or another. And did I really have the time, or want to make time in my already ridiculously overwhelming schedule? What about the healing foundation I was hoping to start, what about my patients, what about my already full waiting list of people like Kim, who were hoping, through me, to connect with their loved ones? What about the new book—this book—and those other million little things I was struggling to make time for? There were a million and ten reasons why I couldn't get involved.

But Kim was good, as of course she would be with the help of her husband and father, and she seemed to know just the right things to say to get me hooked.

"I'm going to Tampa on Saturday to write a piece for the paper on the USS *Victory*, a ship that was used by the Marines in World War II, and which is now being used as a tourist attraction. I'm hoping," she said slyly, a small smile playing around her mouth, "that I might find a ghost story or two. I might even be able to write it up as a ghost ship. You never know. Are you busy on Saturday? I'd loved to have you come if you're not."

Well, of course I was busy on Saturday, and every other day if it came to that, but still I heard myself say, "Let me think about it for a couple of days. Let me see if I can juggle my schedule a little bit."

After Kim left that day, I knew I was going to have to call and say I couldn't make it. True, the idea of a ghost hunt on an old warship was intriguing, and it sounded somewhat fun. Also true, it was an opportunity to get to know Kim better as a friend, and that thought was appealing. But . . . and but, and but, and a million and ten buts more . . . I really couldn't justify taking the day off.

It's a funny thing, working for yourself, and I know that there are so many people who would give anything to be their own boss. But being your own boss, making the rules and then sticking to them, is the only way to ensure that you have a job at all. Not having anyone to tell you what to do, to dictate your every working hour, sounds like a dream come true to most people. In reality, however, when you work for yourself, if you want to be successful or even to simply make a reasonable living, you have to have self-discipline or your life would become a mess. Ruefully I decided, no play planned for Saturday. Why, I wondered, had I even said I might?

I was about to call Kim to say I wouldn't be able to make it when miraculously, as these things happen, my schedule was cleared for me. An appointment was unexpectedly canceled. An overseas visitor, a patient, was not going to make it until Sunday. The person who was flying in to see me had had a flight change. Of course, there were still those other one million and seven things to do, but when I called Kim, I heard myself agreeing to play.

As we drove to Tampa, I felt as if I'd been let out of school early. Neither of us had any idea what the day might bring, but it felt to me as if we were on an adventure, and I realized that it had been way too long since I had had one of those. Would we find ghosts, ghouls, or things that go bump in the night? It didn't seem to matter. We were just two ghost busters, busting to have fun.

There was a tour guide, an old Marine, waiting for Kim when we arrived. As we were being shown around the ship, we listened while he regaled us not only with tales of the USS *Victory* but with his own war stories as well.

"Any ghosts, by any chance?" Kim asked, after a suitable interval. "Anyone heard of any strange happenings aboard?"

"Ghosts?" exclaimed the old Marine, a little confused by the question. "Good Lord, no, this was a cargo ship, went to Russia and back, didn't really see any action, y'know. Anyway, as I was saying . . ." and on he went, telling yet another of his war stories, as we continued around the ship.

It was time for me to move off, make my own inquiries, and see what I could find out for myself. Was I expecting ghosts? No, not really. But

I knew that if walls could talk, this old tug would have plenty to say. Of course, if you know about energy or about psychometry or if you have used psychometry, you know that energy can talk. Energy can tell you everything you need to know.

The energy on that ship was palpable. The energy of every person, every event, every occurrence, every conversation, thought, or deed was present. All I had to do was tap into it. It was an easy thing for me to do.

Sounds came first, muffled but unmistakable, the sound of boots, hundreds of boots hitting the metal of the deck. It sounded like hundreds, if not thousands, of army boots, and I most definitely heard the sound of marching. A moment passed. Then I saw them, row upon row of solders, like phantoms rising up out of the past. Part of their energy had remained onboard decades after they themselves had departed the ship.

When Kim had asked the old marine, he said that this was a cargo ship. He had said, "No action." Now, though, as I watched from my place in that familiar no-man's-land, Grey Eagle began describing to me the human cargo—soldiers, hundreds of them—being taken to fight a war on foreign soil.

As quickly as it had appeared, the scene shifted before my eyes. A new sensation took its place, and I felt the movement as the ship rolled and bucked, although to other eyes—those other visitors who had come to look over the ship, day-trippers on a fun outing—the vessel lay still and safely moored.

More sounds now, and I heard shouting and saw many men running fore and aft. As I watched and listened, as I tuned more fully into the energy of the vessel, I heard the creaks and groans of the ship tossed to and fro in what seemed a raging storm. Those sounds seemed muffled by the louder sounds of raging winds, the crash of waves hitting the deck, slapping hard against the sides of the boat. Then I heard more, I heard the sounds of scared men, brave men, many young and inexperienced, trapped inside the huge tin can, thinking that they were about to face death at the bottom of the ocean, or perhaps on that unknown shore. Some were screaming; some were taking a moment to utter a quick prayer or mutter a curse, or just shout to a friend to hold on.

Still I watched, slowly moving through the ship. The sounds and sights of the past were everywhere I stepped, sounds and sights from a long-ago time in another and far distant place.

Then another sound, though still muffled, it came with such a force that it hurt my ears: a crack so loud, a splitting, tearing noise, and I watched in fascination as part of the ship split open.

I saw the scar of the ship, where the metal had broken open, a scar that few eyes of our world or of our time could see, and it was as it had been in that moment long ago. That scar would never heal, not fully anyway. It would always remain in view for those of us who "see."

"There were many soldiers aboard the ship, during the war." It was more a statement than a question to our tour guide, the old seafarer. There was no doubt in my mind about what I had seen.

"Oh, yes," said the old Marine, unfazed by this. "Yes, it's true, this ship was used to transport our soldiers to Russia toward the latter part of the war."

"The ship was damaged, split apart at one end." Again, more a statement. But if the old Marine was conscious of that fact, he did not show it.

"During one of its voyages I believe the ship was damaged, but not enough to cause any real problem," he replied.

At the very moment he said there were no real problems, I felt a presence, a ghost you might say, one of the soldiers who had been on the ship during that long-ago time, one who could speak for that time, and who wanted to speak for all those who had been onboard.

"I suppose," I heard the soldier whisper in my ear, a distinct chuckle in his voice. "I suppose that would depend on your point of view. My arm was broken. That might seem like a small injury to him perhaps, but let me tell you, it's a hell of a problem when you're trying to stay upright in a storm."

He laughed and so did I, but the old Marine heard not a sound. He just talked on about the glory days, his days at sea, oblivious of the soldier who could have told him so much more.

Kim and I walked on, following our guide, and going down into what seemed to be the bowels of the ship. My new friend, the soldier, followed on our heels. We entered what used to be the sleeping quarters, where row upon row of hammocks, three and four deep had hung from the ceiling. Once again, connecting with all the energy from that time and all those men, I was transported to a most amazing scene.

The conditions were appalling. Bodies were crammed together; the smell of body odor was overpowering. The noise was deafening, as men's voices competed with each other, the sounds of the ship's engines, and the sounds of a storm raging, and it seemed, out of control. Added to that was the sickening roll of the vessel, as it lurched crazily from side to side. The men struggling to stay in their beds, or clinging tightly to whatever solid object they could find that would prevent them from being flung across the room.

"See what I mean," my friend whispered in my ear, the soldier relaying his experience to me as best he could, and yes, as the ghostly sounds of laughter, sounds from the past, came to my ears, I could absolutely see.

Yes, this was a ship, a ghost ship of sorts, but not haunted in the way you might expect. It was a war-torn vessel, holding the energy of that time, the memories of that time, safely and carefully preserving the thoughts, feelings, and emotions of everyone who had ever been onboard. No man was forgotten, no memory erased as if it did not exist. No moment had been a waste of time; every second had been counted and recorded for all time, and there was no life wasted, not one!

There are many such situations, since all buildings, young and old, hold on to energy, an energy that will retain information someone like me can and does tap into. There are few really haunted houses or, in this case, ships, places where one or more people from the spirit world make a regular habit of appearing. In most cases, when I am asked to go ghost hunting, there are no ghosts, no ghouls, no things that go bump in the night, just people like our soldier, with a story to tell. And I am always a willing listener!

Kim and I eventually left the ship, and since that time, we have been on other ghost hunts, as our next story will show. But before the telling of that story, it is important that you are clear about what it is that we are trying to accomplish when we go in search of those experiences. Kim is looking for truth and for history. I am looking for those who might like their voices to be heard or perhaps those who have a need to bring hope and reassurance to someone needing their help. And, of course, in my natural and somewhat insatiable curiosity, I am always looking for something new, which will intrigue and inspire me to explore the unknown possibilities of the world I know exists beyond this world of ours. And you know, when I do connect with "ghosts," it is important to remember that . . . ghosts are people too!

The Golden Apple

This was my third visit to this wonderful old theater, and the play was *Beauty and the Beast*. I had seen this play performed once before, many years ago, when I was in school, and our drama teacher had arranged for a group of us to go out on a school trip. I was fourteen years old, and it was my very first experience of real, live theater, and so the play had a special meaning for me, evoking many memories of that long ago time.

The first time I had visited the Golden Apple, I had gone to see *Cats*. Although I had seen the play in London a few years earlier, for me this was by far the better performance, partly because the Golden Apple is a dinner theater, and the players were able to come out into the audience, which made us feel much more a part of what was going on. Everyone I spoke to that night believed that the theater was haunted. Of course there is a belief among thespians that all theaters are haunted, and this theater was old. It had a history; therefore, it must be haunted, mustn't it? In the last story we have seen that energy, or rather the type of energy that comes in the form of lights, noises, unusual or unaccounted for movement, doesn't necessarily mean ghosts.

It can merely mean that someone is particularly sensitive to the energy around them and is sensing the past, connecting with the vibrations that the building has retained throughout the years.

However, after *Cats,* I had gone backstage to one of the dressing rooms and had seen and spoken to an actor/director, who was reposing on the sofa, very at home in his surroundings, enjoying his anonymity, having come to see the play himself. He was very vocal in his opinions, and I learned later, from those who had known him well, that this would have been just like him. "When he was alive, of course!"

I had gone to see *Beauty and the Beast* with Kim, my ghost-buster friend, who was eager to see what, if anything, I could tell. Was the place really haunted, as everyone thought? Were there actual ghosts roaming about, other than the one I'd seen previously?

In her investigations, Kim had spoken with a number of people from the theater, and many had told her of an experience they'd had, something "spooky." Lights going on and off, shadowy figures passing across the stage, that sort of thing. She was convinced that there was something to those reported sightings. So after the play, she had arranged for me to speak to a couple of people who had their own stories to tell, and for us, once again, we were to have a tour backstage. Maybe, with luck, I would see more ghosts? Kim, I can tell you, was certainly hoping so!

Many of the players were still there, and we were not the only visitors, as people were crowding around them to give their congratulations and to applaud their performances. I found a rickety chair in a dusty corner and sat down, looking about me and taking in the scene. One young man stood out from the others, and I knew that I must find an opportunity to talk to him, although I was not sure why. I leaned over to Kim to ask his name.

"Oh, that's the young man who played Lumiere," she said, referring to one of the characters in the play. "He's one of the ones who had something strange happen to him. I'll see if I can get him to come over and talk to us."

Lumiere, as we will call him, was only too pleased to talk to me once he realized that I was a medium. Like most thespians, he had an unshakable belief in the spooky side of life and a healthy respect for ghosts, ghouls, and poltergeists. In fact, there have been countless sightings and ghostly stories surrounding the theatrical community for as long as theater has been in existence. To put it plainly, ghosts are part of the tradition of theater, and are to be expected!

He began by telling me how one evening not long after he had come to the Golden Apple, he was standing in the wings, next to the closet where all the costumes were hung, waiting to go onstage. All of a sudden, the coat hangers started to rattle together on the rail. He looked around to see who was in the closet, but no one was there. After that first time, it happened often and he became quite used to it, almost expecting it in fact. He told me that many times, sitting at his work station, where he would sit to put on his makeup, through the mirror he would see dark shadows going past. This, he said, had happened several times, and he had become quite used to this as well. But one incident stood out more than the others. It had happened the first night he was to perform at the theater. He had gone to sit at his work station, and needed to switch on the mirror lights. But because he was unfamiliar with his surroundings, he had no idea where the light switch was. Looking around, he couldn't seem to locate it, so assuming that someone might be outside his dressing room, he called out, "Can anyone tell me how I turn on these lights?" A moment later the lights came on, and he called out a thank-you, presuming that someone had heard and obliged. It wasn't until later that he discovered that no one had been outside his dressing room to hear him, and no one had switched on his lights. No one could have you see, as the only light switch for his mirror lights was not located out in the hallway but just to his right, next to the mirror itself!

I listened, fascinated, as Lumiere was speaking, and I smiled to myself when I saw her, a lady who had died of cancer, standing by his side. She was nodding as he spoke, smiling as he recounted his experiences. Turning to me at some point, knowing that I was aware of her presence, she asked, with a twinkle in her eye, "Well, how do you think I did?" I knew she was referring to the phenomena—the rattling coat hangers, the light switch trick, the shadows—although I also knew that not all the shadows had been she. I laughed. "Well," I replied, "you certainly caught his attention, didn't you! So would you like me to let him know that it was you and that you are here now?" I said this with my own twinkle, knowing of course that she had been my reason for talking to him in the first place.

She wanted him to know how much she was still with him, and as she told him about his pending move to New York, how she knew that he was following his dream, she gave him lots of advice. At one point, and pointing to his knee, I said, "Your mother is telling me you injured your knee in a climbing accident." Poor "Lumiere," completely taken aback, gasped. How could I know this? Gently, and with some sympathy, I added, "Your mother says no more rock climbing for you. There are not too many parts in the theater," she warned, "for a young man with a limp." Then, on a roll, having had to wait quite a long time to talk to her son, she went on, "Get that back tooth fixed." Lumiere groaned, telling me how much it hurt but adding that he didn't have dental insurance.

"There are two of them—he has a sister—and I want to send her my love. And"—barely pausing for breath—"take singing lessons! You are not going to get as far as you'd like without them. He is a star," she said, turning back to me, tears in her eyes. This was her final message to her boy: "Shine bright, my shining star, never give up, keep on shining for me."

She was the only "ghost" I saw that night, a mother who had seized the opportunity to speak with her son. She had passed so quickly, within weeks of her cancer being diagnosed and her family had had no time to grasp what was happening. Lumiere cried. His girlfriend, a sweet and talented artist, who had been holding his hand all the while I had been talking to him, also cried. They cried tears of joy, tears of sadness, and tears of hope. Thrilled by their experience, the young couple embraced, and then there were hugs all round, as Kim and I headed out, leaving them to savor the moment.

I smiled as I reached the street, thinking how ironic it was that we who had thought to be "ghost hunting" had been the prey all along. The spirit world, always searching for ways to speak to us, sets its sights on us, and we don't stand a chance. I laughed, and as we drove home, silently I thanked God for being the good hunter that He always is!

A Mother's Voice

After asking for help with this next story, I received this letter from Andrea Galuza, a woman who lost her son to suicide. Her account of her experience with me, in her own words, tells her story better than I can. Because we have only so much room, with Andrea's permission, I have taken out many of the messages that were given. I have chosen what I thought would give those of you who have not had the opportunity that Andrea and her family had, a taste of what a personal consultation is like. The most important thing here is that you should hear this mother's voice.

ANDREA'S STORY

A few weeks after my son Erick died, and in search of reading material, looking for anything, anything that would help this pain, I remembered a book I read when my mother died, titled *The Eagle and the Rose*. The author was Rosemary Altea, and a few years later, I bought a subsequent book of hers titled *You Own the Power*. Well, there it was, still on the shelf, unread, and I believe now that my son had guided me to that book because in it there were incredible messages which helped me enormously.

I checked out Rosemary's website and learned about two retreat weekends that she was holding: one in Vermont and one in Greece.

I decided that Greece sounded wonderfully warm, but I couldn't even think about traveling at that time, as I was in so much pain and the last thing I wanted to do was get on a plane or to travel far from home. So I sent for tickets for Vermont, for myself, my husband, and my sister. It was October 3, and it was "peak season," foliage season, in Vermont. Most of the hotels were almost booked, and the prices were high, even the Holiday Inn was charging $275 a night for a midgrade room, but as it turned out, it was worth every dollar.

Since I'd read Rosemary's books, I already had a sense of what we were in for, but had no idea of what it would be like firsthand to share the experience with so many other people. Friday night Rosemary was speaking and giving messages from the spirit world, Saturday was a healing workshop, with her team from England participating, and Sunday was to be a healing day, where anyone could come to have healing from Rosemary and her team.

The audience on Friday evening was large, and we felt blessed to be there. So many people came, like us, with the hope of connecting with a loved one who had passed, a child who had died, and after a brief introduction, Rosemary opened herself up for questions, saying that we could ask anything we wanted. Well, of course, my husband, Jeff, not at all shy, raised his hand immediately, along with a hundred or more other people, and he was the second person she called on. Jeff asked her if people in the spirit world have an aura, an energy field around them in the same way that we do, and if so, did she see them. She began by describing my husband's energy field in exactly the same way a friend of ours, a healer we'd been working with, described it. Then, without a pause, she said, "I see a fellow" (in her English accent, of course), and my sister Kim and I thought, or hoped, right away that it was my son, Erick. But it was my dad she was connecting to, not my son, and she described him and told us how he died, before moving on to make many other connections, and giving many messages and convincing evidence. The stories we heard through those connections brought tears and laughter to all of us, and we could have stayed in that setting for days, but it lasted three hours and everyone, including Rosemary, was tired by the end of the evening.

On Saturday morning we arrived for the workshop, not really knowing what we had signed up for, but we were game anyway. This was a smaller group, and the entire day was devoted to healing, but in a different way than we thought. Rosemary began by describing energy, energy fields, and soul groups, explaining that we are all born into a certain soul group, a certain type of energy, which influences who we are and how we are in relationship with others. We spent the entire morning learning about the groups and identifying who we are. I learned that I am an Earth sign, a Hunter soul: my husband Jeff is a Fire sign, a Retrospective soul, and that my sister, Kim, is a Water sign.

"The Retrospective soul, a Fire sign, has the most difficult struggle of all of us" she said, "and Earth and Fire signs are the least compatible, and can have a difficult time together."

No kidding, I was thinking all along, but what she said made perfect sense and helped me understand my relationship with my husband, and to have more tolerance.

During the lunch break I got my courage up and went to find her, and asked if it would be possible for me to be able to make an appointment to come and see her. She hesitated a moment and then said, "Yes," and directed me to her secretary so that I could get her phone number. Denise wrote the number on a scrap of paper, tore it off and handed it to me, and I tucked it in a very safe place in my purse, thinking, *OK, now what?*

At the end of the day Rosemary sat at a table signing her books, and Jeff and I, and Kim, waited in line to have our books signed too. The line moved along quite quickly and finally I passed her my book. I bent down and said, "I just wanted to let you know how wonderful this all was." Rosemary smiled up at us, and said, "Bless you." I took a chance and began to explain, "The reason we came is that I lost both of my parents, and this year we lost our son."

The words were hardly out of my mouth, when she looked up at both of us, nodded, and said, "He is here. He is jumping up and down, waving his hands, crying and smiling, and so happy to make the connection. He is saying something about a tooth, and that you had to have some work done on your tooth, that something was taken out and something else was put back in," and speaking quite fast, she added, "He wants me to tell you that he was there with you when you had it done."

After the shock had settled, and nodding that I understood, I managed, "That was me. That was me!" The tears were flowing, as I explained that I had been at the dentist two weeks ago to have a crown replaced, but before I could take a breath, Rosemary went on with more information from our son. Erick described our TV room and the two reclining chairs and told us that he watches the games with Jeff. Then he showed Rosemary something red, a jacket or sweater, she wasn't sure, and told us that he wants us to display it, to put it up on the wall. We knew right away what it was; it was his red jacket, the one he always wore. Then more messages came, and Rosemary told us how we had been arguing about a room we were remodeling, she told us our son was saying that his dad doesn't listen, that he needs to listen, to pay attention, and that he just needs to get it done. We understood it all. A few months before our son died, we had begun an addition on our house, but Jeff had not been able to work on it since Erick had died. There were other messages our son gave us, and finally we thanked her and made our joyous way to the car in the pouring rain, Jeff declaring loudly, "We're coming back."

We have shared our joy with many friends and family, some who were interested in what we had to say, and pleased for us, and probably some who think we have totally lost our minds, but that's OK.

In the third week of November I finally plucked up the courage to call for an appointment, all the time afraid of rejection, and lots of thoughts running through my head. As I heard someone say, "Rosemary Altea's office," my heart began to pound, and I try to explain why I was calling.

"You have lost a child?" the woman on the phone asked, and I said through my tears, "Yes," and she says, "Hold on while I check the schedule." About three minutes later she came back to me. "How about December third?" In shock, I replied, "We don't necessarily have to come that soon." Denise, Rosemary's secretary, said, "Do you know how lucky you are to get this appointment?" and I said, "Yes, we will be there."

I immediately called Jeff on his cell, he actually had it on, and I was crying as I exclaimed, "I called and we have an appointment with Rosemary for December third."

The day of our consultation finally arrived and we were greeted by Denise at the door, plus three dogs; a chocolate Lab, a three-legged springer spaniel, and a black cocker spaniel puppy. Denise sat us in the living room, and the view from the large picture windows was astonishing. The foreground included two ponds and a spectacular view of two mountain ranges, and there was not another house in sight. I looked out, thinking, *We're at her house.* I don't know why, but somehow I thought we were going to her office. A few minutes later, Rosemary came out to greet us, and the dogs were in the middle of everything and everybody. I remember thinking, *This is her, but she didn't look like this the last time I saw her. Then, she was all dressed up, her hair was fixed, she was holding a microphone in front of a crowd. Now she looks more like a regular person, and here we are sitting in her living room.*

Rosemary was great, very natural and easygoing. She asked Denise to fix us tea and then introduced us to her dogs. We chatted briefly, and then we were shown into the sitting room. *This is it,* I thought. *So, we're off.* The time was 10:15 A.M.

Jeff and I shared the sofa, and Rosemary sat in the large chair and set her slippered feet on the ottoman. Taking a pad and pencil in her hand, she asked who we would like to have visit with us.

"I know you want to talk to your son, but is there anyone else?"

Jeff said he would like to talk with his dad, and I asked for my mom and dad. As Rosemary began to tell us there were no guarantees, all of a sudden, moving her head slightly to one side, she said, "They are all here, so we better get started."

First she described Jeff's dad, how he died of a massive heart attack, that he was a large man, and that she saw him standing at Jeff s side. "He has this look about him, he's a bit of a bully, and if I'm not careful, he'll take over this whole session. He's laughing as I say this," and then she chuckled too. Then my dad came, and she described him, just as she had that Friday evening, only in more detail.

"He had problems with his lungs, he tells me, and found it hard to breathe. At the end, he had tubes hooked up to him and the nurses kept fiddling with them. He hated it." Next came my mom, and Rosemary described her and told us how she had died very suddenly of lung cancer, and then, and this is what we were waiting for—"And of course your son is here too."

Our son described to Rosemary how he took his own life, that he had been suffering from serious depression and had felt that he simply didn't want to go on living. This was a sad moment for all of us, and of course we knew that we needed to hear this, but it was still so painful to hear Erick say the words, however, we quickly moved on, and as our son began to speak of other things, we started to feel so much better. There were several messages from Erick, but the first one confused Rosemary a little. "I am not sure what this means, but hopefully you will understand. Erick is talking about a blunt saw, he keeps saying, 'Blunt saw.'"

Jeff, a builder by trade, chuckled, knowing immediately what his son meant. "I always have dull blades in my saws when I am doing carpentry work," he explained, "because I won't take the time to change them."

"The roof needs to be fixed," Erick went on, and "the window isn't centered in the wall."

I turned to Jeff, thinking, *What window didn't you center, and what is wrong with the roof—is it going to leak?*

Jeff burst into hysterical laughter, and I thought he was going to have an asthma attack. When he eventually calmed down, my husband explained that ever since he and Erick had framed up the new addition to the house and installed the windows, he had realized that the atrium window in the angled wall of the addition was not centered, but had tried to convince himself that it didn't matter. However, the Sunday before we had gone to Vermont, he looked at it again from a distance and had thought, "Someday we are going to sell this house, and I'm going to have to explain to someone why this window isn't centered. But, I told myself, the house wall is sided now, the Sheetrock is up, and by the time we trim it out, it won't be that noticeable." Knowing, of course, that no matter what he tells himself, it isn't right.

Erick went on to talk about our kitchen cabinets, saying that I was a cabinet person, and had been obsessing about where to put my bowls. It was, of course, all true. The prior weeks I had been thinking about all my pottery bowls, in fact, actually obsessing about them for some reason, but had never mentioned it to anyone. I laughed, thinking that last year when I had mentioned to Erick that I was thinking of redoing the cabinets, he had said, "Bad idea." Now he was saying it's OK for me to do the kitchen.

Many messages later, and toward the end of the session, Rosemary asked if we would like to ask any questions, and I was surprised. I didn't know we would get to ask questions, but before I could think, Jeff asked if there was any connection to Erick and eagles, as he had had several eagle sightings, many in close proximity. The sightings had begun three days after Erick died, while Jeff sat by the river's edge. They had returned another day, after Jeff had called for them. The eagles had circled around and back, four or five times, circling above him, and Rosemary told us that Erick had described how he flies on eagles' wings, and that when we see eagles, that is Erick, showing us that he is flying high.

Rosemary then looked right at me and said, "Erick tells me you don't want to celebrate Christmas anymore. He is saying that you need to get a big tree, just like always, put a silver star on top of the tree, and each year put another star on the tree. When you see the stars, you will know that he will be there with you."

I asked what my son was doing, wondering about his travels. I have often thought of him traveling, knowing what an adventurer he was. "Well," said Rosemary, "It is not 'Was' but 'Is.' He is still an adventurer," reminding us that Erick is still alive, and Erick explained.

"You mightn't understand, Mom," he said, as he came to stand next to me, and Rosemary described how she could see him as he stroked my hair. "Think of me holding onto a star that carries me with it wherever it goes. When you look up into the sky and you see the brightest star, well, that star is me. I know you feel guilty, but please don't. I had a good childhood, and it was simply my time, and no one's fault. You love me, and I love you."

THE LAST PART of Andrea's letter goes like this:

"We know now," she says, "what our family in the spirit world wants of us, the important message they need for us to hear."

"Take the time to do things well," this family is saying. "Slow down, take notice. Love one another, share." And then . . .

"Do people have to die for us to listen to them? I wonder. Do we all have to die before we recognize what is important in our lives?" Andrea asks as she finishes her account.

"Well," I think, as I wonder about her question. "Well, indeed I hope not. I sincerely hope not!"

September Song

It happened so suddenly and shocked the world, as I suppose all crimes of this nature do. Wars have been raging throughout the centuries in one place or another, and I don't think there has ever been a time of total peace among men on our planet Earth since time here began. And Dark Souls have always been in our midst.

Just like so many others around the world, I was first aware of what happened, what indeed was happening, from the TV. I rarely watch morning TV, but was scanning the channels, looking for a show I was to be on that day, and there it was, too shocking at first to be believed. I sat down hard in the chair, mesmerized, unable to really grasp the enormity of it. As my house was then under construction, pretty soon my living room filled with people. The builder, the painters, Denise and Debbie, my office staff, the plumber and the electrician, all of them gathered around the TV. And none of us spoke. We just watched as the same scene was played over and over again. Then panic, as I realized—New York, New York, my child was there, and very, very close to where it was all happening. And I grabbed the phone, believing in my heart that she was OK but still needing to hear her voice, to make sure that she was safe.

I was one of the lucky ones. There are thousands, as we know, who were not so lucky, whose fathers, mothers, sons and daughters, brothers, sisters, aunts and uncles, friends, fiancés, lovers, cousins, would not make it home that day, or any day after that.

September 11, 2001. A day not one of us who lived through it will forget.

Osama bin Laden. A name we associate with evil, and with evil-doing.

Whether or not bin Laden is a Dark Soul is not for me to say, although I would count him as one in my examples. Was he born of the light, like most of us, and then influenced by, drawn into that dark and sinister evil force that exists? Or was he born a Dark Soul? Only God knows that. But what I do know, what we all know, is that his deeds come from a dark source, a dark energy, which only creates destruction. And there is no light in that at all.

The events of September 11 affected me perhaps differently from how they affected many others. As a spiritual medium and healer who has worked professionally in this field for more than twenty-five years, I had been involved in acts of war where thousands had been killed. This was not the first time I had been asked to help. I have been involved in situations in Ireland, Argentina, Rhodesia (Zimbabwe), South Africa, and other countries. It was not the first time that I was to come up against prejudice and mistrust and, in some instances, the same kind of intolerance, although to a lesser degree, that drove bin Laden to act as he did.

There were so many requests. Faxes and phone calls came in daily, too many to count, too many for me to be constructive in a way that might make a real difference to anyone beyond a few individuals.

Friends and colleagues decided to help. Everyone wanted to be part of making something good happen. A theater in New York was donated for an evening. Now we were on our way. Tickets were free; my time was free. Two thousand people, families of victims, could come and participate in an evening with the spirit world. It would be an evening of communication, of messages, giving proof of survival after death; it would be an evening of inspiration, of learning, and, most of all, an evening of hope. And we were all excited, knowing this was a chance to do something big, a chance to give.

The first hitch came when the chief engineer of the theater asked if I was union. Union? What was he talking about? Then this same man made it clear that if I walked into the theater, he and his crew would walk out. "She is evil, of the devil, and she'll bring evil into the theater," he said. We found out later that he belonged to a particular religious group who were against spiritual mediums. Intolerance . . . intolerance . . . intolerance.

We overcame this hitch and, moving forward, picked a date and got ready to roll. But wait. What about the tickets? How do we choose which families should come? How would they know? Simple, we thought, advertise. "Oh," said the doubters, the skeptics. "So that's what this is all about. She just wants the publicity." "She," of course, meaning me. Maybe they had reasons to mistrust, maybe they were judging by their own actions; maybe they found it hard to believe that there really are people who do something simply because it's the right thing to do.

"Well," I suggested, "what about contacting the organizers of the different help groups and letting them give the information out. We could give each group an allotted number of tickets, and that way my involvement would be more discreet." Great, good idea, let's do it— another hurdle overcome. And so we contacted the help groups, who, full of doubt and suspicion, did not want to get involved, no matter how much good we might do. On and on it went, hurdle after hurdle, until finally we gave up trying, and instead we organized small groups in different areas and in private settings . . . making a difference the best we could.

I had a lawyer ask me, during a court case I will tell you about later, in a cynical and very sarcastic way, "It would seem that you do an awful lot of work for nothing?" And then, in obvious disbelief, with a need to put doubt into the minds of others and with incredulity lacing his words, he said, "So, you're telling us you don't charge for healing?"

Why is it so hard for some people to accept that there are those in the world, many in fact, who really do good deeds for others without thought of something in return, simply because it's the right thing to do?

But since September 11, we have seen example after example of ordinary people doing extraordinary things, and also ordinary things, for no reason other than because it's the right thing to do. We have seen example after example of right behavior and right thinking. And I believe it will always be this way. Good souls, rising to the occasion in times of pain and hardship. Fighting evil, combating evil, and restoring faith in human nature.

It is so hard for us to understand why terrible things happen, and it can be even harder to accept that it is God's will. Yet I have to believe. I have to believe that everything happens for a reason, and that God knows what He is doing. I remember a long time ago, perhaps almost twenty years, at one of my Friday-night classes in Yorkshire, England, where a very wise teacher came through from the spirit world to give us a lesson. My students had been praying for peace and harmony to prevail throughout the world, for the wars and violence to stop and for people to find a good way to live together in a tolerant and unifying way. This wise old woman gave us these words of wisdom as a small gift, a Christmas gift, and I can hear her now, even as I write.

"If I were to give you a gift, I would give you the gift of pain," she said. "And I would give you the gift of heartache and of tears. For it is through these things that you will learn and grow." September 11 was a terrible, terrible tragedy, and it is one that many will never recover from. But as all victims of tragedies will tell you, no matter how severe the pain, there are many small gifts which come from it, if you look for them. And I firmly believe that when God takes something from us, He always gives us something back in return.

The journey in was easy and as relaxing as any car ride can be—four and a half hours, and I slept some of the way. I needed to be fresh and alert for tomorrow. It was important that I do my best.

I arrived on Fifth Avenue in the late afternoon, expecting a quiet evening with a friend, whose apartment I was staying at, but it was not to be.

"I had a call from Aimee. She found out you were coming in, and she has a friend whose daughter just died. She wants to know if you'll see her?" said my friend, as I walked through the door.

Well, of course there wasn't time, since I was tied up all the next day and leaving New York later in the evening. It was just on the tip of my tongue to say so when I felt Grey Eagle's hand on my shoulder. "Well," I heard myself say, "if she can get here in the next two to three hours, I'll see her tonight."

We'll call her Mary Smith, and she came with her mother. When my friend showed them into the living room, they were both flustered and nervous. When Mary's friend Aimee had called her with the news that I would see them, Mary had immediately jumped in the car, picked up her mother, and driven the two hours into the city, determined not to miss the opportunity.

Within minutes of us sitting down, I saw the child, about seven years old, eager and excited at the prospect of talking with her mom. I asked her how she had passed, and she began to tell me about her broken arm. *Now, nobody dies of a broken arm*, I thought, but I let her talk on without interruption, thinking to allow her to relax a little and to get used to the process. But I was wrong, for in an odd sort of way the young girl did die from a broken arm. The bone had been shattered at the elbow and had required surgery. During that surgery an infection set in to the wound and pretty soon was raging through the little girl's system, and eventually into her brain. It happened so fast that there was nothing anyone could do. As I listened, the child described it to me that way, as accurately and precisely as she could.

Mary and her mother listened as I relayed little Emily's words to them, and they held each other and cried, knowing it was all true and knowing also that Emily had survived death, that she was OK, and that she was actually there in the room with us all.

We sat together for another hour, listening as the child relayed more information. She talked about her brother and father, letting us know she was still a part of the family, and she talked of her transition to the spirit world. She told us how the angels had come for her in her final moments, and finally she told us that she was safe and happy. This was what her mother most needed to hear. There were more tears, but these were tears of relief and happiness.

Emily had passed only a few days earlier, less than a week ago, but still she was ready and eager to communicate with her family, and it was my privilege that I was allowed to help.

After Mary and her mother left, my friend and I had a light supper and talked about what we might expect the following day.

It was all set. The ABC network had arranged it all, and the whole thing was being televised. With luck, we would have a true record on film of how the spirit world can give us miracles. I was meeting with a group of mostly women—wives, mothers, sisters, and sweethearts of some of the firemen who had died at the World Trade Center. I knew they had high expectations, and I knew how important it was for me to meet those expectations. But I also knew there were no guarantees, no certainties. I would not know until I began, how clearly, if any, the communications from the spirit world would be.

The day began early, and by the time I arrived at the venue, most of the group were there. There were at least thirty people, maybe more, besides the television crew, all of them eager, excited and perhaps a little scared. "What if she can, what if she can't, what if he does, or what if he doesn't." All the usual what ifs, going around in their minds.

My what ifs had been laid to the side. I was here to do a job, the best I could, and the results would be what they were. I looked around the room and saw ordinary people, victims of an evil force, trying to come to terms with what had happened to them. But how could they? Evil had destroyed their lives, and they were scrambling to find the pieces in order to try to create an existence they could somehow live with.

The camera crew was only partially set up, and from the looks of things it was going to take awhile longer, which meant we all had to wait. My inclination was to go right into the middle of the group, introduce myself, and get going. My energy level was high, as it always is when I'm about to work, especially with larger groups of people, and I could see that there was a crowd in the spirit world, eager and waiting to begin. But this was TV. Among the group, and out there in that future broadcast, would be people watching, who, skeptical and doubting, would use any excuse to debunk my work. Not only was it important that everything be aboveboard, but it was important that it be seen to be aboveboard. Chatting to people before the show could easily be misconstrued as my gleaning information. And so I made myself scarce. I left, went outside and over to the coffee shop across the street, and asked one of the crew to let me know when they were ready.

Drinking my tea, waiting to start, I began to reflect on the reason I was here. I knew that a group of firemen were relying on me, that their passing was extraordinarily tragic, and that the cause of their passing had rocked the world. Would I be able to help? Would I be able to hear well enough, to see, to sense, to feel, to communicate well enough? Self-doubt crept in, and I wondered, as I often did, if I was good enough. As I walked back to the studio, I prayed for light, I prayed for enlightenment, and I prayed for help.

The producer had arranged the women in three rows, all sitting facing a lone chair—mine. All eyes were on me as I walked across the room. Almost everyone there held their breath as I arranged myself in the chair, including me. One last silent prayer, I took a deep breath.

One last silent thought, *Would light in some way prevail over those dark forces, which in many ways were still at work?*

I hoped so. I believed so. And so I began.

It is impossible for me to recount minute by minute or even hour by hour, as we spent many hours, and there was so much, so many messages, some funny, some sad, as one by one those wonderful firemen from Brooklyn's Ladder Company 132 came through to talk to us. Each one recounted how he had died on that day, and each one had a different story to tell of how he had felt, and what it had been like for them as they had faced the destruction and mayhem of the Twin Towers.

One young man talked to his wife about the accident she had just had a few days ago and described an injury to her leg. Tears ran down her face as she realized he was still with her, watching over her as he always had. Another spoke to his wife about their children, sending them all messages of hope and love. One spoke to his girlfriend, saying he would help with the renovations they'd begun before he had died, describing things in detail so she would be in no doubt that he was with her. Message after incredible message was given, everyone paying attention, enthralled and amazed and comforted by what they heard, and each of the women there receiving messages of love and of comfort.

One of the firemen stands out in my mind as I write because he seemed larger than life—not only his stature but his personality as well. He was standing next to his fiancée, tall and broad-shouldered, his hair unruly, his round face and beaming smile very clear to me. I knew at once that despite his seeming macho bravado, he was a gentle and sensitive, caring and thoughtful man, and as he told his story, my heart broke a little more, and then even more as I saw the terrible despair in his fiancée's eyes.

"We were to be married in a week," he quietly said. "Everything was arranged—the church, the reception, everything," and in a flash, as I listened to his words, I was traveling with him, down through the hole, down and back to the place where there are no barriers, where my spirit can come and go at will, where those in the spirit world can show me all. I was in her room, in her home, and I saw her wedding dress as it hung in the closet. I saw the tears in his eyes and heard the agony in his voice as he whispered, "I died just a week before our wedding day."

None of this was new to me. I had done it before, on many, many occasions, too many to count. Working with people in tragic situations is part of my job. I have seen great heartache and heartbreak, and I have watched people die. Why, even the night before I had been with the mother who had just lost her seven-year-old child. So I'm used to it, to hearing the stories, and seeing the pain, I'm as used to it as it is possible to be. But this was different. The tragedy was on a major scale. It has affected all of us in different ways. So many people damaged at one time—not just those who died but, worse, those who were left behind. One blow, one blow from the hand of a Dark Soul, and that blow had caused so much destruction and devastation, calculated and intended harm. And had that Dark force won?

I looked around the room at the women sitting before me. I looked past them toward the camera crew. I looked at the technicians, the many family and friends who had come to help and support, perhaps some on the off chance of receiving some small message themselves. The room was utterly silent save for the quiet sobbing of some. Great sadness filled the air and settled like a dark cloud over us, and yes, it seemed for a moment that those dark forces had indeed won. Then I lifted my eyes and focused my thoughts and attention on those oh-so-brave firefighters, who still had some things left to say and some things left to show me.

Shifting, slowly shifting, I felt myself moving once again, that part of me which has such a powerful connection with the spirit world. Then I was there, right in the thick of it, down and back, down through the hole, as they took me through the wreckage and mayhem that had taken them from us.

There was smoke and dust and sounds like rolling thunder. I saw people screaming, people quietly crying, and many people praying.

"It was a living nightmare," I heard them say. "And then," said the spokesman for the group, "and then an amazing thing happened. It seemed as if the world stood still, and a strange quiet came over us all. People stopped screaming and crying and praying, and at the same time we all became still and listening. At first we were confused as we saw a strange light, bright as sunlight, which seemed to seep through the fog. Weak at first, the light became stronger; the silence became louder and strangely comforting. Then we saw them. They were everywhere—angels filling the rooms. And no one was afraid, and there was only a feeling of incredible joy as we followed them out of the hell, and into a place of light and peace, and into a place of Godliness."

As he spoke, I saw that light. I heard that beautiful silence. I felt them all as they became calmed and comforted, and then I saw angels filling that space with light, where just seconds before it had seemed so dark and so despairing.

Shifting once again and coming back now through the hole, my focus changed, and it was strange—as I recounted the young fireman's words to everyone in the room, and I swear that what I'm about to say is true—there was a light that had entered the room where we all sat, and a quiet descended over us, which was strangely comforting. And I saw them, and they were everywhere . . . angels . . . filling the room with their presence, filling the room with light, where we all sat. And the wives and mothers, the sisters and fiancées of the firemen who had died, for a moment lost their fear, as they felt a holy presence, and there was only a feeling of incredible joy, as we followed their loved ones out of the hell, which was the Twin Towers, and into a place of light and peace. A place we might call heaven.

Did it win, that Dark Soul, that Dark force? I don't think so. It had its moment of victory, oh yes, indeed it had that. But it was only a moment, and although it destroyed lives, it did not—and we must not and will not, allow it to—destroy our hearts, our minds and our souls.

"And angels came and carried us to a place of peace, of light, and of God," I heard the firemen say.

And evil, even in its worst form, will never, never win!

The Last Word

There are thousands of people who go missing each year—men, women, and children who disappear without a trace. Most are never found, like Rose, in our first story, and their families are left wondering, worrying, in a state of limbo, unable to go forward with their lives. There is always that dark cloud hanging over them and a thousand questions never to be answered.

These are the times when I feel that my work is truly valuable, when I can bring closure to a family in torment and when my gift of sight can shine a light on a situation that many may feel hopeless about. The unresolved becomes resolved at last. The doubts and fears, even when realized, become fact, and those terrible times of imagined horrors fade away, for now we know. Whatever the reality might be, whatever dark secrets we may discover, when they become uncovered, they are far better and far easier to deal with than what we believed in our darkest imagination might be true. As a spiritual medium, able to see, to hear, and to sense all that there is or has been, and even what will be in the future, I know that small miracles can happen. With Grey Eagle's help, there are times when we can find that which has been lost, mend that which has been broken, and bring sight to those who have not been able to see. This next story is simply an example of one of those times.

She was in the house, having been out earlier, and was getting ready to settle in for the night. Tired of all the arguing, the court case finally over, she felt easier than she had in a long while. Her granddaughter, who was living with her for a while, was staying over at a friend's house, which meant the evening was hers to do whatever she wanted, and she wanted to settle down for the night and watch a little TV.

We shall call her Margaret, Maggie for short, for the purpose of this story, and we begin this way. . . .

The TV was on but not loud, as I entered the house, which was quite spacious and very cozy. Maggie was only half watching the movie, as she was moving around, not yet settled for the night, doing those small household chores, wiping down the kitchen counters, straightening up the cushions, and opening a bag of chips. *Dinner?* I wondered briefly as I watched her.

The loud banging at the door startled us both, but Maggie, quickly recovering, strode angrily across the room and flung open the door, obviously knowing perfectly well who it was.

"What is it now? Why can't you just go away and leave me alone?" she shouted, furious with the man I could just glimpse from where I stood inside.

He pushed past her, ignoring her protests that he wasn't welcome, trying at first to reason with her, hoping to settle their argument. Her ex-boyfriend told her that he just wanted to talk. Their fight was mainly about the trailer, a trailer that had been his when they had first met. He believed that she had taken it from him through the courts, claiming it was on her property, and therefore hers. Possession, apparently, is nine-tenths of the law. Since it was indeed on her land, in the field next to her house, the courts had awarded her all rights to it. This left the ex-boyfriend with nothing, no home, no place to stay. He felt that she had stolen from him all that he had owned, all that was rightfully his. Maggie would have none of it. She told him to leave, to get out, and to stay out of her life.

"But you've taken everything, everything that was mine," I heard him say. "I only want what was mine before we met," he sobbed, choking back his angry tears, pleading with Maggie to listen to him. She would not. Again she yelled at him to get out, which finally he did, his shoulders slumped in defeat, his head bowed low.

Her mistake was in following him out into the driveway when he left the house. Her mistake was in kicking him when he was down, assuming he was defeated and helpless, and then reveling in victory. When she followed him out into the driveway, I went after her, down the steps and onto the driveway. Maggie just wouldn't stop, and all her pent-up feelings toward him came spilling out of her mouth in a vitriolic diatribe. The more he didn't respond, the more she yelled, and her words were like daggers, cutting and wounding, slicing into him, until finally, unable to stand it any longer, he snapped. Spinning around to face her, taking them both by surprise, he reached out and grabbed at her hair, yanking her toward him. Cursing, he hauled her across the ground. Half stumbling, half running, Maggie had no choice but to let herself be dragged. The pain in her head made her almost blind, as involuntary tears spurted from her eyes.

I watched from the back seat as he half tugged, half pushed her into the car, shoving her so hard she hit her head on the rim of the door. Maggie collapsed, breathless and scared, hugging the seat, holding her head where the hair had been torn from her scalp. Blood stained her fingers, and shock and panic for the moment held her tongue in a vice.

But as we can see, Maggie was not ordinarily a mild-mannered woman; nor was she easily intimidated. If there was one thing she had learned in her fifty-three years, it was that you never let a man put you down. And so, after a while—a long while, it seemed—after we had been driving down dark country roads, winding this way and that and going nowhere, all of us silent and waiting, Maggie let loose again, scream-ing and raging. Her voice grew louder, and once again she became verbally abusive, calling him a creep, a nobody, a has-been.

He had been quiet, brooding, thoroughly shocked at what he had done, and had been wondering how to put things right. But now I could feel him tense up, his shoulders becoming rigid, his breathing more shallow as his anger began to burn again. I tensed too, suspect-ing that the worst was about to happen. But Maggie was on a roll, and just couldn't shut up. She didn't notice when the muscles in his jaw hardened, or see his hand as it curled into a ball. She was unaware of the rocketlike impact of his fist as it hit her in the face, jarring her head back, and she was deaf to the ear-splitting crack of bone as her neck broke in two.

Back in my study, I smiled sadly at the young woman on the other end of the telephone, my voice gentle as I described the last of what I'd seen and heard, all of it not taking more than fifteen minutes. This was my job, to be the eyes and ears and voice of those in the spirit world who had only me to tell their story. Although I will often leave out the worst of the details, unless my communicator insists that I tell it all, I will reveal the secrets, uncover the truth, and shed light on the situa-tion, keeping strictly to the facts. Now Maggie's granddaughter could finally get on with her life, her future, without the shadow of her grandmother's death hanging over her. The unknown was now known, and the relief the young woman felt was immense. I listened to her as she told the rest of the story.

"The next morning, when I returned to the house and found the door still open, at first I thought nothing of it. My grandmother's car was parked in the driveway. Her bag and keys were in the house. Noth-ing was out of place. It was only as the hours ticked by and Maggie did not come back from her walk, or wherever it was that I'd assumed she'd been, that we became worried. By then, though, it had been several hours. Many visitors had come and gone, and any trace of a possible struggle in the driveway had also gone.

"My grandmother went missing in 1986, and it was more than twelve years later, in 1998, that her body was discovered in the attic of an old derelict house, many, many miles from where she lived. No one was ever charged, although the ex-boyfriend was the prime suspect in the ensuing investigation, but by the time Maggie's body was found, there was nothing left of her to tell us what happened, and no evidence of foul play."

It would be a further eight years before Maggie's voice was to be heard again, when her granddaughter came to me for this consultation. As you can see, Maggie had no trouble telling me her story, taking me back to revisit her past, and taking me back to the scene of the crime, so that I could see for myself what had happened. There was no pain or anger, no regret in her voice as we spoke. She was delighted to be able to give all those wonderful messages to her family, which she had waited so long to give. The consultation was a great success for everyone, finally bringing closure to a cold case, which we had been able to solve. The mystery was over. The story had been told.

"It was my fault, y'know," Maggie said, as the consultation came to an end, smiling wryly at the part she had played in her own death. "If I'd just shut up, been more reasonable, kinder, he would never have done it. But I always did want the last word, and you know, Rosemary, I never could leave well enough alone!"

The Boy

Thirteen is a strange number, and one that many people believe to be unlucky. Many hotels and office buildings will deliberately eliminate the number thirteen, going from floor twelve to floor fourteen, in an attempt at avoiding bad luck. Personally, I have never considered the number thirteen unlucky. If I look back on my childhood, however, I could easily associate the number thirteen with my father, and see that as the reason for my highly dysfunctional family, since my father was born on the thirteenth of March and died on the thirteenth of April some seventy years later. I have often thought that strange. Not a believer in mere coincidence, I am prone to giving consideration to such things, but in my father's case, I have never drawn any conclusions.

There are thirteen soul signs, and it will definitely be noted by some that the thirteenth sign is the Dark Soul. Could that be considered a dark number for a dark being, perhaps? If this is so, it was certainly not my intention when I discovered and wrote about them to have it seem that way.

Many people have a number, a lucky number, as I do. Mine is the number seven, and it just happens that when Grey Eagle first gave the soul signs to me, the seventh sign, the Warrior Soul, is my soul sign. My number, my soul sign! Since I don't believe in coincidence, I have to think that there is some meaning to this. Maybe this was my guide's way of helping me to trust this new information, which it certainly did.

Is the number thirteen a powerful universal number? I think it is. Could it be that certain numbers, or some configuration of a number, has energy of its own? Yes, I do believe so, although I have no idea how it works. Is the number thirteen unlucky for some? I am sure that it can be if we believe it is, because our believing gives power to the idea.

Is the number seven a powerful universal number? I personally believe so. Is it lucky for some? Well, it definitely holds a power for me. Why? I don't know why, I only know that it does, partly, I am sure because my belief gives the idea power. But I think there's more to it than that. My daughter was born on the seventh. When I was in my twenties, long after I had begun to collect any and every bus ticket with the number seven on it, I was diagnosed with a rare blood disorder. I was deficient in factor seven. You might explain this as my being psychic, so I must have known, and you might be right. Maybe I knew without knowing that I did. But there is more to it than that, even. It's about belief.

Belief can be a strange and indefinable thing, something we often don't understand or even know why we have it when we do. Although we can't necessarily define what belief is, we feel it nevertheless.

How do I know that there are thirteen soul signs, thirteen different types of soul energy? That's easy—because I have learned through the years to trust Grey Eagle, and it was he who told me. But how do I know that I'm not just hearing voices in my head when I hear his voice? How do I know that I'm not crazy like my grandmother, or that it's not simply my imagination running riot? Again, it is because I believe. And so, why do I believe? What reasons do I have to believe? It is through my experiences, the experiences of a lifetime which tell me so.

I would like to tell you a story, an amazing story. At least it was for me. This is a story which would confirm the belief I already have. If I were ever to need confirmation of my power, and the power of God and the power of the universe, which I must say I do not, then this is the one story that would give me that confirmation.

I was in Italy about three or four years ago. The city was Naples, and my audience that night was a large one. I was getting used to it, and I had decided that I would not be at all nervous. I knew that I could not afford to be, since there were those in the audience who would use anything to discredit me. A fanatical group had begun to mount a campaign against me. My popularity throughout Italy was growing, and there were those who saw me as a threat to the Catholic Church. I openly voiced my beliefs about suicide, about life after death, about the fact that we are all capable of giving healing. To some, my beliefs were unacceptable. They were misconstrued as going against the Church and therefore against God. This could not be further from the truth. Some had made deliberate attempts to mar my good name, smear my reputation, make false reports in certain newspapers about my healing organization. They claimed that I made millions of dollars from sick and dying individuals who were willing to pay for a miracle, and of course, there were attempts to ban me from certain popular television shows. Even though I had been told that the media was present that night, in full force, and even though I could easily have gone into hiding, I knew that this was one of those times when I must take my courage in my hands, when I must live my faith.

There had been so much hype about my visit, so many TV and news appearances, and so much discussion going on in the country about my abilities as a spiritual medium and healer, that it seemed that I was the only thing people were talking about. Was I for real or not? That was the big question, and the buzz was on. Newspeople from all over the country had come to see for themselves and to report whether the claims about my mediumship were real. At another time, perhaps earlier in my career, I would certainly have been a nervous wreck. But over the years I had learned that I am only a human being. I can do only as much as I can do, and no more. I kept reminding myself of this. It was the only way I was able to stop myself from bolting.

So there I was, standing on the stage, living my faith, facing an audience of thousands, trusting that God and Grey Eagle were by my side. Together, I knew we made a formidable and powerful team.

For the sake of the story and to ensure the smoothness of its telling, I will ignore the fact that I speak only a little Italian and that I had a translator working hard by my side that night, and I will tell the tale as if we were all of one mind, one language only, for in truth, we really were.

Such a strong feeling of excitement rippled through the theater as I pushed my way through the curtains. After giving my introduction, I stepped off the stage to walk among my audience, as I usually do. The space between the first row of seats and the stage was narrow, made even narrower at one point as I inched my way around a baby's stroller in which the child lay soundly sleeping. Of course, I could not resist looking down at the sleeping babe; I thought what a perfect child he was. It had taken only a moment's pause, but it was enough, enough for the mother of the child to grab my arm and hold me there. Crying, sobbing loudly, she told us her story. The boy was perfect, she said, perfect in every way, except, for one thing. He could not or would not speak. "We have taken him everywhere," the mother sobbed. "There have been so many doctors, so many tests. No one can find anything wrong. Yet he is three years old and has never uttered one sound, one word."

I could see the pain in the mother's eyes, and in the eyes of the friend who was with her, as she told her story, and I could sense the emotion of my audience as they heard. What was I to do? As I listened to the pleas of the mother, felt her belief in me, and heard her desperate cry for a miracle, I felt Grey Eagle draw close by my side.

The air was electric. My audience wondering what I would do? Would I lay my hands on the child and heal him? The crowd was waiting with baited breath to see what would happen next. I looked down again at the child, his thick dark hair curling around the creamy skin of his face. And I knew that he was indeed perfect, as God had made him. He was a happy child, an intelligent and inquisitive boy able to express himself in so many ways. His lack of speech was not a trial to him, only to his parents, who naturally wanted him to be normal, to be whole.

"How can I help them? Can I help them?" I softly asked Grey Eagle, who then immediately began to guide me.

"It is not the child who needs our help, our prayers," I began, joining my mind, my energy, with my guide, inspired by him as I spoke to my audience and to the child's mother, "for God made him as he is. He is indeed a beautiful and perfect child. It is the parents and family of this boy who need our help and prayers, for they are the ones in great pain and great need of understanding." As I spoke, all the while I connected with Grey Eagle, and inspired, I began to walk up and down the aisles, my audience a sea of faces. I began to talk about healing and asked for everyone in the theater to join hands, to join their energies, and to join with me in sending healing prayers to the parents of the boy. As I spoke, explaining the process of healing and the power of healing prayers, I could feel the power of the audience, their energy, combining with mine, their willingness to participate, the reverence and spirit of God filling the air, saturating each one of us present. Still connected, still united, staying in tune with Grey Eagle, forming a unity with his spirit, uniting our energies and guided by him, I walked, first down one aisle, then another, back and across, up and down, all the time walking, praying, voicing my healing prayers, explaining my beliefs. There was not a doubt in my mind as I passed through the audience that every single person in the theater was participating. Each person, I knew, was thinking only of the child and of the child's parents. Each person was, I knew, combining his or her energy with the others. It was wonderful, unbelievable! Everyone present was of one mind, one heart, and one God.

In all honesty, I must tell you I did not feel pushed or drawn or even in the most remote way led to the man who sat in the aisle at the back of the theater. I did not see a light around or near him; nor was he in any way unusual to look at or striving for my attention. But the energy of his soul and the force of God's power, like a magnet, drew me.

It was like this. I simply stopped in front of him, smiled, reached out, and took his hand. Gently, I asked, "Would you like to help me give healing to the boy?" His surprise that I should be talking to him showed on his face, and for a moment he was overwhelmed. All he was able to do was to bow his head and nod his consent. My next question came, with no thought on my part, in a natural and easy way and was spoken with the greatest compassion. "Can you tell us why you would like to help give healing to the child?" I asked. And the audience, stunned by his reply, gasped in unison, as they heard him say, with tears raining down his cheeks, "Because I am the boy's papa!"

How was it possible, how could it be, that in an audience this large, one man could be found so? It would be like looking for a needle in a haystack.

I made the headlines in most of the papers throughout the country the next day. The big question was, how did I do it? And I will tell you once again, that I did not feel pushed or led. I did not have any signs. There were no lights, no light above his head to show me the way, and no voices to steer me to him. There were no words from my guide. Grey Eagle did not say to me, "This is the one." Indeed, he did not say anything. Yet God's hand was in it, my guide had indeed guided me. The balance of energy was perfect; the power of the universe was at work and in the most remarkable way.

During the rest of the evening, Grey Eagle and I, with God by our side, gave many more examples of spirit communication. All through the theater we worked, hand in hand, giving messages of comfort and hope. A child had died in a car crash; a mother died of cancer; a husband died suddenly of a heart attack . . . and so on, and so on, and so on, for hour after hour after hour, for the next several hours, and each time a message was given, belief was strengthened, belief was confirmed, and lives were changed for the better.

God and Grey Eagle and I, oh yes indeed, we three, and the many others in the spirit world who came that night to help, we were indeed a formidable and powerful team.

And, "Can you tell us why you would like to help give healing to the child?"

"Because I am the boy's papa!"

The father of the boy was now crying openly, for in his eyes and in the eyes of the audience, he had just received a miracle. He had hidden himself at the back of the theater deliberately. Being a shy man, and perhaps not altogether believing as his wife did, he had decided to watch but not participate. But God had found him, and shown him that He had other plans.

I took the man down to the front of the theater and sat him with his wife. They hugged and cried, and the audience cried with them, sharing in their miracle. For had God not shown us all—we can never hide from His eyes. And does He not see everything? And does He not see our pain and suffering, our joys and sorrows? And He shares it all and brings us comfort when He can.

These two people had suffered for the silence of their son, for the fact that he was different from other children, and they worried that he might therefore have less of a life, a marred life. One—the mother—had believed, she had believed in the possibility of a miracle; the other—the father—had not. Had the mother's belief given us the power to produce the miracle, or was it the power of God alone? I don't know. The only thing I do know is that God had shown the parents of this child that He had noticed them and was taking care of them in their suffering. One small simple act, a miracle, was given to them all and to the audience watching.

Belief is a strange and often indefinable thing, and there is no doubt in my mind that it holds energy, a power of its own. Whether you believe in lucky or unlucky numbers, rabbits' feet, lucky pennies, or whether you simply believe in the power of God, I know that those of us who believe in power give more power to ourselves in doing so.

As I have recounted this story, I cannot help remembering my own amazement as I heard the response of the father. The fact is that I was just as astounded by his answer as my audience was. I know that every-one there thought I must have known, for after all, wasn't I the one who found him? But I had no more idea than anyone else—only my belief, my faith, to lead me!

He lay sleeping, I remember, the boy, with his dark, thick hair curling around the creamy silk skin of his face, completely unaware, or so it would seem, of the miracle his parents had been given, and that the rest of us were witness to. He lay quiet and still, a small smile on his lips, his angels close by, peaceful and content, as God watched over us all.

Fire . . . Fire . . . Fire

This was a difficult story for me to write, and I had to make a tough decision about whether I should write it at all, since the last thing I want to do is to confuse you. Let me explain.

There are so many stories, so many experiences that I as a spiritual medium will have on a day-to-day basis that sometimes it's hard for me to separate them, especially when I'm traveling. I'm often exhausted from all the travel, never mind the lectures, workshops, book signings, and the work itself. Things can and do become blurred, mixed together somewhat and confused.

If I have someone traveling with me who is good at taking notes, or holding a tape recorder, it is much easier, of course. Or if I am able to contact all those people whom I give messages to, which is sometimes the case, then they will be able to help, to fill in the gaps in my memory, to remind me of exactly how things happened in their experience with me. But that, of course, is not always the case, and then it is easy for me to confuse one story with another.

I was traveling on a plane, through Canada, going from one city to another, giving a lecture, the next day flying to then another lecture, then another. At each of the lectures there were many messages, many stories that were memorable, and one or two are recounted here. What stood out for me on that trip were the similarities between the messages from one city to another.

Of three cities, three lectures, there were three families who had had tragic losses through fire. Each had been a house fire, each had lost children, and each had left the families devastated. As I have already explained, the similarities between one person's experience and someone else's can be remarkable and shows us how we can often be living parallel lives with a perfect stranger. The similarities among these three families were so great that it was easy for me, later, in compiling my notes, to get their stories mixed, to confuse one family with another, especially since the lectures were so close together. But one thing was easy for me to remember, and that was the pain, the sadness, and the consequent joy of all three families as we were able to connect with their loved ones in the spirit world. All of the children had died tragically at a young age. They were able to give very clear and definitive details about their passing, proving to their parents and to my audiences, beyond a shadow of a doubt, that they had survived death.

Because the experiences of these messages was so powerful, so moving, and so inspirational to all of us who witnessed them, I decided that I could not leave them out of this book. So, to clarify: The following story—told, as you will see, as one episode, one encounter—is in fact a combination of three separate but remarkably similar events. When I might refer to a man, it might have been a woman When I refer to a father, in one case it was a mother. When I refer to the children, it might be a boy rather than a girl or two boys rather than a boy and a girl. But the important thing to remember is that although the names, the place in which the tragedy happened, and certain smaller details are in fact different, many things will be exactly the same in each of the three stories, and the endings are the same, which is why I have tried to combine them in this way.

I was moving, moving through familiar territory, going down and down, and through the hole, to the place I knew I would soon know everything. Used to it, accepting that those who were listening to me, my audience, would have no idea that I was journeying in this way, and even if they did, they would not be able to understand it, I slipped into that nowhere time and drank in the scene.

Smoke was everywhere, thick and black and billowing, permeating through the house and making it almost impossible for anyone to see.

The man was running, as much as he could, going from room to room, down and along the hallways, calling out, crying, desperate and searching, his voice seeming to echo eerily through the fog.

And I watched.

A voice, another, and much younger, this voice filled with fear and panic, seemed to echo through the house, a sound muffled by the smoke. "Dad, Dad, Dad."

And still I watched and listened.

There was no sign yet of the boy, and the man, now desperate beyond words, was running back and forth, back and forth, confused and disoriented by the smoke, blinded and choking, his arms and hands, his hair, his head, burning in the heat of the fire. But he was not giving up; he was refusing to admit defeat, calling out, choking out his child's name. Still searching . . . searching . . . searching.

And still I watched and still I listened, and yes, I prayed.

So hard to see, the smoke blinding, I strained my every sense, peering through the blackness, until finally I saw him, the boy who had been calling for his father.

In a room that might have been a living room or a large bedroom— it was hard for me to tell—I saw the child huddled on the floor, unable to get up, faint and exhausted by his fight to survive. I knew, as I looked at him, that he was dying, but I was helpless to interfere.

I found myself moving back, moving slowly back, into another part of the house, and as I did so, I passed close to the man, still dashing from room to room, who was crazed, choking, screaming frantically for his son, and his terror was palpable. I could taste his fear in my mouth.

I watched, I listened, and I prayed, the silent observer, feeling only, at least for the moment, merely a quiet acceptance of a sort. I was a ghost, simply a ghost, unseen, and in no-man's-land.

It was then, as the man reached out to open the door to one of the many rooms in the house, that I heard another voice, not the voice of the father or the boy but the voice of yet a third. This voice was different, otherworldly it seemed, calming and gentle, soft and clear but somehow commanding, firm in a way that held my attention and demanded to be heard. Only one word rang out, but it was enough. "No!"

The man, who had been about to open the door, heard it too and, without hesitation, quickly pulled his hand away from the doorknob and turned to go to another part of the house. In turning, he paused for just a moment, and there was a slight hesitation. What was it that he should know? What was it that was here with him? Something . . . something . . . but what? He couldn't quite fathom, and mentally shrugging it off, he continued his search.

Still I watched, trying to pay attention to everything around me, seeing more than he could see, knowing more than he could know.

He began running again, dashing from one end of the house to the other, and back again, his hair and arms on fire, searching, searching, searching . . . searching for his children.

I could see the angel quite clearly. It was hard not to, as her light shone out like a beacon despite the dense fog, her figure shimmering and godly in what seemed like an ungodly, unholy, and terrifying place. Had she come to take the child? I wondered mildly.

On and on, on and on, in endless and fruitless circles the father continued his search, ignoring his own pain, his own burning flesh. His pleas, his cries for help seemed useless, for I knew that his son had now passed, and so did he. But still he tried, over and over, not wanting to accept the inevitable, wanting, needing, to save his child, and he continued his search until the firemen came and forcibly removed him from the house, exhausted and sobbing, desperate in his failure.

And still I stayed, and still I watched some more, knowing there was more to see but not yet knowing what.

There were many voices now, as the rescue teams came in to the house, and the smell of smoke was pungent in my nostrils. Now my own emotions began to seep through, and although I tried to remain distant and impartial, I could feel, I could feel the unspeakable terror of the night piercing my heart.

Wanting now to leave, not wanting to see more, not wanting to know more, still I watched, knowing that I must, while I stood in the midst of this terrible nightmare. And as I stood in the center of the heat, the smoke, and the terrible smell of burning, one word reverberated through my head . . . "Fire . . . Fire . . . Fire."

I bowed my head, fighting to hold back the tears, and it was then I saw, just a flicker of movement, reaching across my vision, coming from the left. Out of the corner of my eye I saw it, but oh so briefly, before it disappeared.

And again, not wanting to, but accepting my role, I waited, knowing that I must.

Still, still, being very still, my audiences waited with me, holding their breath, listening as I had narrated my journey into the life of the man, the lives of the three families, as each in turn, on three separate nights, had sat in front of me.

The man, crying, as I had described his nightmare, waited with baited breath for more . . . As he must.

Now, coming back through the hole, back to my audience, I turned my head to the left once more, and then I saw. The small child I had been waiting to see, a girl, just a little thing, not much more than a baby, scampering to my side. I smiled gently, and turned my head to the right, going back and down again through the hole, not wanting to see but needing to see what had happened to her, needing to see how she had died.

I was back in the smoke, back in that dark and unforgiving hell, and I could smell the burning flesh of those I knew were sweet and helpless children. And there, in that terrible place, I could see a small child, a little girl, alone in the midst of the smoke, and she was lying still and unmoving in her crib, such a little thing, suffocated by the filth from the fire.

Another movement, I held my breath, and once more I heard the boy cry out, and shifting my gaze from the crib, I saw him again, watched him again, a rerun of the time I had seen him last. I watched, saw him again, and heard him call out, as he tried helplessly to find his daddy.

"Brother and sister, brother and sister," I heard Grey Eagle say, as I turned my head again, and emerging out and through the hole to the "now," saw my guide, standing by my side.

The "now" was Canada, Edmonton to be precise, the "now" was also Toronto, and the "now" was Montreal, and my audiences were large, eager and excited that they had been given the chance to journey with me for a short time. And we were traveling, through time and space; to places some might think were impossible to go.

As I faced my audience, as I looked to the three families, in my three different audiences, I saw the two children as they now stood by their father . . . their mother . . . their parents . . . their grandfather . . . and I marveled at their resilience, thrilled that they were able to give so many messages to him and to their family, giving proof of their existence after death.

All the while I had watched, I had waited, and I had listened, and all the while I had recounted everything I had seen and heard to my audiences, going back and forth, back and forth, down and through the hole, as the children had relived their passing.

The man, their father . . . was crying with joy and with pain, as he heard my words. The woman, the mother . . . The couple, the parents . . . They were all crying with joy and with pain, as they heard my words.

And so, back through the hole I went, one final time, three final times, to the place of the fire where these children had perished so horribly. I went back to the place where the angel now stood, two small children lifted up into her arms, her wings folded around to protect them as they traveled.

And I waited and watched and listened, for there was more. I knew there was more.

There was noise all around as the rescue teams came in, and the angel stood quietly, not quite ready yet to leave. As I turned my head in the direction she was looking and followed her thoughts down the hallway once more, I came to a room that seemed so familiar and realized at once how I knew it so well. I remembered the father, as he had reached out toward the doorknob, and I remembered that third voice, the voice of the angel, as calmly but firmly she had called out one word, that word, a command, "No!"

Now watching, I saw clearly, as the door to the room opened and as I looked inside I saw them, two more children, a brother and sister, lying safe in their beds.

I turned to the angel, now ready to leave, with her charges held gently in her arms. "If he had opened the door, the room would have filled with smoke, and these two would also be gone," she explained quietly. "It was not their time, not yet their time to go." And then she continued.

"Two children we are taking, and two must stay," she said, and as I heard these words, my heart felt as if it was broken into a million pieces, and I knew I would never fully understand why it had to be this way. For a moment, I bowed my head again, not caring that the tears fell from my eyes; then I looked up. I looked up into the eyes of the angel, and I saw my pain clearly reflected in hers as she smiled at me, a loving and compassionate smile.

Coming back to the now, back through the hole, somehow, and with God's help, and struggling to find my strength, I held back my cry of desperation, understanding that this was not the time for weakness, that there was more work to be done, important work, more messages to give, more connections to make. There were others in my audience,

others who had also had trauma and tragedy in their lives, other people who needed our help, who needed the hope and inspiration from
their loved ones in the spirit world, and they were counting on us to
do our best.

Moving on to the next person, and then to the next, the messages
flowed, as night after night the spirit world made their presence felt.
Each time, understanding how every person's story, every person's
pain, is just as important, just as tragic, just as inspiring, and just as
heartbreaking as the next, and the next, and the next.

Will it ever end? I ask. Will it ever be different? Will the pain ever
stop? And I know that my question is futile, that it will not.

I am a spiritual medium and a healer and am used to seeing terrible heartbreak and pain. But first I am human and cannot help my humanness, no matter how I try. And so the memories stay with me as I
travel my path, and I hold on to them, for they are a precious gift, and
in my saner moments, I know this as a fact.

I will remember the cries of the child as he runs through the house.
I will remember the pain and the terror and the hurt. But mostly, I will
force myself to remember the angel, the three angels, in those three
separate and different yet so similar stories. Or could it be, I tell myself, that it was the same angel each time?

Above all, I am determined to remember the joy and the happiness
of the children, of all of the children as they lay nestled safely in the
arms of their angels. I will remember the look of peace on their faces,
all fear gone, all terror forgotten, as they journeyed heavenward . . .
heavenward . . . to a place of safety . . . to a place of light . . . and yes,
to a place of wonder.

PART IV

A PROMISE IS
A PROMISE

The Age of Enlightenment

It is true that we live in an enlightened age, an age when, in our Western society, we have finally come to accept mediums, psychics, healers, and most forms of alternative medicines and lifestyles as part of our modern culture, even if we don't ourselves necessarily subscribe to it. No longer do people like me have to hide or have to contend with raised eyebrows and sideways glances when we talk about what we do. The world—in part because of the many TV shows, magazine articles, and people like Larry King, with a willingness to be fair and open to the subject—has at last said, "This is real. This is OK." So there is no more sniggering or harsh and cruel judgments, no more fear of being thought crazy, and no more witch hunts. We live in an enlightened age . . . or so we would like to think!

Llewella Day, whom I mentioned in an earlier chapter, came to be my patient when a mutual friend had loaned her my books. After reading them, she had asked if it would be possible to meet me and to have healing, as she had cancer and was recovering from surgery.

On my first visit I took with me a friend and fellow healer, Joan, who happened to be visiting from England at the time. The town of Ira, a place I'd never heard of, was a forty-five-minute drive away, and it was January in Vermont. The snow was thick on the ground as we wound our way up the narrow country lanes, going higher and higher into the mountains, and the roads were treacherous, but we finally reached our destination. The place looked bleak and un-lived-in that cold winter day, and from what I could tell, the farm seemed to consist of an old red-brick house, small, with a rough extension on the side, which was partially falling down. A large barn stood behind the house, and there were some outbuildings, which were barely standing. Scattered every-where I looked were rusting farm machinery and enough piles of old tires to boggle the mind. Across from the brick house, however, stood a small stable, which seemed structurally sound and in good condition. Unlike the rest of the place, the area surrounding it was clean and tidy. This building, I was to learn later, was for Llewella's horses. Higher up on the hill, a small white house stood alone, where Llewella lived, and as we headed on up, it was impossible to ignore more rusting junk, piled dangerously high in places, and more outbuildings in a state of collapse.

Hill House, unaffectionately referred to by Llewella as Hell House, was in a reasonable condition, although it was desperately in need of a paint job and some major repairs. As we pulled up and got out of the car, I couldn't believe how cold it was. I wondered how anyone in their right mind would want to live in such a place.

Inside the house it was warm, but I could immediately see that Llewella was no housekeeper and that very little money had been spent on the place in years. The furniture was sparse, the floors were bare, and the linoleum was cracked and dirty. Dirty dishes were piled high in the sink, and the sofa in the living room was so old and dirty that it was hard for me to look at it. Add to that the overpowering smell of farm animals—a mixture of sheep and cow manure and unwashed dogs.

It soon became clear where the dog smell was coming from. Two enormous white shaggy things suddenly appeared, their coats matted and caked with who knows what. These were huge creatures, that scared

Joan and me half to death. They were Llewella's guard dogs, protecting the farm against any stranger who happened to stray onto their territory. Since Joan and I were most definitely on their territory, we stood very still, barely breathing, until our friend came out from the living room into the kitchen and sent the dogs outside.

A small and seemingly frail figure, she lay on the hospital bed, which was situated at one side of the small living room, next to a window that looked out and down to the horse barn and the brick house below. Wearing dark green coveralls, tied in the middle with string, heavy wool socks on her feet, and tufts of gray hair sprouting from beneath a worn baseball cap, Llewella pushed herself into a sitting position as I entered the room, and thrust out her hand. As I took it, she smiled the biggest and warmest smile I think I have ever seen. No longer was it cold or bleak, for with that one bright smile, life and love and God were breathed into my heart—and there it stays.

The definition of the word *enigma,* according to *Webster's* dictionary, is "a mystery, something which baffles understanding, one of nature's secrets, a contradiction, something obscure, or hard to understand, a puzzle." Llewella was all of those things and more besides. She was valedictorian, summa cum laude, at the University of Vermont and had planned to continue her education and to study English literature. She would have if her brother, also clever and three years older, had taken over the farm after he graduated from the same university. But he had other plans. At the time of his sister's graduation, without telling a soul, he packed his bags and left town, heading for Arizona. Llewella was left to take care of their aging parents, a dairy farm already showing extreme signs of neglect, and all other responsibilities.

Born with an innate sense of doing the right thing, Llewella gave up her dreams of further education and travel, as her brother knew she would, and took care of her parents until they died several years later. In 1938 she gave up dairy farming—it was just too much—but determined to keep the farm and some of the animals, especially her horses.

She got a job as a schoolteacher in the next town, and this worked for a while. The hours were short, the summers were long, and with her small salary and a grueling schedule, she was able to keep some of the livestock and maintain a few of the hayfields. Even so, Llewella worked every minute she could, mending fences, haying fields, tending to her beloved horses.

Somehow, she told herself, *somehow it will work out. Somehow I will manage.*

The years passed and Llewella changed from the naive young woman she had been, with her dreams of seeing the world and connecting with her family in Wales, to an older, much wiser woman with other dreams. Perhaps one day, she often thought, she could turn the farm into a museum or maybe a place of healing for people and for animals. These were her dreams now, and her ideas were endless.

Against all odds, this tough Vermonter hung on to her beloved farm. Now, however, all these years later, neglected from lack of money and manpower, all the buildings except the stables were in disrepair. Filled with more than three generations of junk, they were starting to crumble. However, all the fences were straight and in good repair, the fields she hayed were always plowed and kept in good order, and the animals—thirty or so horses, a few sheep, and half a dozen cows—were well fed. The stable was clean and neat, and nothing in it was out of place.

It had been a choice, and a simple one for Llewella: the well-being of her animals or her own well-being. Something was bound to suffer, and it was not going to be the animals!

Isolated and alone for most of her life, with only her Bible to keep her company, Llewella developed a deep and unrelenting belief that God had given her the farm for a purpose. What that purpose was she didn't yet know, but she trusted that God had a plan and that He would show her what it was, in His own good time.

Llewella eventually traded her teaching job to work nights at a nearby veterinary clinic. She slept on a narrow cot in a tiny room at the back of the clinic. This was by no means a great trade, since the clinic paid her a pittance, but the hours were better for the farm. It meant that she could put in a full day's work on the land or with the horses. She would arrive at the clinic at five P.M., and by eight the next morning she would be back at work on the farm. She ate on the run, but only when she remembered or on the odd occasion when a friend took a plate of something to her at the farm. Sometimes she would stop at the local café for a homemade-bread sandwich and pie, but only very rarely. She never cooked, and she loved doughnuts and M&M's, which became her staple diet.

At some point God lightened up on Llewella a little, and John and Esther came into her life. Llewella and John became like mother and son, and Esther became her best friend. Still life was hard, so very hard, and with age Llewella became more and more cantankerous, earning herself the reputation in the area of being a difficult and some-what ornery woman, given to speaking her mind whether she pleased or offended. It was not unusual for her to be seen driving along the road in her truck, with a sheep sitting in the passenger seat, and over time, she became an enigma. Some thought she was rude, intolerant, and downright impossible. Others knew her as "difficult but honest" and respected her, but all agreed that you'd better watch out. Llewella spoke her mind, gave an opinion asked for or not, and everyone feared her wrath. Her tongue was razor sharp as was her mind, and she used both to full advantage. Llewella Day became a character.

From the first moment I met her, Llewella treated me with respect, which was unusual for her, as she generally looked on strangers with more than a modicum of suspicion and mistrust. Her attitude was that you were worth little of her time until you proved otherwise, as she had very little time to waste. Perhaps it was because she'd read my books, or maybe it was that she instantly recognized a kindred soul, but some-how, Llewella saw in me that same faith in God that she had, and not an easy woman to fool, as I sat with her on the bed that first time, I was aware of her scrutiny as she looked straight into my eyes, finally giving me her wonderful smile.

We became friends immediately, as we were truly soul mates, and over the next few months I visited Llewella at least twice a week. During that time her health improved so much that she was soon back on her beloved tractor, mowing the fields, tending her horses, and anyone not knowing her would never have guessed she was ill. Her gait became strong, and she was back to her old ways and as cantankerous as ever around her friends and colleagues. She went to the clinic, worked nights again, and tended the farm during the day.

Spring turned to summer. Each time I visited, Llewella was stronger, determined to be in control of her life. We would get up in her old truck and she'd drive me around, proudly showing me her property. It was easy to see why she loved the place. The term *breathtaking* did not sufficiently describe the magnificent beauty, even with all that rusting junk and tumble-down buildings.

Not long after I began going up there, Llewella began confiding her plans for the farm after she had passed. John and Esther were to inherit half the farm, and another couple, also horse farmers, whom she had known for only a couple of years, were to inherit the other half. They shared her love of horses and could help John and Esther with expenses and day-to-day running of the farm. Llewella also had a partner with the horses, whose job was to help with breeding the horses and finding buyers for the foals, but although the partnership was ten years old, it wasn't working. Llewella was the one buying the horses, and they had only two foals, and money was running out fast. Still, Llewella wanted her to have the use of the main house and the barns for her lifetime.

"What did you think?" Llewella asked me one day as she talked to me of her plans.

"Well"—I smiled—"I think it's more important to ask what your friends think. I take it you've talked to them about it and they're all in agreement?"

Llewella was a little taken aback at this, as she'd just presumed it was a good plan and that it was the best she could do for the farm. "Well, no," she answered. "Do you think I should?"

I told her it might be a good idea. Maybe her friends might have a different view of things. Maybe the couple with the horse farm might not want to move to Vermont; maybe they might all see things differently than she, perhaps want things done differently.

As usual, Llewella took some time to think about what I'd said, mulling it over before making any decision, and a couple of weeks passed before she brought the subject up again.

"I think you're right," she said one day out of the blue, "you know, about talking to John and the others. I should ask them what they want and not assume that my way is good for them. But first, Rosemary"— and she gave me one of her penetrating looks—"I want you to tell me what you think they'll say."

"Is this a test?" I answered wryly. "Are you testing my psychic ability by any chance?"

"Maybe," she said, laughing, "But I would really like to know what you think."

At first I refused. What I thought was not the issue and might color the way she approached the situation, but after a lot of bullying and pushing, I eventually agreed, making it clear that I could be wrong.

"The couple with the horses [as I referred to them] will not be satisfied with half the farm. They'll want all five hundred acres. Your partner will be angry that she'll only have use of the property and not inherit, and she will sulk for a week or two. John and Esther will say that whatever you want is up to you."

I had, of course, asked Grey Eagle for this information. But Llewella couldn't believe that the couple with the horses would possibly want all the property. I was pleased, for this meant that her approach to them would be fair and unbiased, as it should be.

A few days later Llewella called, very distressed, but wouldn't talk on the phone, and asked if I'd go up to the farm as soon as possible. Her face was stony, as I walked into the kitchen, and it was hard to tell if she was sick or simply mad as hell.

"I called them," she said, tight-lipped and pacing the floor. "You were right. I explained about the will and that I was leaving them half the farm. I'd hardly got the words out before he told me it wasn't enough. He wanted all of it, all of it!" She shoved some papers at me. "Now, look at this. He's written me a letter explaining why over two hundred and fifty acres isn't enough for him. I told her too"—she was referring to her partner—"she screamed at me that it wasn't fair, slammed the phone down and isn't speaking to me. I've tried to call her, but she hasn't called me back."

As she spoke, tears glistened in Llewella's eyes, and I could hear the heartbreak and anger in her voice, anger at herself for being so gullible. "I'm just an old fool! I thought everyone wanted what was best for the farm," she said, plopping down on the sofa, exhausted and disappointed.

"What did John say?" I asked gently, knowing the answer and not surprised when she gave me a wry smile and said that Grey Eagle had been right about everyone.

"John made it clear he doesn't like the others and wouldn't work with them anyway under any circumstances." Then, gazing up at me, dejected, she said, "What am I supposed to do now? I have to do something, protect the farm somehow."

I knew how Llewella felt about John. He was the son she had never had, and it seemed to me that he was the answer she was looking for. But when I suggested it, she told me that the only reason she had included the others in the first place was because John and Esther could never afford the taxes or the expense of running the farm. She'd already asked him anyway, she said wearily, and they both knew it wouldn't work.

Llewella had once told me that over the years she'd looked into various charity organizations, hoping to find one she might leave the farm to, but none had seemed right. During the next weeks this idea became the topic of our conversations. We both knew that time was becoming an issue, although neither of us spoke our thoughts out loud.

"How about the Land Trust or the Nature Conservancy?" I suggested time after time. I always got the same response.

"Don't trust 'em. Don't trust the Land Trust. Never have, never will!"

Then one day in late summer Llewella came to me with what she called the perfect solution.

"What about you?" she said slyly, acting as if she'd thought of it only a day or so earlier. I had known it was coming, had sensed it weeks ago, and had done my best to steer her in any other direction. I didn't want to offend my friend by refusing what most would consider an incredible gift, but I knew that this "gift" came with a price and I didn't want it.

My answer was gentle at first, and thanking her for her trust, I refused. My reasons were many. Mainly, it was obvious to me that such a commitment was a job for life, full-time, leaving little room for anything else. That aside, the amount of money it would take to clear the land, renovate the properties, and make the place workable was overwhelming. I didn't have the money or the time to spend turning the farm into a healing center, which was what Llewella had in mind. "It's not feasible," I'd tell her every time she brought it up, and I made it clear that it wasn't going to happen, at least not with me. The whole idea was crazy. I would be crazy even to consider it and I didn't.

Then something happened that seemed the answer to our prayers. A local man wanted to buy the place, to build an estate for himself and his family. At first Llewella didn't even want to consider the proposition. "I don't want strangers on my land," she said, in that way of hers which meant, "I've made up my mind."

"Well," I replied, "it might at least be worth thinking about. Maybe he'd consider buying part of the land, so you could still stay here but have enough money to keep things going for a while." I was thinking not just of the animals, the land taxes, and day-to-day expenses, I was also thinking of the medical bills. Llewella had a good health plan, but it didn't cover all the medications she was taking, and over the last few months I'd had to cover some of the expenses when the pharmacy had refused to fill the prescriptions. I hadn't burdened Llewella with this. As far as she knew, everything was covered. I wanted it to stay that way, but I knew I couldn't do it for too much longer. If Llewella was to sell part of the land, I reasoned, that would help solve many of her problems.

Over the following week Llewella gave some thought to the idea and decided that she should at least consider it. But there was a catch.

"If I sell half the farm, will you agree to take the other half and turn it into a healing center?"

I knew she had me. She knew she had me, and after much discussion and with ill grace, I agreed to consider the idea, but I knew I really didn't want this millstone around my neck. I was too old, too tired, and too busy. However, under daily pressure from Llewella, and knowing how sick she really was, I eventually agreed, saying I would do my best to build a healing center, and that if I couldn't manage that, then I would do the next best thing.

So Llewella agreed to go ahead with the proposed sale, and it seemed like the perfect solution, and would have been, except for one thing. Llewella was a very private person and had lived on her own, without neighbors, all her life. Her new soon-to-be neighbor had taken to dropping by, walking into her kitchen without knocking, wanting to be friendly, he said, and continually asking if she would sell him the rest of the property at some time in the future. A forceful man with lots of money, used to getting what he wanted, he royally ticked Llewella off. And of course the inevitable happened.

"You know how you told me I could change my mind about the sale at any time," she said, calling me early one morning. "Well, I've changed m'mind. I couldn't sleep all night, thinking about having him for a neighbor, and I can't stand him. So, you'll tell him, won't you? And soon."

There was no discussion. I knew when to keep quiet, and I could understand her reasons. I'd even called the man a couple of weeks before, suggesting he might want to telephone Llewella first before turning up, as she'd begun to complain about him. He hadn't listened, and now it was too late. The sale was off, but I wasn't prepared for what came next.

"Well, you've already agreed to take part of the farm, so you might as well have it all," said Llewella, a satisfied smirk on her face. "And anyway, I don't think I could find anyone better for the job."

I have often wondered if that had been Llewella's plan all along, to back out of the sale, her way of getting her own way and making sure the farm was protected. Now, I'm psychic, remember, so you'd think I would have known. However, mediums don't know everything, especially about themselves, and just because we speak to the spirit world doesn't mean things always work out fine for us. We have the same everyday challenges that everyone else has and are equally capable of messing up our lives. The reason I didn't see this coming, I think, was because I really didn't want to. It was not part of my dream. It was not what I wanted to do with my life.

Llewella recognized she would never change my mind by badgering; we were too much alike in that respect. But she did know my heart, and she believed in me. Strong, tough, and cunning, a true Vermont hill farmer with a will of iron and a heart of gold . . . yes, she knew exactly how to get her own way with me, and indeed she had.

Then, one day I arrived at the farm to give Llewella her healing. As I made my way toward the house, I was practically knocked down by her partner, who'd come storming out the door in a real tear. As soon as she saw me, her rage spilled over. "If you hurt her," she spat at me, "I'll squash you like a bug," and she stormed off down the driveway.

"Well, I told her," said Llewella matter-of-factly, as I came into the house, "and I tell you, she didn't like it one bit. She called you a gold-digger. Said you'd pulled the wool over my eyes. She tried to persuade me to leave the place to her. I told her you were the boss now, and what you say goes." Before I could say a word, she gave me one of her cold, hard looks that said "Don't argue with me," and continued. "Look, Rosemary, this is what I want, this is what I've prayed for, and you have to help me do what's right for this place. So let's not talk about it any-more, at least not today."

I'd been taken off-guard by Llewella's partner's anger toward me, but I understood that she needed someone to blame for everything that had gone wrong between her and Llewella. Some people like to blame others for their own mistakes, and in her mind, I had become the one who'd influenced Llewella against her. I had become the enemy! Less than a month later, the partner, enraged, went to see a lawyer and began the process of contesting Llewella's will.

How she found out, I'll never know, but when Llewella discovered what her partner was up to, she wanted to give me the farm before she died, just hand the deed over. I would have nothing to do with the idea. Part of me was still hoping that she would give the place to the Land Trust or to the Nature Conservancy, but mainly I didn't feel it was right to take the farm away from Llewella. As long as it remained in her name, I felt, she could change her mind, leave it to a cat's home, a horse rescue center, or whatever she felt like. For more than fifty years she'd worked like a slave to keep her farm, and it was only right that her name stayed on the deeds until the day she died, no matter what the consequences would be afterward.

Not one to sit still for long on a problem of any kind, Llewella in-vited some of her neighbors and friends, John and Esther among them, to her house one evening for a meeting. She told them the sit-uation and, introducing me, made it clear that I was to inherit every-thing, and gave her reasons for her decision. She asked if anyone had anything to say against the idea. No one did. She asked if anyone

would like to ask any questions. No one did. Then she asked if anyone would help, when the time came, to ensure that everyone knew
her wishes and that no one would be in any doubt as to what she
wanted to happen to her farm.

It was a strange meeting. Although they were her neighbors and had
known her for years, few had known Llewella well, and they didn't
understand the reasons for the meeting at all. Others knew her only
too well, and they also knew that it would take more than this to avoid
the trouble that was inevitably brewing.

What's in a Name?

Llewella died the next January, having had the most wonderful summer and fall, riding her tractor, helping with the haying, and tending her horses. We'd spent many hours discussing what would happen to the horses after she was gone, since she knew I couldn't keep them at the farm. November turned to December, and Llewella began to fail just a little, although if you hadn't known her you'd never have believed she was ill, as she still insisted on doing many of the farm chores. She made a list of all the horses, and instructions as to what I was to do with them after she was gone.

Leaving nothing to chance, Llewella had given me her instructions for her burial and her wishes for her remains. She also left instructions about the remains of her dog, the only one now left whom she knew would not survive without her. We were to put him down as soon as we could after she passed, she had said. Fortunately, she had given this task to John.

Her final words to me, as I held her hand as she lay, once again, on the hospital bed, which we'd placed by the window overlooking the field where the horses were, as it had been when I first met her, her

214

final words were these. "You made me a promise, you know, and I know you'll do your best to keep it. I love you."

Hundreds of people turned up at the funeral. After all, Llewella was something of a legend, but although I was grateful for the turnout, a little part of me couldn't help wondering where all these people had been over the years, when my friend had been so lonely, when she had been in such need of company and good friends. I wondered where they'd all been this last year, when she'd been ill. John, I know, was wondering the same thing. Were we just being cynical? Or were we just sad that so much good-heartedness from so many good people had amounted to so little when Llewella had been alive?

It was early the next morning when I received the phone call from Llewella's cousin, who'd been staying at the farm for the funeral. "What should I do?" she said breathlessly, knowing that she'd be unable to stop them but wanting to try for Llewella, knowing that what was happening was expressly against Llewella's wishes. "They're taking the horses. They have a couple of big horse trailers, and they're loading them all up."

I didn't need to be told who "they" were. *Oh God,* I thought, *the battle has begun.* What was I to do?

No one in their right mind wants to get involved in litigation, but I'd been left no choice. This was my first step, my first real step onto the battlefield. My father, a soldier all his life, had taught me a few things about war, and the first rule he instilled in me was never to step onto a battlefield unless you're sure you can win.

"Life is full of battles of one sort or another," he would say. "Learn to pick the ones you can win. Don't waste your time on those you know you're going to lose."

Sound advice, and advice I had mostly paid attention to over the years. Now, though, having paid my first visit to the lawyer, heard everything he had to say, and realizing how uncertain things were—that because I was a spiritual medium, I was more vulnerable—I felt totally out of my depth.

"They're going to say that you unduly influenced her, that you used your gift, your position, and her vulnerability, to persuade her to leave the farm to you," my lawyer said. I knew he was right, and I knew there would be many who'd believe it to be true. There would be a court case, a trial. My name, my reputation, and everything I believed in would be questioned. My intentions, my ethics, my work, would all be scrutinized and ridiculed by some. I knew that honesty and good intentions didn't necessarily mean a thing, that I could still lose a trial by jury. *I'm British*, I thought, *a foreigner and, worse, a woman who talks to the dead. What chance do I have of winning?*

The lawyer made all this plain, leaving no doubt of the consequences if I was to continue to fight. "We have a good case," he had assured me, "but that doesn't necessarily count in a jury trial."

The lawyer made it clear that I had only a fifty-fifty chance, and that no matter what, a trial was an extremely costly process, and it was much more than I could afford. So, again, I wondered, *What am I supposed to do?*

I talked at length with my daughter, who wanted me to simply let "them" have it all. "You don't need this, Mum," she said, several times. "Who cares about the stupid farm? It's not your concern anymore, and anyway, nothing is worth what this would put you through. Just drop it . . . please," she had pleaded. My good friends all advised the same thing, and I knew they were right. If I went ahead with it, the cost alone could break me, even if I did win. It wasn't worth it . . . was it?

Now I know that, as you read this, you might be wondering what happened to my psychic abilities? What happened to my talking to the dead? You may be expecting me to tell you that I had spoken to Grey Eagle or to Llewella and they told me what to do. Well, you'd be wrong, as I had decided after Llewella died that no matter what happened, right or wrong, I wouldn't burden her. Still trying to protect my patient, I decided that this was my problem now. Of course, I asked Grey Eagle at least a thousand times, but wise as he is and not wanting to influence my decision, he told me it was up to me, that I had to decide for myself.

I'd never wanted the farm in the first place, so it was easy for me to agree with Samantha, that it was no longer my problem. I knew that Llewella, although she might not like it, would totally understand why I had to let it go. I knew it would be OK with Grey Eagle. This, I decided, was not just the easiest way out but the most sensible by far, for everyone's sake.

It felt good to finally make up my mind. It felt right for everyone, right for my child, right for my other patients, who needed my time and attention, and it felt right for my friends who cared about me and who didn't want to see me hurt. It just felt right, and part of my training as a spiritual medium and healer had taught me that I must never ignore my feelings. And yet . . .

"A promise is a promise." Those five little words kept going around and around in my head.

We can all convince ourselves that we're doing the right thing, I suppose, even when we're not. We tell ourselves it's OK; we find the right words to make us feel better about our decisions. The trouble is that we can't convince our heart; we cannot stop the guilt, even if we can learn to ignore it.

"A promise is a promise," my heart was saying, and I tried so hard to make the voice of my conscience go away.

As a girl in Sunday school, I was always fascinated by those incredible Bible stories. Stories of Jesus and his disciples, stories of water turned to wine, the loaves and the fishes, the Good Samaritan, Christ walking on water. My imagination would soar, and I would become inspired by the courage and the faith of the characters. I would listen, spellbound, always wanting to hear more. I was especially inspired by the stories of Daniel in the lions' den, and how the Christians, having only to denounce Christ to escape being thrown to the lions, would not turn against Him to save themselves. I had wondered, as I'd listened to the stories, what I would have done. Would I have been brave enough, risked everything? Would my faith have been strong enough? Of course, in my imagination, I'd bravely fought the lions, even knowing I couldn't win, even though I was terrified. I always imagined I'd have done the right thing, and a small part of me envied those Christians their opportunity to have their faith so tested and to be found not wanting . . . and envy is a terrible thing and can lead to all sorts of trouble, now can't it?

There really was no choice in the end, of course, not for me. Not if my life, my work, my beliefs, really meant anything to me. So here I was, like Daniel, facing the lions' den, and despite my father's warnings, I was going to fight, no matter what the cost. It didn't matter, I realized, whether I won or lost. It only mattered that I tried, as I had promised I would do. After all, a promise is a promise!

Daniel in the Lions' Den

When the phone rang at nine, I'd been up for a while and working in the office, going through some of the letters from my patients. It was my lawyer.

"Well," he said, "it's begun. Did you see the *Rutland Herald* this morning? Did you see the headlines?" As he was saying this, my secretary, Denise, walked in carrying the paper, and thrust it under my nose, and there it was, blazing right across the front page, in bold print: "Bequest to Spiritualist Contested, Final Will by Ira Woman Leaves Family Out." Reading on, I thought, *What family?* Well, so much for a fair trial. I guess the witch hunt is on.

The story, playing on all the old suspicions, all the old recriminations and negative attitude toward spiritualists, was a one-sided account of how I'd taken advantage of a sick old woman, using my psychic abilities to influence her. I was used to it, had come across it before, but that bigoted attitude was long gone. We lived in a new age! New Age books, TV shows, and talk shows were popular, and the stigma that used to be attached to the subject had disappeared, or so I had thought.

The news article was just the beginning. My enemy knew exactly how to exploit the media hype. Going door to door, they canvassed the neighbors where the farm was located, starting rumors that I was going to sell the land to build a housing project. They told how I'd used the fear of a sick and dying woman to persuade her to leave her property to me. The fact that I was a spiritual medium was so damning that it was easy for them to be believed. I was "that" woman . . . the woman who talks to the dead, and that very fact drew suspicion. It implied that I was the kind of person who took advantage of people at their most vulnerable. I was being judged without a trial, and as far as many people were concerned, I was already guilty.

I knew the things that were being said about me, and I felt the stigma as I'd never felt it before. People, even good people, were giving me a wide berth. No one wanted to be tainted. No one wanted to be seen mixing with me. After all, what if I was found guilty? What if the court ruled against me? Who would want to know me then?

My world began to shrink. Fewer and fewer invitations came. More and more people turned away if they saw me in the grocery store or out in the street. I began to feel as if I had a mark on my forehead, just as it was in the old days when a person was branded a harlot or some such. I still had friends of course, people who were supportive and kind. But even they were worried about the outcome of the trial, and most could not understand why I was fighting. "Is the farm really worth it?" I was asked again and again. "Is all this really worth risking your reputation for?"

I couldn't make them understand. Even my daughter was against my involvement, continually trying to persuade me to quit.

Many years earlier, in the beginning, my good friend Mick McGuire had told me that the price of good mediumship was loneliness. Through the years I've understood, more than I have wanted to, exactly what he meant. Now, the loneliness and emptiness I felt, and the struggle of day-to-day living, was overwhelming. Every day I felt more lost and more and more tempted to give in, to ask Llewella to let me out of my commitment. But I could not. Each time I felt alone, I would remind myself of the loneliness she had endured all her life. Each time I felt my courage failing, I would remind myself of the courage she had shown her entire lifetime, to keep the farm going. Each time I felt my strength and commitment waning, I would remind myself of the years and years of brutal winters, when she would struggle down to the stables to feed her horses, sometimes in snow so deep it must have come almost to her shoulders. I would remind myself of the price she paid, sitting alone night after night, year after year for more than fifty years, with no one to talk to, hardly anyone to confide in. Her price had been greater than any I would have to pay. I had made her a promise, and it had not been an idle one. I had known, at the end, what keeping that promise might mean. I had looked at Llewella, and I had seen her goodness and her purity, and I had recognized a need in her. So I tried to be that good Samaritan. I tried to live my faith, to hold on to the belief that God would not let me down. "If I had to be one person," I decided, "strong enough to keep my promise, then I would be a Daniel, a smaller and much less brave Christian than he, and I would walk, if necessary, into the lions' den!"

Can Money Buy Everything?

The deposition was the worst so far, I thought, as I sat with my lawyer, directly across from the opposition. I knew that all I had to do was tell the truth, but I also knew they were going to try to trip me up, to get me to say something they could use against me. They had investigated me thoroughly, looking for anything I may have been trying to hide. I wasn't worried about that, but even so, anyone who has been in my position will understand that no matter how innocent you are, a good lawyer can make you seem like a criminal. I was on my guard. Yet I was surprised by some of the questions. What kind of car did I drive? Was it true that I took gifts to Llewella on a regular basis? What were those gifts? At first I was confused by that question, as the only "gifts" I had taken were a down comforter, some new sheets and pillowcases, and new pillows for Llewella's bed. These gifts had been prompted by the fact that I'd made Llewella's bed for her one day and discovered her sheets were threadbare; her blanket, made of harsh wool, was like an army blanket; and the pillows, stained with sweat and tears, should have been thrown out years ago. But I realized they were trying to make it sound as if I'd tried to buy her. My answer to the lawyer was simply, "A down comforter and bedding."

Well," he replied, with exaggerated patience, "didn't you also take food?"

I was stunned and then angry at the question but answered calmly. "Yes, it had become my practice to take groceries each week and to make up a batch of chili, one of Llewella's favorite dishes, for her to put in the freezer. Then there were the jelly doughnuts," I added, "and a couple of large bags of M&M's. As you can see," I explained, "Llewella had a sweet tooth and very little time to sit and eat, so it was important to make sure that any food I took could be easily prepared and eaten on the run. Otherwise she wouldn't touch it and would give it to the dogs."

The lawyer's response was sarcastic. "So it could be said that you came bearing gifts!" A statement rather than a question.

"You've been a healer and medium for more than twenty years"—he began his next question—"so how many times over those years have you been the beneficiary of a will or a personal gift of money or property?"

That was an easy one. "Just once," I replied.

"And exactly what was the value of your inheritance?"

I had to think, to convert pounds to dollars, and began making my calculations out loud. "Let me see," I muttered, "a hundred pounds equals one hundred and fifty dollars, I think." As I said this, I realized that the lawyers were sitting just a little straighter, paying more attention, and I smiled to myself, knowing exactly what they were thinking. "Yes, a hundred is equal to one fifty," I said, deliberately drawing it out. "Yes, I think that's right, it would be a total of one hundred and fifty—" I paused and the lawyer jumped in, barely containing his excitement. "So you inherited one hundred and fifty thousand dollars. Could you give us the details, please?"

I knew that I shouldn't have done it, but I just couldn't help myself. "Well"—I took my time, pretending to think back—"well, no, no, it wasn't one hundred and fifty thousand, and it was not left to me personally but to my organization. It was left to us by a patient of ours who died of cancer, and actually, sorry if I gave the wrong impression. It was not one hundred and fifty thousand dollars but one hundred and fifty dollars."

The lawyer's eyes grew wide in surprise. He laughed out loud. "One hundred and fifty dollars," he spat out incredulously, "one hundred and fifty dollars?" It was obvious he thought it was a joke.

"Well," I replied sweetly, "that's a great deal of money to a lot of people, you know."

On and on it went, lasting the whole day, and finally ended with the lawyer, in frustration, making yet another snide remark.

"It seems to me," he said, in the most sarcastic and derisive tone, and perhaps trying for one last cut. "It seems to me that you do an awful lot for free, for charity, that is?"

There was no winner that day, and it made me sad to think that even the simplest kindnesses are looked upon by some with suspicion, and it made me realize how sad our world has become.

It is often said that we judge by our own standards, and throughout the coming months I realized how easily good people can seem to lower their standards for money, how money can and does corrupt. I watched basically good people present a version of the facts, under oath, with their hand on the Bible, that I found to be a distortion of the truth. You might call me naïve, but I was shocked by it. However, I'm getting ahead of myself.

Vermont law demands that before you can go to trial, all parties must sit down with a mediator and try to resolve their issues. So there I was at the offices of the mediating lawyer early one Saturday morning with my secretary and my lawyer. We were shown into the office downstairs, and my opponents were upstairs, quite a few of them apparently, and we were all ready to begin. At this point, I was more than willing to work on a settlement, as the costs had already skyrocketed, and a trial would make it worse. If we could come to some fair and reasonable compromise, we could all go home and finally get on with our lives, I thought. Of course, I knew that I would be going against Llewella's wishes, but I'd had enough. For over three years I had tried my best, I reasoned, and that was all I could do. We were already past the three-year mark, and I was not prepared to live the next three years the same way.

Back and forth the mediator went, up and down the stairs between us, first with one suggestion then another. My lawyer had advised me to stay calm, reasonable, and to consider every suggestion thoroughly before responding. I was taking his advice. When we were asked to give up everything, I thought carefully about my response. When we were asked to consider splitting the land, we came up with an alternative suggestion, which was to sell the land to the Land Trust, but to each have use of ten acres for our different projects, my healing center and their therapeutic riding center. When they came back and said they wanted the most prime piece of property, I said no, but they could have any other site on the five hundred acres. Finally, we agreed, and then we discussed the money the Land Trust would give for the land. The legal fees to be paid first, then to split the rest between us, right down the middle. I accepted this but insisted the money be kept in escrow, to be given only for our individual projects and that proof of expenditure must be given in the form of receipts, etc., before we could access the money. They refused, but I wouldn't budge, and on and on the negotiations went, hour after hour. Each time it seemed that we were close to an agreement, they wanted something else. At one point the mediator came into the room, his exasperation undisguised, and almost forgetting that I was in the room, he spoke with my lawyer of his frustration. "You would not believe what is going on up there," he said. "They're fighting among themselves. One wants one thing, another disagrees, wants something different. It's unbelievable. You have to see it to believe it."

My lawyer looked at me and raised an eyebrow. Having dealt with these people for the last few years, neither of us was surprised. We believed that they were influenced by money only, which was why I'd agreed to give them half but which was also why I'd insisted the money could be accessed only on condition of its proper use. Now I was tired, and we had been at this all day. I had done my best to be reasonable, and we had come close to a settlement several times. Now I wanted to finish it.

"The use of ten acres for each party! Ten for them, specifically for a riding center, ten for me, specifically for a healing center. If after three years either party has failed to make any progress in their particular venture, the land will automatically be given back to the Land Trust. Monies from the Land Trust to first pay all legal expenses, then the remainder, if any, to be split equally but to be held in escrow, and to be given only upon proof of use for our respective ventures. This," I added, to the mediator and to my lawyer, "seems more than fair and is my final offer. I cannot and will not negotiate any further."

Both lawyers looked at me and agreed that this was indeed the best possible resolution and that no one could possibly have a reason to disagree. All parties would go home satisfied.

While we waited for the mediator to return, my lawyer took the opportunity to tell me how well I'd done. He thought I had shown myself to be above reproach and more than reasonable. It crossed my mind and only briefly that Llewella might not agree, but what else could I have done? I just wanted to go home and put it all behind me.

It was five o'clock, and we had been there since nine that morning. I signaled to Denise, who had been sitting quietly in the corner all day taking notes, that we would soon be leaving. Finally, the mediator returned, a tired and frustrated look on his face.

"After long discussions, and much arguing, they have all agreed to everything." He sighed. "Even putting the money into escrow, which they were initially adamantly against."

Relieved, exhausted, I pushed back my chair to stand, thinking that it was over at last, but the mediator was not finished.

"There is just one thing." He hesitated, looking at my lawyer and shaking his head as I sat back down. "I have tried, but I cannot change their minds. This for them is a deal breaker. They want it all. They want all of it, the money. They refuse to split it. They want it all."

I had heard the expression "black rage," but had not really understood its meaning until now. My head seemed to explode with heat and yet I remained like ice. For a few moments I stayed very still, not wanting to make a mistake or to overreact. My mind could only register their greed, their unbelievable and appalling greed. What had I been thinking? How could I have been fooled into thinking that I could possibly negotiate with these people? These people who had knowingly and seemingly without conscience begun these proceedings while Llewella was still alive, having been told by her in the most explicit way what her wishes were, deliberately going against those wishes, claiming that their only reasons had been to protect her and her interests. These people, none of them her family, had told themselves and each other that they knew what was best for her. They had convinced themselves they had the right to intervene, even though they knew her well enough to know, without a doubt, that Llewella had never allowed anyone to tell her what she must do. And now they had been fighting with each other all day, and for what? For more! For better! For bigger! Where were Llewella's best interests served here? How was it in Llewella's best interest that the land should be split up, given to the Land Trust, in which they knew she had no faith? How was it in Llewella's best interest that the Trust should get all the money? How could I have been so stupid as to believe that I could ever have reached a fair and reasonable compromise with these people?

Black rage! It seemed to blind me for a moment, to consume me, yet my body was ice cold. It was there inside me, held for a moment, and then it was gone in a flash. Pushing my chair back, I stood and at the same time my hand came down hard, my palm flat on the table, taking us all by surprise.

"I'm done," I said coldly, turning to my lawyer. "I'm done with these people." My voice was quiet but firm, and there was no mistaking my resolve. "I will not sit for one more moment and listen to any more. They are greedy, just purely greedy, and I will not negotiate anymore. We will go to trial, win or lose, I don't care. I take back everything so far that I've agreed to. It was a mistake. I would rather risk losing everything than spend one more second, one more breath, doing any kind of a deal with them!"

My lawyer, confused as to how to handle me, began to try to reason with me, wanting to salvage some of the day's negotiations. I could see why. He was trying to protect my interests. What if we did lose? At least this way I could still have my healing center, at least something could be gained. But it was too late. I had made up my mind. The lions were waiting, and for better or worse I would fight them. Win or lose, I would fight, for it was the only right thing to do.

Finally, the End

It was a cold February morning and the drive to the courthouse was a little treacherous, with plenty of snow and ice on the road. My daughter was with me, and a friend, and as we drove the forty-five minutes there, none of us talked much. After all, what was there to say? Samantha had been disappointed that I hadn't settled out of court, yet she understood the reasons why and was in full support of my decision. By this time, however, she had come to hate the farm and everything about it. She had always been very protective of me, so I could fully understand why. This millstone was all but strangling me, and it was threatening to destroy everything I'd worked so hard to achieve, mainly the reputation I had so carefully and so meticulously earned over the years.

We were the first to arrive, but before long two of my lawyers and an assistant turned up, and we were shown into a small room, which we were to use for the next ten days.

Going over last-minute things, being reassured by my lawyers that everything that could be done had been done, I was able to stay calm, to put on a brave face, as much for my daughter as for any other reason. Finally we got the word that it was time. As we walked into the courtroom, I must admit to being more than a little shocked at the number of people there, most of them sitting on the side of my adversaries. They had obviously gathered their troops in support, and as we walked in, there was a lot of laughter, finger pointing in my direction, and sniggering. It seemed as if they were already celebrating their victory. It quite shocked me, as I suppose it was intended to do, and when I looked over my shoulder at my own little group, I saw my daughter's face, pale and angry. I could see she was a little unnerved. I flashed a smile her way, my way of telling her not to let them get to her. She gave me a weak smile in return.

I was first on the stand, and I was questioned for a day and a half, a grueling experience for anyone. It became obvious very quickly that I was on trial for who I was, not for what I was supposed to have done. Again and again I was questioned about my work. Could I really talk to the dead? Wasn't I, after all, just scamming people, taking advantage of their vulnerability? Hadn't I simply seen an old, vulnerable, sick, and lonely woman and wormed my way into her life in order to influence her to leave me everything she had? Repeatedly, my credentials as a spiritual medium and a healer were put on trial. The idea that anyone could possibly talk to the dead, or have the ability to heal, was brought into question, belittled, made less of, dismissed as nothing more than preying on the weak. The only thing I knew to do was tell the truth, but I knew that because truth is sometimes stranger than fiction, I just might be giving the enemy more ammunition against me.

I do not exaggerate when I say that it was like being in the Dark Ages, or being at the center of the Inquisition, when people like me were considered heretics, witches, and burned at the stake. Gone, it seemed, was the age of enlightenment. Gone was the fact that the world has finally accepted the fact that mediumship exists in a good way, that the ability to talk to the dead is an amazing and incredible gift. Gone was the tolerance. As I sat, hour after hour, bombarded with questions, insinuations, and insults, all I could do was to live my faith and to retain my dignity and my honesty. At the end of my testimony, my lawyers were wonderful, allowing me to explain many of the facts that had been deliberately misconstrued or twisted. But who knew if the jury was prepared to listen to me?

When I was finally allowed to leave the stand, my lawyers told me how well I'd done and reassured me that this was only the beginning, that our turn would come. But as Samantha and I drove home on that second day, we were both very despondent. We had lived through this kind of thing before, in the beginning, more than twenty-five years ago, when I was ridiculed, called bad names, accused of going against God, even accosted in public places. My daughter had been my greatest supporter and friend during those times, even though she was very young, and over the years, we had watched the world change for the better—or so we had thought. Now we were back there, back to that gut-aching time when the whole world seems against you, ready to condemn you for who you are. Once again my daughter was my greatest supporter, my best and most loyal friend. But as I looked at her, I wondered how unfair was I being to her? It was all very well doing the right thing for someone else, but was I doing the right thing for my child? However, it was too late for these thoughts now, and all I could do was hold her hand and tell her that it would be OK.

During the next days, my opponents produced their witnesses, about ten in all, and as I listened to their testimony, to my astonishment, all but two seemed to have a totally different and utterly distorted version of the facts of the case. Since they had given their oath, had sworn on the Bible to tell the truth, I expected the truth. My lawyers came into their own, ruthlessly pounding out the facts, revealing again and again the inconsistences in their testimonies. I'd had no idea how naive I was until now, listening as my enemies told their stories, appalled at their audacity. I had truly believed that when people swear on the Bible to tell the truth, the whole truth, and nothing but the truth, so help me God, that, if only out of fear of reprisal, they are going to do just what they say. Time after time I listened, my mouth open as they spun their version of the facts, time after time I listened as their web became unraveled.

Eventually, I could see the greed, the distortions, the meanness, all begin to show, and the case against me seemed from my perception to be falling apart. But perhaps it was obvious only to me. We had a jury, ten in all, ten people who might see me in the same light as my enemy had, and I had been painted as a cheat and a charlatan. Whom would they believe?

On the tenth and final day, the court was adjourned at twelve-thirty. The jury was given instructions by the judge, and there was nothing more to do but file out and pray for a positive ending. All through the trial I had reminded myself that this was not about winning, and as my lawyers and I, Samantha, and my friend went to lunch, I reminded myself again. None of us could say what the outcome would be, and as I pushed my food around on the plate, I wondered how long we would have to wait for the phone call that would bring us back to the court-room to hear the verdict. I knew the jury would take at least half an hour for lunch, and then they would have to sift through the evidence, look at all the paperwork, debate among themselves, and so I was shocked when after an hour and a half we were called back to the court-house. This could mean only one thing. The jury had heard enough evidence throughout the trial for them to have made up their mind be-fore hand. It was a fast and unanimous decision, which could be very good for us, or very bad.

Throughout it all, I had conducted myself well, staying calm and centered, focusing on the trial, seeming, I knew, even to those who knew me well, to be ready for whatever came.

The jury filed in, but I kept my head down, not wanting to betray my emotions now that the end had finally come. I knew that if I lost, I must remain at all costs, dignified. I would not let my enemy see me broken, of this I was sure. I would be like Daniel and would stand proud, knowing that I had kept my promise, that I had kept my faith.

We all rose as the judge made his entrance. Still, I kept my eyes down. I stood between my two lawyers and felt their hands on my elbows. I could feel my heart begin to pound a little as the judge asked the jury for their verdict.

"We find for the plaintive," said the small woman, the spokesperson for the jury.

I stood there emotionless, waiting, confused for the moment and wondering, *Which am I? Am I the plaintive or am I the other?* My mind had gone entirely blank. Then the lawyers, both together, grabbed hold of me and began hugging me. "We've won, we've won, Rosemary, we've won!"

It's funny how, in crisis, we can hold ourselves together, and at the precise moment the crisis is over, we fold. This is exactly what I did. In all my years I have never cried so loudly, so publicly, and for so long. It was something to see, I can tell you.

Each time the judge tried to thank the jury and to dismiss them, he would have to stop. I was making such a noise. Each time I would gather my poise, bite my lip, force myself to be in control, but then I would lose it again. The judge was very patient and so, it seemed, were the jury. But try as I might, it took several minutes before I could stop making those awful sounds, long enough for the judge to finish up. My lawyers were amazed at my lack of composure, I know, and the effect it had on them and everyone else who was there in support of me was gratifying. Pretty soon, we were all crying. And yes, I know, it's hard to believe, but YES, even the lawyers themselves!

So now, here we were, the two of us, making our way home, the nightmare finally over. Now we could get on with our lives. I drove slowly, still shaken at my response to the verdict and still a little embarrassed, to say the least. We were both quiet, both lost in our own thoughts, both letting go in our own way. Then, after about thirty minutes, my daughter spoke.

"You know, Mum . . ." She paused, looking, I thought, for the right way to say whatever it was she needed to say. I reached over to take her hand. "You know," she continued, then paused again for just a moment longer. "You know, you made ever such a lot of noise. You were really, really loud!"

I turned to look at her, shame-faced, and she turned to look at me, then grinned. I grinned back, and we both began to laugh!*

*To learn more about the court case, consult the Rutland County Court records department. To learn more about the Rosemary Altea Healing and Educational Foundation, go to www.rosemaryaltea.com.

PART V

THE GOOD, THE BAD,
AND THE BEAUTIFUL

Life Takes Funny Turns

There are times, we all know, when it is so very, very hard, indeed almost impossible, to let our loved ones go, especially if they are young or healthy and we're not expecting them to leave us. In these times, life can seem so unfair, is unfair, and we flounder, confused, hurt, trying to deal with our grief. Many people presume that as a medium and having a direct line to the spirit world, I would find the loss of a loved one easier than most. They are wrong. In times of loss I suffer just as much as the next person. I complain about the unfairness of God, just like everyone else, and am sometimes left feeling bereft, just as others might be. My psychic abilities protect me no more or less than anyone else. This next story is about one of those times.

Sheldon had worked for me for over four years, taking care of my house and grounds, a big task but one he loved. Truly an outdoors person, no matter what the weather, Sheldon would be hard at work and loving every minute of it.

He did everything: mowed lawns, cut trails, chopped logs, and cleaned out the brush. If I saw something on the property that needed doing, by the time I mentioned it to Sheldon, he would give me one of his wry smiles and say, "I did it yesterday," or, "Oh, yes, just finished doing that." He was always ahead of me, no matter what, and over the years we developed a real closeness.

On winter days he would come into the house to take a break and would talk about his life, his home, his wife and son. Often he would tell me his troubles, and I almost always made time to listen, as I found Sheldon to be one of the most sensitive and gentle of men. His great humility impressed me. He never talked about his skills with a rifle or his championship wins at bowling, and he never tried to impress me by ever mentioning all the cups, the accolades, he'd received as a sportsman, or the fact that his peers held him in the greatest esteem. I was to learn of those things later, from others who had loved him even more than I.

Quiet, unassuming, dedicated, loyal, and naturally protective, over the years Sheldon became protective of me, and took the utmost care of me in every way he could. As he went about his work, day after day, Sheldon acquired a helpmate, or should I say, more accurately, a playmate.

Sheldon was Niño's favorite and helper, and the two of them could be seen any day of the week out in the grounds, having a good time together. Next to me, Sheldon was Niño's love, and my puppy was always excited to see him.

I was planning a trip to Europe when Sheldon's own dog, a fifteen-year-old mix, really beautiful, died. His wife, Mary, was devastated, as was Sheldon, although the dog was old and they'd known for quite a while that he wouldn't last forever.

A couple of weeks passed. My trip to Europe was now imminent, and Sheldon came to talk to me about the possibility of getting another puppy for his wife. "I was thinking that perhaps we could get a chocolate Labrador, like Niño," he said. "Do you think you could call the kennel you got him from, Rosemary, and see if they're expecting a litter?" We decided to wait until I got back from my trip, as I was leaving the next day, but life, as we know, takes funny turns and our tomorrows are not always as we think they will be.

While I was gone, halfway through my tour, Sheldon went into hospital for a planned minor surgery. He had polyps in his nose and needed his nasal passages cleaned out. The surgery was to last two hours, maybe less, with another two hours of recovery time, after which he could go home. Since the procedure was so simple, Sheldon went to the hospital by himself and had arranged to call his wife when he was ready to be picked up. He could see no sense in her waiting around while he was under.

When the phone rang, Mary was surprised that the hospital was calling quite so soon. She thought it would have taken at least a little longer, and she was not at all prepared for what was to come.

"Mrs. Taft, can you please come right away. Something went wrong. Your husband had a seizure, and we need you to come in right away."

He had been on life support for two days when I arrived back from Italy, and I went straight from the airport to the hospital. Every day I visited, giving healing to Sheldon and his family, praying for a miracle and asking for God's help to accept His will. But two weeks later Sheldon was gone, just like that, and although I know better, I was devastated.

His family had allowed me the privilege of being by his side when they took him off the machines. Mary and her son, Sheldon Jr., sat on one side of the bed, holding Sheldon's hand, and I sat opposite them, with the rest of the family all around. The end was peaceful and in some ways an anticlimax to the drama that had been playing out for the previous three weeks. It was also a blessing and a good conclusion for Sheldon himself, because we'd been told that if he had recovered, the damage to his brain would have been extensive. I knew this, of course. I knew that he would be safe, and I knew that he was in a far, far better place, that he was truly healed and in the light. But still, I was left feeling bereft, as if I'd been abandoned by my friend. "What," I asked, of nobody in particular, as I drove home, "what am I going to do now?"

Christmas was less than two weeks away, and my heart was simply not in it at all. I had looked for Sheldon and had not seen him anywhere at all. I'd thought that maybe at the funeral he would come through to let me know he was OK, but no, I didn't see him there either. I was determined not to pester him. I was determined not to ask him my thousand and one questions, at least not until he was ready to talk to me. But it was so hard for me to let him go. I had to use all my self-discipline, all my lessons, not to call on him for my own selfish reasons. I knew, I hoped, that I would hear from him soon.

It was the morning after the funeral that I heard him first, just as I was waking up from a deep, exhausted sleep. His voice, faint at first, became stronger.

"Mary, Mary," I heard him say. "Rosemary, you have to get Mary the gift."

It took me a few minutes to realize what was happening, and in that time Sheldon must have repeated those words at least half a dozen times.

"Tell me again, Sheldon, tell me again," I said, finally fully awake and able to pay attention, searching the room for any visible sign of him.

There was no visible sign, but it didn't matter because his voice was now perfectly clear, and there was no mistaking what he said.

"A puppy! A puppy! A Niño puppy! Get one for Mary for Christmas," he said. "You have to get Mary a Niño for Christmas!"

I sighed, took a deep breath, and promised that I would, and with that, my friend was gone.

Twelve days. I had twelve days to come up with a Niño. "Well," I reasoned, "if he asked me to do it, then that means it can be done. Somewhere out there is a puppy for Mary, so I'd better start looking right now."

I called all the kennels I knew, and then all the ones within a fifty-mile radius. No one had a puppy, not a chocolate Lab anyway, so I got my group to help, who also called the kennels they knew. But we could

find nothing. Days passed. Among us we made more than three hundred phone calls, but still we could find nothing—only black Labs or
goldens. Now, with less than a week to go until Christmas, I was getting desperate.

Then one morning my now-much-depleted list of phone numbers
for kennels in my hand and only five more places to try, I began to
make the calls. "No, no, no, no," and "I'm awfully sorry, but no!"

But there must be, I thought, desperately muttering my displeasure
at Sheldon's lack of help, and feeling now, as I listened to the kind
woman, my very last hope, as she suggested I might want to take a look
at the golden Lab she had for sale, that perhaps this was what I
should do.

Yet I had heard him so clearly and I was confused. "Get a Niño for
Mary," he had said, and I knew what that meant. And this was the time
to trust.

"It's really kind of you, but I must have a chocolate," I replied, saying with a sigh, "I'll just have to keep looking until I find one."

"Well, I'm sorry I can't help further—but wait a minute, there might
just be one chance. There's a woman who lives quite close by whose
chocolate Lab recently had a litter of four, but she could've sold them
by now, as they're more than eight weeks old. Let me give you her
name and phone number. It can't hurt to call her." As she spoke, I felt
my heart skip a beat and wondered, *Could this be it?*

It was now ten in the morning, and I just had time to make the call
before I headed out to the hospital to see a patient, but all I got was the
answer machine, so I left a message and my name and number.

Throughout the day I made several more calls to the woman; still, I
got the machine and left more messages. If there was a chocolate
Labrador puppy out there, it was going to be mine.

I spent the day at the hospital, and when I arrived home at nine that
night, the phone was ringing as I came through the door.

"I'm so sorry I wasn't in to take your calls," said my caller, "but I've
been at the hospital all day with my husband."

"Perhaps I should call back tomorrow," I suggested, apologizing for the number of messages I'd left.

"Oh, no, it's OK," she said, laughing. "Yes, I do have two puppies left, both female and both beautiful of course. The only difference between them is that one has a more pointed nose than the other."

"I'll take one," I said quickly, hardly daring to believe I had finally found Sheldon's Niño. I surprised myself, because usually I would want to see the puppy before making such a decision.

"How far away are you?" We compared notes and realized that her home was a five-hour drive away, and tomorrow's weather forecast was for major snowstorms, which posed a real problem for me.

She explained that she too, liked to meet with prospective buyers. "I don't like my puppies to go to just anyone," she said. And of course I understood perfectly.

"It's for a friend who lost her husband two weeks ago," I explained, hoping that I wouldn't sound too bizarre, and at that moment I heard someone in the background calling out. The young woman excused herself for a moment, coming back to apologize, explaining that her husband had needed his pain medication.

"I'm so sorry. Is he all right?" I asked.

"It's just that he had surgery today, only minor, his nasal passages, but it's very painful for him."

"Nasal surgery?" I could feel the heat prickle the back of my neck as she described her husband's condition. He'd had polyps and had had surgery that day to remove them, she told me, and then she went on to explain in more detail what her husband's problem had been. When she finished, I knew absolutely and without question that Sheldon had led me here, that it was no coincidence that I'd found a puppy whose owner had just gone through the identical surgery that he'd had.

I looked to Grey Eagle, who simply smiled, and at that very moment, I felt Sheldon's presence in the room. I recounted his experience to the stranger on the other end of the telephone, and she gasped at the amazing "coincidence" of it all. But I knew better, and anyway, I don't believe in coincidence.

My friend Gary drove through the snowstorm the next day, as he lived closer than I, and even so, it took him almost nine hours to pick up the puppy and bring her to me. I kept her at home for the next three days until Christmas Eve, when I took her to Mary, with a big yellow bow around her neck and a card from Sheldon; after all, it was his gift to her, not mine.

When we ask for a miracle, sometimes it's the instant miracle, the rise-up-and-walk kind of miracle. But more often miracles take time, and we don't always see them because they happen in the most subtle ways. I knew that this new puppy, this miracle, was the beginning of Mary's healing, that Sheldon had found a way for Mary to survive the pain of his passing, and as I watched Mary gather the puppy up in her arms, I smiled, knowing that everything would be OK.

Not quite a Niño, I thought, as I smiled at them both, more a Niña, a little girl puppy, and her name is Angel, a gift from above.

There's a Serial Killer on the Loose

Part I

Every story you have read so far shows us that God is ever-present, that our angels are close by, and that we are protected by the love and grace of the Almighty, which we are. But this book would not be complete without the telling of another force, a force of darkness and evil, which, whether we like it or not, does exist and can creep into our lives and change us forever. This, then, is the one story that shows us the dark side of our universe, and which, as you will see, illustrates quite clearly the battle of good and evil, a battle which has been fought since time began.

There's a serial killer on the loose. A serial killer connected to at least twenty-three murders, and with the next intended victim already chosen. Seemingly very ordinary, apparently happily married, and living a simple and somewhat ordinary life in Florida, but a person of secrets, terrible and dark secrets, which were soon to emerge.

Our story begins with Carl and Teresa Brandt. Carl was a technical engineer, living in the Florida Keys, whose house was damaged by the hurricanes in 2004, as were so many others. Whole towns, whole communities, were almost wiped out. People lost their homes, their belongings, and some people lost their lives.

"Why don't you both come and stay with me for a few months until your house is fixed?" Michelle suggested to her aunt Teresa. "I'm on my own, and there's plenty of space. It wouldn't be an inconvenience at all; in fact, having you around would be fun."

Michelle was an outgoing girl, and very friendly, with a great personality. In her mid-thirties, she had a wonderful relationship with her mom and also with her closest friend, Debbie. Debbie and Michelle went almost everywhere and did almost everything together, told each other their utmost secrets, and were more like sisters than friends, so naturally, the first weekend Uncle Carl and Aunt Teresa arrived, Michelle planned a welcome dinner and invited Debbie to come along.

Friday evening was great, the food was good, maybe a little too much wine, but no one was going anywhere. The four sat around the table until late, telling stories, laughing, joking, and making plans for the next couple of days. Debbie had agreed to stay the whole weekend, and they were just going to have fun.

On Saturday morning Debbie woke early and, for reasons she still doesn't understand, decided to head home. Quietly, so as not to wake the household, she slipped out, leaving a note for Michelle that she needed to get back to her husband and kids.

Later that day, Debbie called Michelle, and so, apparently, did Michelle's mom. They got the answer machine but thought nothing of it. They would be out and about.

On Sunday they called again, and again they got the machine. Debbie presumed that her friend had taken her visitors out to show them around, but Michelle's mom began to worry. She and her daughter always spoke on Sundays, no matter what. Where could she possibly be that she couldn't call, at least to say hi? It was their ritual, their unspoken rule, a mother-daughter thing. Something was wrong; something was very wrong. Michelle's mother began to be afraid.

Debbie lived just fifteen minutes away from Michelle, and when

Michelle's mom called and asked her to go over to the house to check things out, it seemed a reasonable request. Debbie had no problem. She had a key to Michelle's house, and she was sure that Michelle's mom was worrying for no reason. It was only when she pulled up outside the house that Debbie started to get strange vibes. Trying to shrug them off, telling herself she was being ridiculous, Debbie walked to the door and rang the bell. No answer. Strange, the cars were parked in the driveway, someone must be home. Maybe they were out in the garden. But a really creepy sensation overtook Debbie as she put the key in the lock and tried to open the door. The key stuck, wouldn't turn— and was it her imagination or was it just a little too quiet in the house?

Turning, she ran up the driveway and crossed the street to a neighbor's house. The neighbor must have thought how odd it was that this young woman, obviously on the verge of tears, was asking him to go with her, to try the key. She was babbling that she thought something seemed wrong.

Together they went back to the house, and he tried the key, which didn't work for him either. Trying to calm Debbie and knowing that there must be a good explanation, he suggested they go around to the back of the house. He was sure they'd be there. It was as they passed the side of the garage and he looked in through the window that the neighbor pushed Debbie, knocking her to the ground, not wanting her to see what he had seen. But it was too late—they had both seen it.

Uncle Carl, his neck in a noose, hanging from the rafters . . . and very, very dead.

Part II

atching was no fun at all, but I was used to it. I had learned over the years to remain detached when I went down and through the hole and entered that space between time where I can view, or be part of, an act that has already taken place and that has nothing to do with me. That's what was happening now as I stood in the corner of Michelle's bedroom, an impartial observer, listening to her crying, soft mewing sounds. She lay on the bed, unable to move, barely breathing but conscious and aware of what was happening.

She had been rendered helpless. The cut in her belly was long and deep, deep enough to draw blood, deep enough to stifle any resistance, a cut made by a professional, someone who had done this many times before.

Michelle's hands lay limply on her stomach, any attempt to escape made useless by her inability to move. Blood was slowly spilling onto the sheets as she tried feebly and unsuccessfully to stop the bleeding. But her strength had been drained, and all she could do was lie there and listen to the screaming and fighting coming from another part of the house. Strangely, the pain was gone, at least for the time being, but the fear, that terrifying and all-consuming fear remained. She knew the worst was yet to come.

They were arguing, she could tell, but she was too faint to understand the words. Perhaps she wouldn't die, after all. But as soon as that thought came into her head, the screaming became worse, petrifying, unbearable, the voices rising to another and even more intense level. Another scream and then another and another, and then silence, a most deafening and terrible silence.

Michelle waited, a small ray of hope beginning to creep through the fear. Dare she hope? Was it possible maybe that they were both dead? But then footsteps, slow and purposeful, loud on the hard floor, coming closer and closer. Her fear was increasing, her head began to pound. The monster was coming back, coming to finish what he had already begun. The chilling realization hit her. She knew that she was going to die. She was going to die a horrible, horrible death.

I stood in the corner of the bedroom, waiting, those heart-stopping and terrifyingly slow footsteps loud in my head. I too knew that this beautiful young woman was going to die.

Part III

Our Father God,
  Who art in heaven,
All hallowed be Thy name,
Thy kingdom come,
Thy will be done . . . the words and music going around and around
in my head, spilling out of my mouth, my heart pounding so loudly in
my chest that it hurt to breathe.

What was I doing here?

No, no, that wasn't the question at all. I knew what I was doing here.
I had come willingly. But the danger was all around, all-consuming.
The monster was hiding, playing the waiting game. I could hear its
voice in my ear. "I'm going to get her and then . . ." Those words would
be followed by a mean and evil chuckle, a sound that left no doubt in
my mind that we were in the presence of a devil. "And then, oh yes,
and then I'm coming for you!" it continued.

When I had first walked into the apartment, there had been nothing to indicate an evil presence of any kind, although Debbie had no
doubt of it. Gina, my friend Gerry's daughter, and a friend of Deb-

bie's, the one responsible for bringing us together, sat with Debbie on one sofa, and Gerry and I sat on the other, the four of us holding hands, none of us knowing what to expect.

That morning, in the bathroom, as I was putting on my makeup, I had pretty well convinced myself that this was not really going to be my area of expertise. From what Gina had already told me about the situation, the chances were that Debbie had been so traumatized by her friend's death and the manner of that death, that she was having terrifying nightmares, hallucinations and visions, caused by that trauma. She was convinced that the monster was in the house, had come to get her.

Both she and her husband, a total nonbeliever of anything remotely connected to the paranormal, had heard the footsteps on the stairs on many occasions. Both had seen the shadowy figure as it glided through the house, and both were petrified, thinking that it was coming for them. I was not so sure. Naturally skeptical, but trying to keep an open mind, I was leaning toward the assumption that a psychiatrist or psychotherapist was more what Debbie needed. That was until I heard Grey Eagle's voice. "Pay attention, pay attention, things are not as they might appear to be. Don't be complacent, Rosemary, be careful. Don't be complacent."

That Saturday morning when I went to meet Debbie, I was still unsure as to how much of this was her imagination and how much was real. Debbie was distraught, shaking uncontrollably, crying incessantly as she told the story. Very aware of how the mind can play tricks, I was not yet ready to be convinced. Grey Eagle had said not to be complacent, so the only thing to do was keep an open mind and investigate for myself.

I had walked into the apartment cautiously, used to ghost hunting, used to coming up empty-handed, but I was never complacent. You just never know what's around the corner.

Walking to the stairs, I stood quietly and listened, all my senses alert. . . . . Nothing!

I went into the hallway through to the kitchen . . . still listening, paying close attention, but still I sensed nothing.

The apartment was new—no dusty corners, no darkness or dampness. Everything in the place was clean. The surfaces were bright and shiny, the walls freshly painted. All the rooms were light and airy, with half-open blinds at the windows, the sun streaming through. Not at all a place where you might imagine a ghost to reside. Debbie and her husband had had it built as guest quarters and had been living there while the main house was being built, but they had moved into the main house before completion because they had become convinced that some evil thing, the monster, was haunting them there.

As I continued my search, Debbie, Gerry, and Gina stood by the door watching, hardly daring to breathe, afraid of what I would find. I had spoken to Gerry beforehand and had explained the procedure, and what would happen if Debbie and her husband were right, if there was some kind of evil in the house.

"You'll know something's wrong if I start to take off my jewelry," I had said in the car, when we had parked in front of the house. I explained further that if by any remote chance I should go into a trance state, then the buildup of energy in my body could be strong enough, coming into contact with metal, that it could burn my skin.

Trance mediumship is rare these days, and there is little reason for its use. In the first few years of my training with Grey Eagle, if I had to do any rescue work for someone in the spirit world who might be stuck for any reason, or if someone needed to use my body and my vocal cords to connect with the Earth world, to express themselves in a more powerful way, then I would move out or, more precisely, my spirit would vacate its host, allowing the spirit world to use my body. A strange concept, I know, but one that has been used successfully for centuries, especially in the United Kingdom, where trance mediums were very common during and after the First and Second World Wars.

So, not knowing, and absolutely not complacent, I thought it would be best to warn my friend of all possibilities.

Did this scare her? Yes, it did. But Gerry and I have known each other for many years, and she and her family have had many consultations during that time. She trusts me emphatically, she trusts Grey Eagle, and she trusts God.

"If anything happens, just pray," I told her, "and keep on praying for light and for our angels to be present. That way you'll help keep us safe."

So here I was, having checked the stairs, the kitchen, the hallway, and I had not seen or felt anything that might be of concern. So far, nothing!

"Don't be complacent. Don't be complacent," I kept on reminding myself as I headed across the living room toward the bedrooms. Then, suddenly, as I passed the sofa . . . WHAM, right in the stomach, then again . . . WHAM, as if someone had thrown a heavy football, hard and fast, right at me.

Somehow I kept moving, going past the sofa and into the bedroom, where the energy was now back to normal, except, that is, for the sound behind me, a low rumbling, almost echoing sound.

Out of sight of the others, I stopped, took a huge breath, then another. Debbie was right . . . something evil was lurking in this place, something hidden, something waiting, something terrible . . . waiting for me!

I came back into the living room and slowly began to take off my jewelry.

Part IV

When the four of us were seated on the sofa, I told them my findings. Yes, there was indeed, most definitely, a presence in the room which was decidedly unfriendly, but as yet it was impossible to tell who or what it was. Above all, we must not jump to conclusions but wait and see what happens. I also explained to them the danger they would be placing me in if they decided to bolt. "Once we begin this," I said, "you must not leave until it's over. If I do go into a trance state, it is very important that we stay together, no matter what, so that I can rely on and use your energy if I need to. If there is a Dark Soul here with us, we can show no sign of weakness, no break in our collective power. We must at all costs stick together. So if you feel you cannot do this, say so now; don't back out later."

As everyone nodded agreement, I saw that we were not just four in the room. Michelle had come to stand beside her friend Debbie, and one other had come to stand beside me. Grey Eagle was present, standing to my right side, as always, and I was comforted, knowing that no matter what happened, he would protect and keep us safe.

We were ready, at least as ready as we were going to be. I was not surprised to see Michelle. In fact, I would have been surprised had she not been there, as I had presumed that she would want to connect with Debbie and her mom. I lifted my head, took one last look around the room, and I smiled as I saw them, the small crowd, clustered together at the far side of the room. Thank goodness our angels were present. But one thing puzzled me. They were turned away, their backs to us. I realized that whatever was to take place here, our angels were not to interfere. Whatever it was that needed to be done would be a matter of free will. We four—Gerry, Gina, Debbie, and I—would decide the outcome, we four, plus Michelle and, yes, that evil entity.

Could this be true? I looked to Grey Eagle for the answer.

"When we die, we have choices, we can choose to go to the light, we can choose to go to a place of darkness, or we can choose to go nowhere, to stay in a no-man's-land, holding on to old issues, old hurts and anger, to hold on to those worldly experiences, those worldly issues that we have not resolved. Michelle," Grey Eagle continued, "is holding on to the past, she is hurt and confused, and she is in fear. Help her, Rosemary. Show her the choices she has."

I smiled at Michelle, but there was no returning smile. Instead, her eyes, like hard flints of stone, stared back at me. Her mouth set in a thin tight line showed both anger and fear. I knew in an instant that this young woman was in trouble and needed me. This was why I was here. I had seen it before, and I knew that I would need my wits about me, my strength, and my faith. But there was something else I needed too, for even as I looked at Michelle, I was trying to find the source of the energy, which had now become palpable, a disgusting taste in my mouth, and which was pervading the room, a foul odor, like decaying rotted meat. I needed to find the enemy, to seek it out, to come face to face with the monster I was to do battle with. And there was no doubt that it would be a battle, for even now I could feel the pressure in my head, a force trying to push its way into my mind, into my brain, as we four women held hands and began to recite the Lord's Prayer . . . Our Father God.

Part V

Our Father God,
    Who art in heaven,
All hallowed be thy name.
Thy kingdom come,
Thy will be done . . . the words and music going around and around in my head, spilling out of my mouth, my heart pounding so loudly in my chest that it hurt to breathe.

The monster was hiding, and although I could feel its presence, I couldn't find it, couldn't see it. Somewhere behind me I knew that a dark shadow lurked, the same dark shadow that Debbie and her husband had seen moving through the house. The same dark shadow whose footsteps they had heard so many times on the stairs. They had known who it was then. They had known that it was Michelle's killer, and Debbie had known that she was next.

It was playing the game—pushing its way in, pushing *his* way in, trying to find my weak spot; for he knew that at this moment I was the most dangerous one in the room as far as he was concerned. Somehow he needed to render me helpless, to defuse my energy and destroy my power. Using scare tactics to instill fear into me was part of the plan. Fear was something that he could use, had used so many times. It was an energy that he could feed off to get the upper hand. It had always worked before, and he was in no doubt that it would work again. He was right. We were afraid. I was afraid. Anyone in his or her right mind would be afraid.

I had met evil before, had fought it, and knew the power of it. I had been devastated by the knowledge that such a thing as a Dark Soul, born from an evil force, could and did exist. Knowing this, I would be plainly stupid if I was not scared stiff. And I was! I also knew that this was the monster's ace card, the only card he had to play. Fear, anger, resentment—any and all types of negative energy—fed him, made him strong, and gave him his power. I began to understand how he had been able to wield that power and to ensure that Debbie would become powerless against him.

Michelle was full of anger, resentment, and fear. Debbie, too, was also full of anger that she had lost her best friend. Through his visitations, the monster had created in her a great and terrible fear, which had fed his lust and allowed him the power to destroy. He had fed on Michelle's anger, used what had been done to her to gain power over Debbie. And it had worked.

Now here he was, and the pounding in my chest hurt so badly that I could hardly breathe.

He was good, very good. My brain seemed to be on fire. The pressure in my head so strong, and I felt as if it were going to explode. Trying as hard as I could, I fought to get him out. At the same time, I felt myself slipping and becoming weaker. I felt his energy bouncing around in my head. I knew he was trying to take me over, to control my mind, and I knew that I must not let him do it. I must stay in control no matter what happened, and I must overcome my fear. I must not under any circumstances feed the monster . . . and as we fought, he and I, I heard his voice—mean, cruel, a harsh and eerie whisper in my ear . . . "I'm going to get her, and then I'm going to get you!"

Here was the serial killer, definitely on the loose, refusing to allow a little thing like dying to curtail his activities. He had had a plan to, first, take sweet, wonderful Michelle, full of life, full of fun, ready to play . . . and they had played.

This was not the first time he had struck. He had lost count of the number; they all seemed to merge together in his head. They were all like his mother, except that his mother had been pregnant. But what of Debbie and Michelle? His plan had been to take them both together. After all, they always did everything else together. But then Debbie had left, ruining his plan, ruining his fantasy. Now, that wouldn't do. She was his and he would have her. He would not be thwarted again. Yes, first he would have Debbie, and then he would show this interfering bitch who thought she could stop him. No one was going to stop him, least of all some woman who thought she had more power than he. His mother had thought the same thing, and look what he had done to her.

He had been thirteen when he'd shot and killed his mother and her unborn baby. He had tried to kill his stepfather and sister as well, but that plan had failed too. Sent to a psychiatric hospital, he was treated and let go after a year for good behavior. For the next few years, as an outpatient, he had fooled them all, had even got married, and had played the loving husband to cover his tracks. Until now, all his many plans had worked out perfectly well, in fact, very, very well.

None of those women would ever have babies; he had made sure of that. Michelle would never have babies. And Debbie, what about Debbie? He would make sure that she would never have another baby. Nothing was going to stop him, nothing.

We were his next intended victims, first Debbie, and then me!

"Stay in control, stay in control. . . . Our Father God, Who art in heaven, help me now. Help me stay in control, help me fight the demon."

Part VI

Not all killers are evil, not all killers are Dark Souls, but Carl Brandt most definitely was. Some would call him insane but not me. I knew his soul was infused with and created from a dark force and that his actions were calculated to cause harm whenever and wherever he could. This had been his life, and for more than thirty years he had gotten away with it. He was not about to stop now!

The four of us—Gerry, Gina, Debbie, and I—sat in a small circle, holding hands tightly, praying hard, as the monster crawled around inside my head, trying to force me to submit to his power.

I managed to push him out, but he forced his way back. I pushed again, but he pushed right back in, his laugh, a deep chuckle in my throat, his voice now loud inside my head, telling me that he was here to stay, that there was nothing I could do about it.

The sound of his voice, oozing out of my mouth, was smug and full of slime, as each word he spoke dripped darkly from my tongue. All the while he worked to force his will onto me.

Now the real work began. I knew that the warrior in me must fight;

the knight must slay the dragon. But I was no knight; I was just one little person on a huge, huge battlefield.

"Be like David, fighting Goliath, dare to stand up to the giant. Find the monster's weak spot, his Achilles' heel, and do not feed him with your fear."

This was another voice, quiet but firm and full of love. This was the voice of Grey Eagle as he whispered softly in my ear, and this was the voice that for one brief moment drowned out the monster, the voice that reminded me that I had a job to do, and that I was giving far too much credit and power to my enemy.

I lifted my head and looked to where Michelle stood. She had something to say, something to tell us, and as afraid as she was of him, I knew she was determined to do it. I also realized that in order for her to tell us her story, I had to make myself vulnerable, open . . . which meant that I would be open to Carl too.

"So," I asked myself, "where was the monster's Achilles' heel? What was the killer's weakness? How should I fight the enemy?"

My father, a professional soldier, had taught me two very important things a good warrior needs to remember, two things that any good general takes into account before stepping on to the battlefield.

First, confuse your enemy.

Second, keep your enemies closest to you.

So be it. I knew this was the only way. I would stop fighting and let things happen, at least for a while. I would give up control and trust in the process. I knew that this would confuse Carl Brandt. He would see me as weakening, my strength ebbing, my determination faltering. After all, this was what he was used to. His intimidation tactics had never failed. And here was his Achilles' heel: He believed too much in his own invincibility, he was certain he could win, and he underestimated his enemy.

Many generals have lost many battles over the years, making the very same mistake. Who would win this battle, this battle of good over evil?

As long as we were not complacent, as long as I did not make the same mistake, I knew we had a chance.

Michelle read my thoughts and was ready to do battle with me. He was inside me now, certain of his victory. I gave one more tremendous push, finally moving the monster out, just long enough for Michelle to move right in to the place he had occupied.

My trance state now complete, I allowed Michelle to take me down and through the hole, moving fast, down and down, through time and space, and back into her bedroom. I was her witness, a silent witness so far, to the horrors of that terrible day when she was so brutally murdered.

Slowly, slowly, there came the sound of footsteps returning, coming closer and closer, until the monster appeared in the doorway, a bucket swinging loosely from his hand.

Michelle was too weak to lift her head, but she knew he was there, and she heard her own screams reverberating inside her head.

Now, using my voice box, she began to tell us the things he did, recounting the horror. Tears were raining down her face—my face. Her voice—my voice box—filled with terror as she relived the experience.

He had cut her deeply and had taken her organs—heart, lungs, liver, kidneys, and intestines—placing them carefully in the bucket one at a time. At some point Michelle had passed. But still in her spirit form, her etheric body remained present, unable or unwilling to let go, watching with me in the bedroom as he violated her body in the worst way, mutilating her, defiling her, until there was nothing remaining but her torso, which he then dressed in Victoria's Secret underwear. This was how the police found Michelle on that fateful day, after Debbie and the neighbor had found Carl hanging in the garage and called 911.

But our monster had finally made a mistake. His lust and his greed had been so overwhelming that for the first time in more than thirty years, he had allowed himself to get out of control. And so he had been caught . . . by his wife, Teresa.

She had discovered him in Michelle's room, where she had tried to stop him. He dragged her into another part of the house, and a great argument had ensued, she, screaming that he was a madman, he, at first, trying to reason with her and figure a way out of his predicament. Finally, in anger and frustration, stabbing her several times, he returned to Michelle, to finish what he had begun.

The only reason he had hung himself was because he knew the game was over. His murderous and vile lifestyle could be no longer.

Now Michelle began to recount more, using my voice box. She was crying and angry, still afraid, but determined to tell it all. On and on she went, going into the most intimate and horrific detail, as is usual under these circumstances, and I watched and saw it all, as if it were happening right at that very moment. Now, unable to remain undetached, as sometimes happens, my own tears became mingled with Michelle's, and no one would tell the difference, as I watched and listened as her words came tumbling out of my mouth.

It was unexpected, although it shouldn't have been. All of a sudden he came upon me with such force that for a second Michelle was knocked away, long enough for the monster to reappear, and to take her place inside me. But now I found my strength forcing him back, and then a strange thing happened. Not only did I become a host for him . . . I became a host for her too. Michelle had forced her way back in. Now they were both inside, fighting, struggling, both voices speaking at once, the sounds, their words, coming from my mouth like a slowed-down broken record. "Michelle, Michelle"—my voice broke in—"turn to your angels. Forget him. Don't fight him. It's time to move on. Turn to your angels; turn to your angels. They are waiting for you now."

Fury, pure and fiendish, pounded against my brain, as they fought. Michelle was determined to fight as she had been unable to before, refusing to be his victim any longer. Carl Brandt was also determined to remain in control, and so a battle of wills had commenced, their anger spilling over and into me, as they clashed.

Michelle was determined to fight back, to somehow undo what had been done to her. In her anger she refused to listen to me, ignoring everything I tried to say. But she was no match for him. As she weakened, he began to overpower her once more. As the battle raged on, it was fearsome and terrifying. Loud footsteps sounded on the stairs, as if someone was running up and down them. The shutters at the windows swung out and away from the walls, banging furiously. The cabinet door flew open, a thick gray haze filled the room, making it dark. The air became freezing cold, and loud banging noises started up behind the sofa.

It sounded and felt as if an army had come in and was trashing the place. My friends were terrified. With every bang or slam, Gina and Debbie leaped out of their skin, shivering with fear and cold, holding on to each other more tightly. Gerry sat very still on the sofa, next to me, our hands gripped together tightly, her head bowed, deep in prayer. But I was ignoring all this. I was on the battlefield . . . and it was time for me to fight!

Part VII

The storm raged on, the sounds of banging and crashing increasing by the minute. I had to get Michelle out. I had to get her to stop fighting and to understand that if she let it go, she would not be in danger anymore. I had to make her understand that by holding on, she was giving him power over her.

"Look to the light, Michelle. Please, look to the light."

Now my voice was joining with both of theirs and sounding like something out of a bad horror movie, almost like talking heads. There were three voices, connecting and disconnecting, each of them wanting their say. "Get out. Get out," I screamed at the monster. "I am not afraid of you. I have no fear of you or your threats. Get out. Get out and stay out."

My outburst was startling, and I felt the monster shift inside me, surprised by my sudden and obvious strength and lack of fear. I felt his uncertainty, his confusion, at this unexpected turn of events. I had found the monster's Achilles' heel and, giving him no time to recover, quickly took the advantage.

"Get out," I yelled again, this time with more authority, sensing the change. Now I was more certain that I did indeed have the upper hand. "Get out and stay out. Stay away. We don't want you here. You mean nothing to us." As I said this, I felt light streaming into me, forcing out the monster, bathing me, washing me clean. Michelle felt it to and began to cry, feeling the love and warmth of that God force as it washed over her.

"Michelle, Michelle," I whispered softly, "these are your choices. You can hold on to the monster and continue to be a victim, continue to give him power over you. And if you do that, you will stay in that terrible dark place. Or you can look up. You can look to the light. Look to the light, Michelle. Look to your angels and let them help you, let them take care of you, let them take you to the light."

As I spoke, my voice was gentle but firm. The sounds in the room began to lessen and the monster's power was beginning to wane. As I looked on, I felt Michelle slowly letting go.

I turned my attention to Carl Brandt, who I could now clearly see was standing beside me. There was no place for him to hide. The room was now bathed in light.

"You have no power, no power over us," I quietly said, "for we are of God, and your evil is useless here." Then, for the last time, I said emphatically, "NOW GET OUT."

We all felt him go, his energy becoming as nothing. It was as if he had never been there . . . but of course, we all knew that he had.

Michelle was smiling now as I looked at her. She, in turn, was looking to her angels, who were now facing her, their arms outstretched, waiting for her to come to them. Michelle had made her choice, and she had chosen well.

"Can I have just a few more minutes?" she asked her angels. Then looking to her friend, Debbie, Michelle sighed and, smiling wide, said, "Could you please tell my mom that I'm OK now? Can you tell her I'm with my angels? And Debbie, I will always be with you too."

"Lift up your head, Michelle," I softly said, knowing that it was time for her to go. "Lift up your head. Look up, look up, and reach out your arms. You are safe now, Michelle. You are safe."

It was over. It was finally over, and my body slumped down into the sofa, exhaustion from the battle overtaking me. Tears flooded my eyes. I had seen the devil, I had fought the evil, and with the help of Grey Eagle, with the help of my angels, and with help from God, we had won. But it was not a victory that I would celebrate, this I knew, for how can you celebrate the existence of evil, no matter what the triumph?

Arms came around me, the arms of my friend, Gerry, and slowly I came back to life. I wiped away my tears, blew my nose, grateful for the light that was still all around us.

At last I looked up, my job done, or so I thought. It was then that I saw her—Debbie's mom, standing next to her daughter. For the next thirty or so minutes I gave messages of love and comfort from a mother to a daughter, a daughter who had been through a terrible kind of hell. Finally, the nightmare was over.

Later, several months later in fact, I asked Gina bow she felt about the whole experience. These are her words.

"I remember feeling very safe," she writes, "because of Rosemary and Grey Eagle, but at the same time knowing that there was a battle going on in that room—a battle between good and evil. The room was ice-cold, and a haze covered it. I heard footsteps going up and down the stairs, but there was no one there. That experience made a profound impact on me. It is one of those experiences where you can remember every detail like it happened yesterday."

Part VIII

I was home in Vermont, having left Florida several weeks before. My daughter had been extremely sick, and so for the last few weeks I had been living my own kind of nightmare, having almost lost Samantha after what should have been a simple surgery. Her recovery had been slow, and although I did not know it at the time, there were more health problems to come.

Carl Brandt, although not forgotten, was the last thing on my mind. The situation had been dealt with, and now, for me, his was just another story to be told. My focus had been, and would continue for some time, to be on my child. But for now, for these next couple of weeks, I could take a break, relax, and enjoy the mountain air.

It was perhaps two or three in the morning when something woke me. The room was dark, as I opened my eyes, and I immediately knew that I was not alone. . . . Carl Brandt was standing next to my bed, looking down at me, evil filling the space around him . . . and I began to pray.

Our Father God,
Who art in heaven,
All hallowed be thy name,
Thy kingdom come,
Thy will be done . . . the words and music going around, and around, and around, in my head. . . .*

*To learn more about Charles (Carl) Brandt, consult the FBI criminal libraries.

I'll Name Her Angela

The idea that Dark Souls exist at all is frightening, but as scary as the last story is, it shows us that our angels are all around us, always there for us in our times of need. I believe that our angels will always save us from any and all evil and will even save us from ourselves when necessary. The presence and power of those angels is remarkable, as we've seen, and their appearance in our lives will often come in the most unexpected ways. Here now is a story that brings light, hope, wonder and awe, even to the most skeptical of us. As perhaps no other story can, it shows us quite clearly that God really does work in the most mysterious and remarkable ways.

I first met Michael, Dr. Michael J. Brescia, that is, at Calvary Hospital in the Bronx, New York. A good friend of mine, Tamar Wallace, had told him about me. He had seen me on *Larry King Live* and had expressed a desire to meet me. At the time of our first meeting, he remarked that I was lovelier in person than I appeared on TV. As you can see, our relationship was off to a good start.

Tamar had told me quite a bit about Michael before we met, about his extraordinary compassion and dedication to his patients. She had

said she'd never met anyone like him. Michael is the co-founder and
executive medical director at Calvary Hospital, where patients who are
considered to be dying are taken in and cared for physically, emotionally, and spiritually. I had been intrigued by Michael's story and
by Tamar's obvious respect for him, but I was even more intrigued by
the stories he had to tell. It isn't often that you come across so emi-
nent a man as he, a renowned and extraordinarily respected physician,
with a reputation above and beyond incredible, whose life's work is
documented and who is looked upon with awe by so many, and who is
so open to talking about his remarkable experiences with those who are
on the very verge of life and death.

As I sat with Dr. Brescia, listening to his accounts of the miracles he
personally had witnessed, I forgot that he was the executive medical director of his hospital. All I wanted was to hear more, and the more I
heard, the more in awe of him I became—of Michael J. Brescia the man.

Michael J. Brescia, M.D.: Renowned throughout the world for co-
inventing the Brescia-Cimino fistula, a device that has saved the lives
of tens of thousands of people with chronic kidney disease each year
by allowing them to undergo long-term dialysis. Just a young man at
the time of his invention, Dr. Brescia released the device for use without a patent, thus making it available quickly to those who needed it for
survival. The result was thousands of additional lives saved—and tens
of millions of dollars lost by Dr. Brescia and his co-inventor, Dr.
James E. Cimino. Shortly thereafter, Dr. Brescia stunned his friends
and colleagues by leaving the world of nephrology and medical science
to care for those who are sick and dying.

When I met with Dr. Brescia at Calvary Hospital, he told me countless miraculous tales of life and death. One that touched me pro-
foundly was that of Angela . . . and this is her story.

Dr. Brescia was in Washington, D.C., advocating for legislation to
protect and care for people who were dying, when he received a call
from Calvary. He was told about a young woman who had been found
along New York's West Side Highway in shocking condition and with

no apparent resources or identification. Wearing very little clothing, she had a widespread fungal infection of the skin and rotted infected teeth, and was completely unresponsive. She was also HIV positive.

The young woman was taken to Calvary Hospital, where under Dr. Brescia's leadership, no patient, no matter how sick, or how poor, is ever turned away. Learning from the phone call that she was dying and alone, the good doctor returned to New York immediately to care for her personally, and he named her Angela.

Despite their best efforts, Dr. Brescia and the staff at Calvary could not locate anyone who knew Angela, and so, while Dr. Brescia's team at Calvary tended to Angela's physical needs, he cared for her spirit.

Every day he sat at her bedside. "Who are you, Angela?" he would ask. "Did you wear pink ribbons when you were a little girl? Did you sit on your daddy's knee? Did someone care for you? Who are you, Angela? Tell me who you are," he would plead. Every day . . . every day, every day he would ask her to tell him who she was!

The weeks passed, and he had learned nothing more about her; she had said not one word to anyone. Then one gray winter morning Dr. Brescia noticed that Angela's condition seemed to be deteriorating. He sat with her all day long, talking to her, holding her hand, reassuring her again and again. "Everything's OK, Angela! We love you, Angela! Tell me who you are?" Asking all the usual questions, Dr. Brescia continued trying to get through to his patient, but Angela remained unresponsive.

Early that evening, with an ice storm approaching, Dr. Brescia went home to get some rest, but he couldn't sleep. His every instinct was telling him to go back to the hospital. He felt that Angela needed him. Finally, in the middle of the ice storm, Dr. Brescia headed back to her bedside.

When he arrived, her breathing was labored, and knowing it would not be long, he began his questions again. "Angela, we love you," he said. "Who are you, Angela? Did you wear pink ribbons in your hair when you were a little girl? Who are you?" he asked again. And this time there was a small movement. Miraculously Angela slowly opened her eyes. Speaking in a clear voice and calling him by name, she said, "Doctor Michael, in a few hours I will speak your name to God."

Dr. Brescia could not believe his ears. "What did you say, Angela, what did you say? Could you say that again?" And then, "Who are you, Angela? *Who are you?*" But there was no answer. Angela lay still and was unresponsive again.

Later that evening Angela died. Michael Brescia, exhausted and weary, went home. But haunted by what Angela had said to him, he returned to the hospital a couple of hours later to see her body. When he arrived, Angela had already been taken to the morgue, but Michael knew he just had to see her one last time. He arrived at the morgue, and asked to see his patient, and this is where things became more complex than ever. . . . For the body of Angela was nowhere to be found!

Her patient file indicated that Angela's body had been taken by the Marin Funeral Home. It was odd, Michael thought, that the funeral home would come so quickly and strange that they would come in the middle of an ice storm. And who had called them? It had already been established that there was no family to have called on Angela's behalf. Even more strange, was the fact that, upon investigation by Michael and his staff, there was no Marin Funeral Home to be found in the entire New York area!

What then had happened to Angela's body? Who was Angela, and where did she go? These are questions that many who know the story have asked.

Michael Brescia believes that Angela was a gift. He believes that Angela is an angel, an angel who was sent to teach him, to teach all of us, about dying . . . and about living.

AS I WRITE this story, I marvel at the courage it must have taken over the years for Michael Brescia to care for those who are dying, day in and day out, and to share his extraordinary and miraculous experiences with the rest of us. His decision to leave his work in nephrology was controversial at the time, some even called him crazy. But what of Dr. Brescia? What does he believe?

Dr. Brescia believes that he is blessed, and so, without a doubt, do I. But I also believe something more. I believe that God sometimes sends us an "earth angel," an angel in human form, who lives a human existence, performing small miracles, and who sometimes does spectacular and miraculous things. I believe that Dr Brescia could well be one of God's earth angels. His life is always about the matter of life and death. He is certainly an angel of mercy as far as his patients are concerned. And yes, he was surely an angel of mercy as he brought love and compassion and the spirit of God and of all things that are good into the life of the angel we know as Angela!*

*You can read more about Dr. Brescia and his life in the upcoming biography by Tamar Wallace.

Grey Eagle Speaks

So far, in the stories that have been told, we have had examples of pain, heartache, fear, despair, hope, strength, and courage. Basically, we have had examples of the many different trials that life brings to us, and we have seen how as human beings we are able to overcome those trials.

For some of us it is easier to fight, to be strong. For others it is more difficult. In many ways, it seems that the easier our lives were when we were children, the harder it is to overcome the problems we have to encounter later on.

I was lucky in that way, for in my upbringing and through all the adversities I had to face as a child, I was forced to grow, to become a fighter.

My father was a soldier and not just when he was in uniform. This way of life had been ingrained in him since he was thirteen years old, when he joined the army, lying about his age. From then on, he was taught only about the discipline, the way a soldier must think, and even the way a soldier must feel or not feel. He spent his whole life as a soldier, leaving the army only when he was forced to retire at the age of fifty-five.

When I was a young girl, seventeen years old, and heartsick for a boy, I would often moon about like a typical teenager. My father came to me one day as I was playing the piano, a tragic love song no doubt. He asked me to come out into the hallway. He had something he wanted to show me, he said. Nervous, believing I was in trouble for some reason, I went out to see what was wrong.

"Hold out your hand," he commanded, in his best sergeant major voice, and without thinking twice, I did.

"Here," he muttered gruffly. Looking down in surprise and confusion, I saw he had placed in my hand a round, smooth, medium-sized stone. "Make your heart like that stone," he said. "Make your heart as hard as that!"

As I looked down at the stone and absorbed my father's words, I knew that he was trying, in his soldier's way, to help me. I also instinctively knew that it was bad advice but that he was only trying to protect me, to make sure that I didn't get hurt.

A warrior in every sense, both on the battlefield and off, my spirit guide Grey Eagle is also a soldier. In his time on the earth plane, Grey Eagle was a Native American Indian, an Apache, a Shaman, a healer and teacher to his people, and one of the leaders of his tribe. Born into this culture, my guide learned many things during his human experience which enhanced his spiritual growth, brought enlightenment and meaning to his soul, and which helped make him a powerful, worthy, and highly evolved spiritual entity.

I still remember the first time I saw him clearly, one cold Wednesday evening in February—the eleventh, to be precise, in 1981. My daughter, Samantha, just ten years old, was tucked into bed, fast asleep. My development group was gathered in my living room for our regular Wednesday meeting, the purpose of which was to help me develop my psychic abilities.

I had glimpsed him on and off for several weeks and had realized that a strong presence was around me. At first I had wondered whether it was my father but quickly dismissed the idea, as it didn't feel right, and then I became very curious as to who this new entity might be, and what purpose he had (for I could tell that it was definitely a male energy) in wanting to be with me. Nervous and excited at the same time, I instinctively knew that his appearance at this time meant that my life would change in a big way, but I was yet to understand how big those changes would be, and what this would mean to me.

When I was in a trance state on February 11, 1981, Grey Eagle first made himself known to me and to my group. Using my body, my voice box, he entered my life, and nothing, I knew, would ever be the same again. Standing outside of my body, in a mild state of trance, I was able to see and hear everything, and I watched my physical shape changing form. Fascinated, I watched it move, slowly at first, then with more certainty, as if whoever or whatever was inside it was trying it on for size. Then, quickly and easily, *he* stood up. I was no longer looking at an image of me but of someone much taller, with wide shoulders set back and straight, his arms folded across his chest. His very presence in the room was electric, and an incredible power seemed to emanate from his very core. Standing straight and proud, a tall man, and broad, he had dark skin, shoulder-length black hair, and the most startling and beautiful eyes. His voice, when he spoke, held that same indescribable power, strong and vibrant yet with a softness and gentleness I had never heard before from anyone.

"My name," he said, addressing everyone in the room, "is Grey Eagle, and I am Apache.

"From now on you will know me as guide, teacher, and mentor to your medium.

"Together we will work in spiritual harmony, she and I. Your medium will learn many things, and her progress will be great.

"We will achieve much.

"My little flower is weak and exhausted from her many earthly trials. She needs water, food, and sustenance, which I, as her spirit guide and protector, will give. . . . Which I will always give."

It was the first time I heard my guide call me his little flower, and I had no idea whom he was referring to until later. Since that time Grey Eagle has kept his promise, and has been by my side in all things, even in those times when I have been deaf to his words, and when I have ignored him.

In the work that he chose to do, which is to mentor me, to steer and guide, to aid me in my spirit communications and the many other things we do together, he is always on the battlefield. There are always wars of one kind or another to be fought, always situations that require courage and bravery, strength and determination. Fighting for the rights of others, standing firm for those in the spirit world who need us to be strong and to pay attention to them, my guide inspires me to dare to be.

As a warrior, an Apache, and a highly evolved spiritual entity, Grey Eagle uses weapons that are not made of steel. They are not weapons of destruction meant to harm and to kill. Unlike most soldiers, he carries with him no guns, no cannons, no swords or knives to cut, to maim, no drugs or awful germicidal packages, no threatening devices.

Reading this, one might ask how it is possible for anyone to step onto any battlefield, to fight, to win any war, or to create any kind of peace. Surely that is the role of a true warrior and is the reason that any war is fought at all. And yet Grey Eagle's way, the way of the silent warrior, the gentle warrior, the compassionate warrior, is the only way to peace—the only way!

No true warrior wants to fight, although he will stand ready on the field and will fight when he must. As my spirit guide, Grey Eagle must always be prepared to fight. And he has always fought for what he believes is right. What then, I have asked him, are the weapons you take with you onto the battlefield?

He smiles, as he always does. His patience with me is a palpable thing. His knowing that these are the questions I have asked so many times before, and will ask so many times again, only seems to make him more patient still.

"The weapons of a true warrior are a quick mind; the ability to think on your feet; the art of being courageous; the need in you for gentleness; the 'knowing' that speaks to you from your soul; the instinct of your beating heart; the understanding that you cannot die; the acceptance of fear; the imagination to embrace your enemy as if he were your friend; the compassion you apply in all things."

1. A quick mind
2. Thinking on your feet
3. Courage
4. Gentleness
5. Knowing
6. Instinct
7. Understanding
8. Acceptance
9. Imagination
10. Compassion

"And these are not only the true weapons of war; they are the only weapons any of us will ever need."

Tolstoy once wrote, "Everyone wants to change the world, but no one wants to change themselves."

I don't think that's true. At least I hope it isn't true, not in these new days of enlightenment. But still I wonder! And as I do, I turn my head to look to my guide for hope and for inspiration, for comfort and for guidance. In a voice strong and sure, he asks me to ask some of those questions which have crossed my mind as I have been writing this book and which will appear on the page even as I write. His words, I know, will give us all the courage to speak out against the wagers of war, to stand firm against the injustices of our human race, and to find hope for a better future for us all.

QUESTION: Grey Eagle, why is there so much hatred and so much evil done in the name of religion?

ANSWER: There is so much confusion in your world. Confusion brought about by man and man alone. There are many living in your world who choose to deny responsibility for their own actions. And, so, they will hold out in front of them, like a banner, a religious belief, a tenet, a way of life. And, they will shout out loud that this is the way that it should be.

There are those who like to control, and whose will it is to control others, perhaps of weaker mind. And they will shout the loudest, believing that they will be heard the most.

And, then, the next man, fearing that his word will not be heard, will shout also, and confusion begins.

But, as I have said to you before, God hears the smallest whisper, as well as the loudest call. And, we who are the listeners, we are saddened by your confusion.

And we are saddened by the denial of many to accept responsibility of their own selves, and to leave the responsibility of others to themselves.

And, we fear, there are some who will never listen, who will never stay quiet, who choose to live in confusion, believing that they control and are in control, not only of themselves, but of others also . . . forgetting that there is only one hand that controls. And, even that hand does not control in the way that you would understand it.

For that hand is a gentle hand . . . and a guiding hand, and controls only the natural order of things . . . and this is God's hand.

And when the fighting is done, and the shouting is over, and the blood is spilled on the ground . . . and pain is felt by the many . . .

God's hand will still be there, for all . . . not for one side or the other . . .

And, that hand, which knows always gentleness, will be gentle still.

QUESTION: Grey Eagle, why were your people permitted to be almost obliterated, despite the fact that they were extremely spiritual, respecting the earth and all things of it?

ANSWER: This is a question which is close to my heart, for in asking this question, you ask of my ancestors, my own people. But in answering this question, I now have to remind you that there were many ancient cultures that have existed on your earth, who respected your earth, they respected the spirit nature, and were gentle with it, and nurturing of it.

And . . . why should it surprise you that these people are no more on your earth plane? For in asking your question, you make it seem like a punishment, that those souls who have learned and grown should have now returned to the universe.

To understand better, first you must realize that death is a beautiful thing and seen as a gift. It is a rebirth and an opportunity which all souls cry out for.

There are many on the earth plane who I know speak of the loss of these ancient cultures with sadness, but, there is no need. For you have your history books, which of course do not always repeat the way that things were, but will, if you examine them closely, give you an insight into some of the truths of the past, and of past ages.

And, if you will learn from our existence, and, if you will know of our beliefs, and, if you will try to begin to understand the ways of the ancients, and, if you will use what you have learned to propel you forward on your path, more enlightened by our existence, then, indeed, you also have a gift, a wondrous thing, for you will have discovered in our being, in our very existence, a lesson.

And, do not grieve at our loss, the loss of the many nations. For souls depart the earth plane, not to wander aimlessly, but with purpose, and with discovery in mind.

And, I say this to you, and from my heart . . . and you will know it even as I speak to you . . . that the ancients are not lost to you . . . nor is any soul who has walked upon this earth . . . for indeed, am I not here to talk with you, and to remind you of this.

QUESTION: Grey Eagle, why do good things happen to bad people and bad things happen to good people?

ANSWER: Here we differ with our understanding, with our language barrier, which I will attempt to overcome.

You give me the words "good" and "bad." And who is to say what is good and what is bad.

Would you say that a "good" person should be exempt from a learning process?

Would you say that a "bad" person should be given more trials and more difficulties to overcome?

And how do you recognize "good" and "bad" . . . the person or the deed? How are you to judge?

Many trials and many difficulties are placed in the path of every human being, every individual. They are not put there for cruel reasons or for punishment. They are given truly as a gift, although with your limited vision, we who watch you understand and accept your inability to see this, and we are not unsympathetic.

But pain and tears are part of your learning process. For how can you truly discover compassion within yourself until you have learned the need of it for yourself?

And how can you truly recognize pain in others until you have truly felt it for yourself?

If you were not given these gifts, which are pain and despair and heartache, how would you ever feel at one and in empathy with another who feels these things?

And if you truly did not from time to time suffer these pains and anxieties, would you not just be an empty shell . . . never knowing or understanding your deeper feelings, and your capacity to love?

And so my child, I say to you, indeed from my heart, and truly . . . do not judge so harshly, and use your labels "good" and "bad," but learn to accept that gifts come in many forms.

And, your tears are truly a gift . . .

QUESTION: Grey Eagle, would you explain what happens to those souls who commit suicide?

ANSWER: When death occurs, death as you know it, the universe embraces you and takes you to its heart.

When you cross the void which separates the two worlds, and you enter the "death" state, you will enter the light.

And the light, which is love and the love of God . . . God force, will embrace you.

There are those souls who choose to turn away from the light, and it is their choice to do so. For the universe demands nothing other than that which you would like to give.

For many reasons, there are those of you on the earth plane who would take their own life, confused, hurt, angry, bitter, sick, dying, feeling unable to cope with that which life insists they must deal with, feeling unable to cope with circumstances or situations.

But there is only one true reason why a human being should take his or her own life . . . and that reason is the feeling of being unable to cope with one's own self, being unable to cope with one's own feelings of despair.

The universe is not a cruel place, and there is no punishment meted out . . . and not one soul is cast aside, except that soul which chooses to be so.

And when the cry of the soul, in pain and in desperation is heard, and the call for help is acknowledged, then it is brought into the light, and embraced.

And help and loving and compassion is given.

QUESTION: Grey Eagle, can someone die before or after their designated time?

ANSWER: It is said that each human being has a book. And in this book is contained the many events and circumstances of your life.

This book has a beginning . . . a middle . . . and an end.

For some, their book is very long and very full. For others, their book is shorter. And for some, their book is very short.

To glimpse the contents of your book would tell you many things. The secrets of this book are contained within the soul.

There are some on earth who have the gift to see . . . to glimpse, not just their own book, but that of others, too, and the contents therein. These you would refer to as tellers of fortune, or psychics.

Each of you has the power, owns the power, to see his or her own book, to read the contents, which are entered within . . . this knowledge lies within each soul. Each book has a beginning, a middle, and yes, indeed, it is written, an end.

But there are, for some, choices, and there are those of you who would wish not to continue with your lives. For some of these, this is an ending which has been written . . . determined. For others, there are choices, for you do, indeed, have a free will.

If, my child, you seek for answers which are black and white, then you seek confusion. And, if in your frustration, you demand that I should answer your questions yes or no, then I would take away from you your learning process . . . which I must not do.

So I seek to answer your questions more often with questions that you must ask yourself . . . and again, repeat to you that the answers lie within yourself.

QUESTION: Grey Eagle, how do you feel about taking people off life support, when doing so will certainly end their lives?

ANSWER: In your world you have built many scientific things, and in many instances, machine overtakes the man . . . the machine that has no regard for the soul . . . for the sensitivity of the soul . . . for the learning of the soul . . . the machine which man uses willingly.

You ask the question not what are my feelings about life support machines, but what are my feelings concerning machine overtaking man, with no regard for nature and the natural order of things.

The universe, and all it encompasses, holds vast resources. Man is part of that universe. And in the center of each man, there are vast resources.

There is, within the machine, no soul, no understanding, no heart which throbs in tune with that of nature.

The ancients, the Grandfathers, knew of their time to die, and would go into the Wilderness and sit and wait for heaven to come and claim them.

Your machine does not support life . . . but only breath.

We of the universe have no wish to interfere with your choice to use this machine, for you have a free will, and must use it.

But, one small movement of God's hand will disregard the science of man. And, when God's hand is ready to move, then your machines will become invalid.

We have no wish to interfere with your destruction of nature, for it is your choice. We can only gaze upon you with despair and compassion for the joys which you are missing.

You see death as punishment. But we, who are of another world, will know death only as a gift.

QUESTION: Grey Eagle, why are we born to this earth?

ANSWER: Learning. Mortal beings, placed on earth, begin a learning process.

Growth, self growth, is an intimate thing; it is between you and your soul;

The heart of the soul throbs;

The heart of the soul is light;

As the heart of the soul throbs . . . pulsates . . . it shows the life of the soul, and the light of the soul . . . and only shadows cross its path. Dim shadows making patterns on the soul's heart. . . . Dim and fleeting shadows . . . which you will call pain;

And when your eyes meet the eyes of your soul . . . and you recognize the light, then the shadows will become less.

You are placed upon the earth so you may recognize this truth . . . which will feed the soul and will help the heart of the soul to continue to beat strong and true.

As I listen again to the wise and wonderful words of Grey Eagle, and as I ponder his teachings, it gives me great comfort to know that there is no harsh judgment of how we human beings live our lives. It gives me comfort that death is something we should not be afraid of, that it is a beautiful thing, a gift. When it is our time to go, each of us will embrace it joyfully. Grey Eagle has also taught me that while death is something we can embrace, that we should also embrace our lives here on earth, that life here on this earth plane is also a gift and a most beautiful thing. He has taught me that we should treasure the gift of life and that we should make the most of its beauty every day, that we should value our life and savor our life experiences. *We should not hurry toward death;* only see it as a continuing of the path that we are already on, when finally it comes to us.

He has taught me that as we embrace each day, we should never deliberately or intentionally harm or hurt another human being, never take another's life or indeed the life of another living thing. He teaches that we should value all of God's creations, believing them to be of God and here with us on this earth because God wills that it should be that way. That it is God and God alone who decides these things.

In my life and in my work I try to remember one thing, one prayer, which my guide in his wisdom has taught me: Dear God, I will to thy will. . . .

War and Peace

The lecture was in Rutland in October of 2002, and my audience was totally with me, asking many questions. Each question was different and moving in its own way, but there is one that stands out in my mind.

"My brother," said the questioner, "I need to know if he suffered, and is he safe?"

I found myself going down, down and down and through the hole, and although fully aware of my audience, still I was in another place. I heard a noise, a droning sound, and looking up into a darkening sky, saw a small plane—or was it a chopper? I wasn't sure. At one moment the sky seemed filled with aircraft and in another moment it seemed that I saw just one plane. "Which was it?" I wondered aloud, as, struggling for clarity, standing at once both with my audience and also in that faraway place where time can be repeated as if the years between the "then" and the "now" simply don't exist. As I tried to explain what I was seeing, the man, my questioner, nodded, saying he understood.

As I moved back in time, every one of my senses alert, I could smell something dank and musty. Down and through the hole I went again and found myself in what appeared to be a rain forest. There was nothing beautiful about this place. I shivered as the oppressive and threatening atmosphere of the jungle closed over me like a thick black shroud. Then I saw him among a group of others, torrential rain pouring down on them, mud up to their waists, struggling to stay upright under the weight of—what was it that they were carrying on their backs?

"We were taken in a plane, a carrier," I heard him say, as coming back to the now I saw the young soldier standing next to his brother, a huge grin on his face, eager to tell me more. Before I had time to grasp the situation, back I went, but this time the scene was a little different. The noise was deafening, almost unbearable, and as explosions and gunfire mingled together with the sounds of men shouting, the sounds of screaming and dying soldiers, I realized that I was in the middle of a war zone. I was in Vietnam!

This was by no means the first time I had experienced war this way, but that didn't make the horror less real or easier to deal with. Watching from my vantage point of safety of my place in that no-man's-land, where all things are seen, but none can harm me, I sighed the sigh of the hopeless, for here I was again, an unseen witness to another war, just as bloody as the others had been, just as useless . . . and nothing, it seemed, had ever changed.

War is war, and since time began there has been war in one part of our world or another. At the end of each of those wars, the same sentiments are spoken. "This is the last . . . This was the war to end all wars. . . . We have finally won our freedom, and . . . We will never be enslaved again. . . ." And each war is always fought for the people, or this is what we're told . . . again and again and again, and it is endless. Shame on us, shame on our human race, SHAME, SHAME, SHAME ON US!

I watched from my very safe place, as the sky rained down, bringing with it the bodies of the young men who had been fighting for their good cause, doing their duty, not even understanding what the war was really about. I saw the sky filled with the limbs, the arms and legs, the feet and hands, of what used to be laughing, crying, and oh-so-brave young soldiers, our young men who had been sent to war to fight in a battle that could never be won. The smell, now an acrid burning of choking fumes, mingled with the smell of burning flesh, and death was all around.

But that's OK, isn't it, for I am the medium and I don't believe in death. So why does death affect me so?

I came back to the now, sighing the sigh of the hopeless, and smiling sadly at the soldier who was so full of hope, who was laughing and crying, and talking to me about the wonderful changes that death had brought to him.

"I was MIA," he said. Seeing my puzzled expression, he explained. "Missing in action. They never found out what happened to me, my family, you know, and they have suffered so much, Rosemary, imagining the worst, that I might be in a camp somewhere, or that I had a horrible and painful death. But it was easy really, we were blown to pieces, and I never felt a thing."

You might imagine the joy, not just for the brother, but a joy that the whole audience felt on hearing this. But then, hardly giving me time to catch my breath again, my brave young soldier began reminiscing about the old days, when he and his brothers, five in all, used to go fishing together when they were lads.

"Tell him what you see, Rosemary," the soldier said, as quickly we went again down and through the hole to that halfway place. It was a different place than before and so opposite of everything I'd seen so far.

Once again there were trees, but this time there was a peace about the place, a calm and a harmony, as nature lent us its beauty. I heard the river before I saw its sparkle, sunlight breaking out over the water, its voice a gurgling song, mingled with the sounds of five young boys standing on the great flat rock, the perfect platform for all their fishing gear and the picnic baskets.

"This was our place, our fishing hole," whispered the soldier, "and this was our secret. We had so much fun and life was good. We caught lots of fish . . . well, most of us did, anyway." Then laughing, and giving his brother a playful shove, he said, "He wasn't the best fisherman, you know, but we still enjoyed ourselves. I used to think of that place, and all of us there together when I was in 'Nam, and it kept me sane. We would sit together, my buddies and me, when the fighting stopped, waiting for it to begin again, and we'd tell stories. I'd always talk about our secret place, and the *huge* fish we used to catch.

"Dying didn't hurt, and I don't want anyone to be sad for me because it was my time and I'm safe now." Then, looking to me one last time, our hero added, "Tell him I want them to go back to our secret place, to fish again, like we used to do, and to remember that when he gets that big fish on his hook, that it's really mine, as I'll be helping him—my way of letting my family know that I'm still around . . . and still the best fisherman of them all!"

We must be encouraged by this story. Like many others, it shows us that no matter what the circumstances of our death, we overcome the horrors of our lives and find peace at last. But even as I write, I am aware of another war, the war in Iraq, and I wonder about those who have lost their sons and daughters in a struggle that must seem so futile, even to those who agree that war is necessary. And shame on us, for it seems that peace is an illusion, that man cannot survive without the need to fight, to kill, to maim. I hear those who give their fine reasons and excuses, and I might even agree with some of them. But I sigh as I write this chapter, remembering that terrible jungle where so many young men died in vain, and my sigh is the sigh of hopelessness, and I surrender to the fact that nothing much will change. There will always be war in one country or another, and young men and women will die for some politician's cause, some madman's idea of right and wrong, and innocents on both sides will suffer.

I am a soldier's daughter, and as I was growing up, I was forced to live a soldier's life, to occasionally hear the tales of war from my father, all of them gruesome. It made me proud to think of my father fighting for his country. It makes me proud still. I am both sad for and proud of the young men and women who put their lives on the line for the rest of us. But still I say: Shame on us, shame on the politicians that they cannot find a better way, and shame on our human race that we still find it so necessary to have to fight, to maim and kill, and to destroy ourselves.

But peace, I've realized, has to begin at home. It has to begin by our finding a way to have harmony and love in our own individual lives.

There are wars being fought of one sort or another in most people's families, and we all have our own personal demons. The truth is that many of us are at war with ourselves.

I was speaking with a woman this morning who wished to connect to her mother, who had died of cancer and who was waiting eagerly to communicate. In fact, there were two women waiting, one the mother and one a sister who had passed, also due to cancer. As I described the latter, my client, immediately recognizing her sister, said very matter-of-factly, "Oh yes, but you know, Rosemary, she's a Dark Soul, a bad person, and I never had much to do with her."

Later, when my client's mother began talking of another sister still on this earth plane, my client once again informed me that this sister also was a bad person. It was easy for me to recognize that I was dealing with a very sad and dysfunctional family, just as mine had been. My client was a very unhappy individual, who was very lost in her own misery and confusion. Hers was a family at war, just as mine had been. Just like so many of us, hers was a family that had for years lived in a war zone, almost intentionally determined to destroy itself and not even realizing it.

This is what war of any kind does to us. It confuses us, and if we're not careful, it destroys us. Each time there is a war, whether a personal one or one that the whole world is involved in, no one wins. There are no true victors. Everybody loses. Everybody pays the price.

Another lecture, another time, just a year or two ago, and the audience was as surprised as I was at the speed with which I began. My first

communicator was a young man, a soldier in full uniform, coming toward me from the back of the room. No one in his family was in the
audience, the young man knew, but as he gave his name and explained
that before the war he had been a policeman, many people in the audience gasped. "I joined the army and was killed in action," he said,
and as I repeated his words, the crowd nodded in recognition. I had
known nothing about this, since this was not my local area. But I discovered later that the story had been on the evening news, and the
whole town had been devastated. One of their own, a young man who
had grown up with them, gone to the local school, gone out with the
local kids, had been killed the day before in the war in Iraq!

"Tell them what happened," the young soldier asked those there
who knew him, meaning his family, who were home, grieving the loss
of him. "Tell them I was here tonight to show them I'm OK and to let
you all know that I'm safe again and at peace now. There is no more
fighting here, only love."

"There is no more fighting, only love," the brave young soldier had
said, and I wish it were the same for all of us. But I know that for some
reason, it will never be. Yes, it seems to me that there will always be war.
There will always be killing, and our young will always be at risk. But
at the end, for those who must die so that the rest of us can live in freedom, rest assured that for them, they will always find peace!

But at what cost do we fight our wars? At what cost do we send our
young men and women to fight for us? And well we know that the
price we all pay is always much too high . . . !

I listened recently to a mother whose son is fighting in Iraq, who
has had to pay seventy dollars, she told me, thirty-five for her son
and thirty-five for the boy who shares a tent with him, so that they can
get Internet service. Naively I asked how that could be. Weren't they
fighting for their country, risking their lives for world peace? Could
it be true that our governments, our politicians, would allow such
a thing?

"Well," the mother said, "he sent me an e-mail, telling me how bad things were, saying they had run out of bullets and had had to borrow from the British, which was OK, except that they didn't quite fit the guns, and after firing once, the guns would jam."

No! No! No! Surely this cannot be? But it is and the rage I feel when I think of it is overshadowed only by the sadness and heartbreak I feel that there should be a war at all. It is bad enough that we should have to fight but to neglect the safety and well-being of those men and women who fight to keep us safe is criminal. And so I shout out . . . SHAME ON YOU. Shame on all the politicians, all the leaders of our armed forces who send out our young, ill equipped for battle, in the direct line of fire. Shame, shame, shame on you!

Ben . . .

Thursday, 10:00 A.M.

Ask for Denise—she'll tell you what to do. All Rosemary knows about you is that you are on leave. She'll ask you what you would like to know and your name. (Just tell her Ben—that's enough.)

Ideas for you to ask her:

• Is there anyone on the other side that would like to talk to me?
• What does my future hold?
• Who is my spirit guide?

I have never talked to Rosemary (not yet) many people wait years to get this chance to talk to a world-famous psychic/medium. She has been on Oprah, Larry King, *w/Diane Sawyer, etc., and hopefully this will be a very mind-opening experience for you.*

Write down anything you might want to recall if you feel like it. While I am praying your dad comes forward, nothing is guaranteed. Spirits after all have varying degrees of abilities at transmitting energy. Regardless of this, she definitely possesses the gift of being psychic and can shed light on our path and our choices or opportunities. My hope is that you begin to search for a faith system that will sustain you through-

out your life and that will begin to answer the important questions we all have.

That can be a great source of comfort when we need it most.

Should the recorder not work, write down names—even if you don't know who they are. I might or Uncle Bob. (Many times previously passed family members guide us—as well as unrelated souls.) I believe your father is with you. ☺

As you know, my prayers always are.

He had begun the conversation somewhat nervously so I tried to guide him through the process, asking him who in the spirit world he would like to speak to and what were the questions he would like to ask. Ben stated that he wanted to talk to his dad, and then, a little confused as to what to say next, he began reading out loud the first couple of lines from the letter.

"What are you reading?" I asked curiously, hoping to help this young man through his nervousness.

"A letter from my mom," he replied shyly. "She just put a few suggestions down. I haven't done this kind of thing before."

"Why don't you read it out to me?" I suggested. "It might help."

"What, all of it?" the young man exclaimed. I laughed and said, "Why not?"

It was not true that the only thing I knew about Ben was that he was on leave. I also knew that he was a soldier on leave from the war in Iraq, that he was fighting in Iraq, and that his time back home was short, just a few days. His mother had explained this to Denise when she had called to try to get an appointment with me for her son, believing that it was a long shot but trying anyway.

It was no surprise to me, although Ben's mom was a little shocked that a cancellation had just come up, and only days later we were able to fit Ben in on the first day of his leave, less than two weeks after she had first made the call.

As Ben read out the letter from his mom, I listened quietly, inspired and moved by this mother's love for her boy. Afraid for him, wanting him to take back to the war something special, something that would sustain him, she had reached out with all her faith, with all that she believed in, and had prayed that Ben's father would be able to do for her son what she herself could not do.

As I looked around, I hoped and prayed for the same thing. Already aware of Ben's vulnerability, I knew that this communication, if indeed there was to be one, had better be better than good. I also knew that I must be prepared to tell this boy the truth of what I saw and heard, even if it was not what he might want to hear. Was I ready for that? I knew that I had to be!

Ben's father was ready to begin, even before his son had finished reading the letter, and had come to stand by my right side, waiting patiently, listening to his son's voice. He knew of my anxieties, and within a few short moments, he put my mind at ease. But just as I was about to begin, I saw another man standing in front of me. He was talking to me about how he had been killed in an accident. I was a little confused with how to start. Should I begin by talking to this man first or to Ben's father? As I listened, again the man in front of me told me quite clearly how he had been killed in an accident. An accident on a farm, he said. I looked at Ben's father, and he nodded. "Yes," he said, "we used to have a farm." I asked Ben if he knew of a family farm.

"My uncle, my dad's brother, he had a farm—"

"Yes," his dad interrupted, "but we were a family of farmers. Dad, Granddad, a couple of generations back."

"That's right," replied Ben, "on my dad's side."

"I have your dad here, Ben, talking to me about the farm, and he's telling me about your teeth, about a problem with your teeth."

"No," said Ben, "there's nothing wrong with my teeth."

"Oh, yes," I said, and I see Ben's father nodding vigorously. "He had quite a problem with his teeth." "And Ben," I said, as I continued to explain what his father was talking about, "your father is describing a dog, a really scruffy-looking dog you had when you were a boy." I described the color and size, as I can now see the dog standing next to me. "Your dad says that when you were younger, this was your dog. He tells me that at this time in your life, you were having terrible trouble with your teeth and that you hated wearing those braces."

For a moment there was silence on the other end of the phone while Ben tried to figure out how I knew about the dog, but finally offered a clear, "Yes, that's right." His voice a little stronger now, Ben began to believe that maybe this was real.

"I see your dad quite clearly, but what stands out most is how big he is, what a big personality he has, and he's quite a bully. He keeps poking me in the shoulder every time I hesitate to repeat what he's saying. I don't think I'm talking fast enough." I chuckled.

Ben laughed and said that it sounded just like his dad.

"He's telling me how he passed . . . cancer, he says," and I hear Ben's voice again, down the phone, "Yes!"

"It was very fast, barely time to get used to the idea, and then he was gone."

"Yes."

Then Ben's father began to talk about his son and his son's army career. "He's done two years, has eighteen months to go, and just got a promotion, which means he's going to be in charge of a few other kids."

"Yes," Ben said again, loud and clear.

Describing the mosque that is close to where Ben's company is located, and the tower, the buildings, it was clear to both Ben and me that his father had been with him. But just in case he was not getting the message, Ben's dad gave him a message which was designed to let his son know not only that his dad was around, watching, guiding and protecting him but that he could really help in the situation Ben was in.

"I'm with you, son. I see how scared you are. When I was around and when the boys were younger," he said, now looking at me, "I taught them that they shouldn't be afraid of anything, that a man is never afraid of anything. I was wrong, Ben," he said, heartbroken at his own insensitivity. "When I was sick, I was so scared. I was even scared of letting anyone know that I was, so I kept it to myself. I couldn't talk to anyone about it. I know, Ben, that you're scared when you're out there, and those young kids you'll be looking after will be scared too. They are going to need someone to talk to, to confide in. Don't be like me, Ben. Tell these kids that you're scared. Let them know. Let them see that it's OK to be afraid, that you're all afraid. But that if you stay together as a group, as a team, then you'll be OK."

Ben was on the phone with me for almost an hour and a half, and his dad, as you can imagine, had a lot more to say about his son's life, his future, and his future plans. When our time was finally up, Ben was overwhelmed but happy. He gave me his permission to write his story.

Just to be certain that it was OK, the next day I called Ben's mother, who had left her phone number with us in case there was a chance for her son to have a consultation. I first asked how Ben was after speaking with me.

"He's just so overwhelmed, and can't get over the fact that he was able to talk to his dad," she said.

I explained what I wanted to do; saying how much I thought her son's story and her letter would help so many others in the same or similar situation. She was delighted, thrilled to be a part of something that might help a lot of other people.

"My son is so young, only twenty years old, and I just wanted him to have something to take back with him, something to hold on to for the rest of his life. He knows now that his dad is with him, keeping him safe, taking care of him. That is all I wanted for my son, and, Rosemary, it has already made a difference in him. I can see it and I'm so grateful."

"WHILE I AM PRAYING your dad comes forward," this wonderful mother wrote in her letter to her son, "nothing is guaranteed."

My hope is that you begin to search for a faith system that will sustain you throughout your life and that will begin to answer the important questions we all have.

That can be a great source of comfort when we need it most. I believe your father is with you. ☺

As you know, my prayers always are.

As Grey Eagle has told us, no true warrior wants to fight and fights only when he must. As my guide has also taught me, when we are on the battlefield and even when we must use our guns, our man-made tools of war, to protect ourselves and to safeguard the lives of others, there are other weapons that we should also take with us when we have a need to fight. It is these weapons that will ultimately help us win.

In Grey Eagle's words then and for Ben and for all those brave young soldiers of war, who need more than we on this earth plane can give, who need to know that they are invincible, that their soul calls out to them and will find for them the courage that they need, that they are protected by their loved ones in the spirit world, that God's eyes see all. His is an energy that is ever present!

"The weapons of a true warrior are a quick mind; the ability to think on your feet; the art of being courageous; the need in you for gentleness; the knowing that speaks to you from your soul; the instinct of your beating heart; the understanding that you cannot die; the acceptance of fear; the imagination to embrace your enemy as if he were your friend; the compassion you apply in all things."

From Grey Eagle, and from your father, Ben, a gift . . . a gift of love . . .

The Child

The ambulance raced through the streets of New York City, its sirens blasting, urging everyone to clear a path, to get over to the side of the road. Someone might be dying here, in fact, in all probability they were. So move out, the sirens screamed, move over, move over. . . . JUST GET OUT OF THE WAY!

She was bleeding badly, the blood pushing up under her ribcage, forcing her lungs up into her chest, and she could hardly breathe, even though a mask had been placed firmly over her mouth. She was still conscious, barely, and the fear crept slowly into her brain. Was she going to die? *"Am I going to die?"*

Peter was with her, holding her hand as the ambulance sped toward the hospital, and the same fear gripped him too, as he gazed down at her face. White, white skin, all color drained away, she looked almost dead, a corpse already, and he tried to focus on them getting to the hospital in time to save her . . . and they would, he thought. He knew they would, for any other outcome was inconceivable to him right now.

Was it only yesterday that they had been at the hospital, that she had had her surgery, a minor op with no complications, they'd been told.

Was it only last night that they had brought her home, helped her to bed, told her to try to get some sleep? Was it only last night that she had told them that she couldn't breathe, that she felt a tightness in her chest? The nurse had said that it was normal, that it was just stress, that all her vital signs were fine, and that they should just take her home. The doctor had signed off, giving the order to release her. So what had happened? What in God's name was happening to her now?

Arriving at the hospital, she was immediately rushed into surgery, leaving a bewildered Peter to call her mother.

"You'd better come," he said, his hand shaking a little as he held the cell phone. "She's bleeding, and they don't seem to know from where."

Her mother was tough, an in-charge kind of person, especially when it came to dealing with crisis of any kind. As she got out of the taxi, questions came pouring out, and she reached out to Peter, who had been waiting for her at the door, her tough exterior began to crumble with every word.

Remaining calm, Peter took her by the arm and guided her through the miles of hospital corridors to a waiting room. He explained that "she" was still in surgery and that they would have to wait.

The clock ticked . . . one hour, then two, and four slow hours went by. The two sat side by side, saying very little, both engrossed in their own thoughts, neither daring to voice those thoughts, for fear that their fear would show through . . . and the clock just kept on ticking.

It was an endless wait, but eventually the two were shown into a small cramped office, where a young woman sat, the doctor, a solemn look on her face.

"We've managed to stop the bleeding, and we can see where it was coming from. But we don't know why it happened, and she's lost a lot of blood. She's stable for now, and hopefully we'll know more after we do some tests tomorrow."

Peter and the girl's mother glanced at each other, and then back to the doctor. They had both caught it. . . . "She is stable for now!"

"Where is she?" the mother said, the first to speak. "When can we see her?"

"She's in intensive care, and you can go and see her for just a few minutes. But you can't stay long—she needs her rest," the doctor said matter-of-factly, and then, a little more gently, as she must have realized how she sounded, she said, "I'll have a nurse take you up there."

They stood by her bed, one on either side of her. Both of them shocked at the sight that met them. Silent tears fell as the mother reached out and took her child's hand in her own. It felt so small, and the girl looked so small and frail and still, her eyes closed, white bandages wrapped around her head, holding all the breathing apparatus in place.

Prayer is a funny thing. As so often happens, many of us only pray when we need to, when we are in trauma, in a crisis situation. Peter was not one for praying. He was not a particularly spiritual person. He went to church only if there was a wedding, a funeral, or a christening. If he prayed, as he stood by the girl's bedside, he never said so. The mother, however, was very different. She had no trouble talking about God, about prayer, and about the power of prayer. She was a great believer, had prayed all her life. Prayer came to her easily. It was a natural thing for her to do. But there were no prayers in her as she stood looking down at her daughter. There were no prayers, no words, no thoughts forming in her mind, no begging, no bargaining and no pleas for help. There were only tears, only silent tears, hot and wet, raining down her cheeks.

A nurse appeared and asked them to leave, telling them they could come back at four o'clock. "Four hours from now," she said. Silent in their grief, the two of them made their way to the elevators, trying hard to hold themselves together. Then, as they waited, the mother, unable to stay strong any longer, collapsed, her legs buckling, and as Peter caught her before she fell, they clung to each other sobbing pitifully, neither speaking, neither saying a word, for what was there to say?

At ten minutes to four, the child's mother was at the door, waiting to be let in to the IC unit. Peter had gone home to get some rest, as he had been up all night and needed to sleep.

She was only half awake and groggy, but as her mother took her hand, she gave a watery smile. Stroking her hair, concern furrowing her brow, the mother bent down to kiss her child.

"A pain," the child managed to mutter, "I've got a pain, Mummy, in my stomach, and I can't, I can't"—gasping—"I can't breathe."

"Nurse, nurse," called the mother, and as the nurse appeared, she said, "Get a doctor. Get a doctor. My daughter can't breathe."

It was an amazing thing and something that many of us have experienced, although we would never expect to, especially in a situation like this. The mother's eyes widened as the nurse shrugged her shoulders, indifferent to her obvious concern, and told her that she would have to wait. The doctor was on her rounds and would be at least another hour.

Mentally shaking her head, trying to take in what she'd just heard but refusing to accept it, the mother quietly and urgently asked the nurse if she was aware of her daughter's history, that she had bled out, had almost died, and that there was a possibility that it could be happening again.

"You'll have to wait for the doctor. We can't do anything until she's finished her rounds," the nurse said snottily, used to being in charge and to giving the orders, at least when the doctors weren't around.

It has been said that the child's mother was a tough and an in-charge kind of person, although so far, in this situation, there had been no evidence of it. When she had been speaking to the nurse, explaining her daughter's condition, she had spoken quietly, believing that the young woman must have just come on duty and therefore was not aware of the extent of her daughter's medical history. Now, for the first time since the crisis had begun, she came awake, her brain clicked in, her natural protective instincts rose to the surface. Her voice, still soft, still seemingly mild, acquired an edge to it that would have made the hairs on anyone's neck prickle. Her eyes as hard as stone, she replied, "I'm giving you two minutes. You have two minutes to get the sonography machine in here, two minutes to get a doctor, two minutes to move your butt, and don't, please don't"—she held up her hand and spoke in an even quieter but much more deadly voice—"please do not even think about arguing with me."

The nurse stared for just a second, weighing her options. She then turned on her heel and left. Seconds later a doctor appeared, a young intern, and as the mother explained the situation again, she strode into action. The scanning machine was sent for, the primary doctor was sent for, and when she arrived minutes later, a portable X-ray machine was wheeled in. It was all systems go. Yet as the mother stood by, watching over her daughter like a lion watching over her cub, still she did not pray. Still she did not ask for help, and still she did not reach out, for all her belief, to the God she had known and prayed to all her life.

The following day the child was taken out of the ICU, no longer in immediate danger but still very sick. Having lost an enormous amount of blood, and very weak, she sat sleepily in the chair by her bed as her mother gently brushed her hair. Her doctor had been in earlier, and so had a slew of others, and she said that the tests they had done so far were not conclusive but that they were waiting for the final results from the hematologist.

Dr. Greene arrived later that morning and sat on the child's bed, holding her hand lightly as he looked over at her mother. "Well," he said, raising a quizzical eyebrow, after explaining that he was the long-awaited hematologist, "we've finally figured it out, so do you want the good news or the bad news?"

The child inched closer to her mother, a frightened look on her face, and a tear slipped down her cheek. "We'll take the bad news first," the mother said, bracing herself for what was to come and squeezing her daughter's hand reassuringly.

"You have a very rare blood condition," Dr. Greene said, nodding toward the child, "and it took us a while to find it. It's hereditary and it's a type of hemophilia, only rarer, as rare as hens' teeth, in fact, and is potentially more dangerous, as you don't know you have it until you bleed out, which," he said, nodding toward the bed, "is what happened to you. The good news," he said, sounding much more positive, "is that now we know you have it, we can protect you in the future."

A rare blood condition, hereditary, he'd said, and rarer than hens' teeth, and suddenly the mother remembered another time, a time long past, when she too had been sick, and had almost bled out on the operating table during a serious surgical procedure that had almost cost her her life. She had been young, younger than her daughter was now, and had not really understood when she too had been told about her condition. She had been given a card, she remembered, to carry around in her purse. It had said that in case of emergency to give her plasma—plasma, the blood-clotting agent that had saved her daughter's life, the blood-clotting agent that had saved her life all those years ago.

"It's me," gasped the mother. "I didn't understand," and guilt swept over her as she realized that her daughter was like this because of her.

"So, you're the guilty one," Dr. Greene quipped, not realizing how hard the news had hit. Then seeing the mother's stricken face, he added gently, "Don't worry, we've caught it now. But when you're better, young lady," he said, smiling widely at the child, "I will want to see you both in my office. We have more tests to do."

A year went by, and it was a year of trauma, desperation, and fear; a year of tests, more tests, and pills and then more pills. Each hour seemed like a day, each day like an eternity, and life was agonizing and became merely a matter of survival for them all, the three of them trying to get through each day minute by minute. Gradually, and painfully slowly, the child began to improve in health, and everyone began to relax a little, though she was far from recovered. Afraid to sleep on her own, scared to be left by herself for even a short time, knowing how silly that seemed but unable to help it, she was aware that Peter and her mother were stressed to the limit. The girl tried to overcome her anxiety but just couldn't. When you come that close to dying, the stress and the fear, no matter how unreasonable or unfounded it seems, can remain with you for a long, long time. To make matters worse, less than two months after she came out of hospital, the child was rushed in again with an appendectomy, a fairly simple surgery—until you remember that no surgery for this child will ever be other than a risk.

It was strange how the mother—in her greatest time of need, you might say—did not reach out to God. It was strange how not one prayer, one utterance, crossed her lips at any time or even crossed her mind, not in all the time her child was sick. She prayed for others, she prayed for the world, for the young men and women who were caught up in the war. She prayed for her students and her patients who needed her prayers but not once did she pray for her daughter or for herself. And she pondered the strangeness of this, at times wondering if she had lost her faith. She knew she had not, even as such thoughts crossed her mind.

But as I write this story, and having had more than a year to think on things, it doesn't seem strange to me at all anymore.

It was Christmas, and the child's mother had tried everything she knew to make life better for her child, but nothing had seemed to work. She had screamed and she had raged, had wept and despaired, and then despaired some more. And then, one day . . . there was the voice she knew so well! It was the same voice she had heard when she was working, helping others with their problems. She had known he was there all along, but she had not consciously heard any words of wisdom or comfort for herself. It was the same voice that had always guided her, advised her, and had always led her to safety.

"A puppy. Get her a puppy," I heard Grey Eagle say clearly. As I thought of my child and later spoke to Peter, her husband, I realized that maybe all my daughter needed right now was her own little someone to love and to take care of.

It worked, and now, instead of her being eaten up by fear, Samantha concentrates her time and energy on Piper, the little black spaniel puppy who has saved all our lives and our sanity. If only, I wish with all my heart, that all our problems could be solved so easily.

I know how lucky I am that my daughter did not die. I will be forever grateful and even more aware of the pain of those who lose their children. I realize that our soul's journey is simply a matter of life and death. We are born, we live, and then we die. That is what this world of ours is all about, that is what we are all about, and in between the living and the dying, most of us try to do the best we can.

When I look back on the last year or so and remember everything my daughter has had to suffer and all her husband, Peter, has been through, all that we have come through together, I thank God for his protection and love. . . .

If anyone had asked me before this had all happened, what, in my worst nightmare, would my first action be, I would not have hesitated. My answer would have been automatic. I have always trusted in the power of prayer, and I would have said just that. But in my hour of need, in those many hours of need, when prayer might have been my comfort and my salvation, I did not once call on God or Grey Eagle or the spirit world for their help. Why? I can only tell you that there seemed to be no need in me to do so, for unknowingly I was filled up with their presence, and their prayers filled my head to the point that I heard nothing but silence, a great and paralyzing silence that pounded in my heart . . . and which reached down deep in my soul.

I thank God with all of my heart for showing me his mercy, for showing me how to live, for showing me how to use my gift in a way that is right, and good, and true, and now I will share the only prayer I have left to say: Dear God, for heaven's sake, may I always want to live my faith and may I always find the strength to do so.

EPILOGUE

So many things have changed for me in the last three years, the negative energy that seemed to have surrounded me is gone, leaving me free to get on with my life and my work without having to pay attention to unnecessary dramas and hurt feelings, which were only a distraction from what is really important in my life. This sounds harsh, I know, but it is true that we can all get caught up in other people's lives to the point where we have no life of our own. We begin to live vicariously through others, aiding and assisting them and ignoring our own needs, and that's not good. It was hard for me to let go of the negativity, as this meant that I had to say good-bye to some people it was hard for me to lose. But for my own sanity, I knew it had to be done, and having done it, my days are filled with light again, and I no longer have that awful knot in my stomach, waiting for the next drama and the next, which used to be so much a part of my life.

Now my efforts and energy can be centered on the things which are important to me. Building on the things I know I'm good at, creating a place for seminars, teaching, communicating with the spirit world, and the development of my healing foundation. Making a place where we can provide healing for the sick, where people can come to learn about healing and about all things connected to spiritual growth.

Our programs include art therapy, healing for the sick and dying, animal healing, creating a program for kids to learn about how to nurture our earth, and creating a Camp Over the Rainbow for sick kids. These are only some of the wonderful things we have planned. Needless to say, I will be writing more about those experiences in my next book, along with more stories from the spirit world, of course.

For now, though, I will leave you with this last message:

None of us can walk through life alone, and none of us truly wants to. I am fortunate in that I have many who walk with me. I have God and I have Christ. I have Grey Eagle, without whose help I could not have written this book. Nor, without him, would I have any stories to tell. I have friends, and, most important of all, I have my child, I am blessed.

We, all of us, even the most lonely, have those who walk with us through our lives. We have God in whatever form we see Him. We have all those in the spirit world—some we will know and some we won't—who are there to guide and steer us and to keep us safe.

And yes, we have our angels, too, and I thank God for them and I send my love to them, and wish them well, as I send my love to you, and wish you well . . . until we meet again.

To Learn More About Rosemary and Her Work

For more information about Rosemary's books, meditation tapes, media appearances, lecture schedule, newsletter, correspondence course, private consultations, and healing work, please log on to:

www.rosemaryaltea.com.

To email Rosemary personally, address your correspondence to:

raltea@vermontel.com.

THE ROSEMARY ALTEA HEALING AND EDUCATIONAL FOUNDATION

Rosemary Altea recently formed this not-for-profit organization, based in Vermont, which provides healing for people and animals worldwide, free of charge. All donations to RAHEF are tax-deductible. To learn more about weekly hands-on healing and the annual Fall Weekend at the RAHEF healing center in Vermont, go to the website mentioned above.

The Inspiring True Story That Will
Convince You of Life After Death